Master Student

Guide to Academic Success

Teaching Tools for Instructors

Instructor's Resource Manual (0-618-38257-7)
by Robert Onorato, Sacred Heart University, CT

The Instructor's Resource Manual serves as a comprehensive overview and how-to guide for using this unique text in any classroom. The IRM provides directions for creating a syllabus and information on how to adapt the text to a variety of student populations and course structures, especially for learning communities. Chapter-by-chapter tips, activities, and quizzes provide instructors with all they need to use this text effectively. Contact your local Houghton Mifflin Company sales representative to order your copy today!

Instructor's Web Site

The instructor's web site provides more of the valuable tools found in the Instructor's Resource Manual, along with links to additional resources and an online discussion group. Log on to the Master Student Guide to Academic Success Web site at http://masterstudent.college.hmco.com

College Survival Consulting Services

Houghton Mifflin's College Survival Consulting Group is the leading source of student success course expertise and support services. For the past twenty years, College Survival has provided consultation for the design and implementation of student success and first-year courses. College Survival also offers conferences and workshops throughout the year designed to equip instructors with ideas and activities to enliven the teaching and learning experience.

For more information, contact College Survival at 1-800-528-8323 or collegesurvival@hmco.com.

Master Student

Guide to
Academic Success

Doug Toft
Contributing Editor

HOUGHTON MIFFLIN COMPANY   BOSTON   NEW YORK

Editor-in-Chief, Humanities: Patricia A. Coryell
Senior Sponsoring Editor: Mary Finch
Development Editor: Shani B. Fisher
Editorial Associate: Andrew Sylvester
Senior Project Editor: Fred Burns
Editorial Assistant: Lisa Goodman
Manufacturing Manager: Florence Cadran
Senior Art and Design Coordinator: Jill Haber
Senior Composition Buyer: Sarah Ambrose

Printed in the U.S.A.

Library of Congress Control Number: 2003110162

ISBN: 0-618-38256-9

1 2 3 4 5 6 7 8 9—VHG—08 07 06 05 04

Brief Contents

Contents

Introduction: Getting the Most from This Book

Use This Book as a Reference and More

You can read this entire book straight through, or simply turn to se-lected chapters or sections for information on specific topics.

You're free to take multiple paths through this book by using four el-ements in the text—specific ways to locate the ideas and information that you want. These elements are numbered here in the order in which they appear. However, you can use them in any order or combination you like.

1. Use the table of contents

The table of contents starting on page v includes every major head-ing in the text. Note that the book is organized into the following major sections:

- Making Successful Transitions
- Thinking Critically and Creatively
- Planning to Succeed
- Reading and Note-Taking with a Purpose
- Building Memory and Test Taking Skills
- Developing and Presenting Ideas
- Succeeding in Math and Science

2. Use the tabs

On each tab, you'll find a table of contents for the chapters that fol-low. On the pages immediately after each tab is a quick reference guide for those chapters. These guides offer a detailed summary of each chapter that goes a step beyond the table of contents.

3. Read and use the boxes

Located in boxes throughout the text are checklists, examples, and other sidebars. Each offers ways to take ideas "off" the page and ap-ply them in daily life.

4. Use the index

For a complete list of topics presented in alphabetical order, see the index starting on page 331.

Do a Book Reconnaissance

Start producing value from this book by searching for ideas that you can use. Scan the table of contents. Next, look at every page in the book. Move quickly. Skim for headlines, examples, and checklists. Stop on any page to read for more detail. In any case, find suggestions that you can apply to specific situations in your academic life right now.

The following chart lists selected topics from the text that commonly interest students in higher education. Add your own topics and page numbers in the blank spaces provided.

Making successful transitions	Page
Finding ways to pay for your education and manage money	14
Building job contacts and starting a résumé	19
Discovering your learning styles	24
Thinking critically and creatively	**Page**
Thinking critically by spotting fallacies in logic	42
Expanding your creativity with brainstorming	48
Making more effective decisions	59
Planning to succeed	**Page**
Writing goals	73
Using a calendar and to-do list	82
Managing time to create balance in your life	86
Overcoming procrastination	90
Choosing a major	93
Creating a career plan	99
Reading and note-taking with a purpose	**Page**
Previewing what you read	112
Increasing your reading speed	124
Building your vocabulary	130
Listening more effectively	140

MAKING SUCCESSFUL TRANSITIONS

Chapter 1   Entering the Culture of Higher Education
Chapter 2   Using the Cycle of Learning

Quick Reference Guide to MAKING SUCCESSFUL TRANSITIONS

1. ENTERING THE CULTURE OF HIGHER EDUCATION

The transition to higher education is just one example of the major transitions you will experience during your lifetime.

1. **Reflect on the art of transition (page7)**
   To make transitions with more skill:
   - Remember that you always have the option to do something constructive—no matter how you feel about the change taking place in your life.
   - Learn to talk about change in more optimistic ways. (See the sidebar on page 8.)
   - Reduce negative emotions by keeping your focus on the present moment.
   - Balance change in one area of your life with stability in another.
   - "Practice" the change—for example, walk through your first day's schedule with a classmate or friend.
   - Remember ways that you successfully managed change in the past. (See the sidebar on page 9.)

2. **Make the personal transition to higher education (page 9)**
   Review some basic differences between high school and higher education and plan to cope with them:
   - You'll probably find that teachers expect you to study more than you did in high school—even while they give you less guidance about *what* or *how* to study.
   - Build support systems into your life by cultivating new friendships.
   - Take advantage of student services. (See the sidebar on page 10.)
   - Show up for class—mentally as well as physically.
   - Use the cost of each class as an incentive to participate actively. (See the checklist on page 12.)
   - Get involved in campus organizations and events.
   - Thrive among diversity by becoming aware of differences between people. Learn about ways in which cultures differ. (See the sidebar on page 13.)

3. **Make the financial transition to higher education (page 14)**
   Create a plan up front for funding your entire education:
   - Find many sources to help pay education expenses. (See the sidebar on page 15.)
   - Manage your expenses, no matter how much money you make.
   - Avoid the pitfalls of credit cards that many students experience. (See the checklist on page 16.)

4. **Handle the health demands of transition (page 17)**
   Maintain the personal resources needed to succeed in higher education by staying healthy:
   - Maximize your enjoyment of eating by monitoring the quantity and quality of food you consume.
   - Find a form of exercise you enjoy and do it regularly. (See the sidebar on page 17.)
   - Use self-help techniques to manage stress—and get help if they don't work.
   - Know when to get help for a problem with alcohol or other drugs. (See the sidebar on page 19.)

5. **Make the transition from education to work (page 19)**
   See career planning as something you do continuously throughout higher education:
   - Draft a résumé and continually update it as a way to record your skills and achievements. (See the checklist on page 21.)
   - Start a portfolio by keeping tangible evidence of your achievements, such as certificates, licenses, and awards. (See the checklist on page 21.)
   - Sustain relationships with people who could serve as references, sources of recommendation letters, and contacts for part-time or permanent jobs.

2. USING THE CYCLE OF LEARNING

Use an understanding of different learning styles to promote your success in higher education.

1. **Look for differences in perception and processing (page 22)**

   Remember that the concept of *learning styles* acknowledges that people vary in how they prefer to perceive and process information:

   ◆ Discover your own learning styles. (See the checklist on page 24.)

2. **Build the complete cycle of learning into your courses (page 24)**

   Include a variety of approaches to learning:

   ◆ Make use of concrete experience, reflective observation, abstract conceptualization, and active experimentation. (See the sidebar on page 26.)

   ◆ Approach any learning task with four questions: Why? What? How? What if? (See the sidebar on page 27.)

   ◆ Accept the occasional discomfort that comes with learning in new ways.

   ◆ Learn from any teachers you have—no matter what *their* learning styles.

3. **Relate to people with differing learning styles (page 28)**

   Learn to survive—and thrive—among people whose learning styles differ from yours:

   ◆ Become aware of how your friends, family members, and coworkers prefer to learn.

   ◆ Once you've discovered differences in learning styles, look for ways to accommodate them.

   ◆ Use your understanding of learning styles to prevent and resolve conflict.

   ◆ Use "I" messages as a way to defuse conflict. (See the sidebar on page 31.)

Entering the Culture of Higher Education

You share one thing in common with other students at your vocational school, college, or university: Entering higher education represents a change in your life. You've joined a new culture with its own set of rules, both spoken and unspoken. The skills you practice in making this transition can apply to any transition in life—from beginning a new job to starting a new relationship.

Reflect on the Art of Transition

One of the few constants in life is change. Transitions in your life can take you from high school to college, from being a freshman to tackling upper-level courses, from being a part-time student to becoming a full-time employee or business owner. These are just a few examples.

To be in transition means to stand between two worlds. The world of your immediate past is still familiar but fading in importance. Yet the new world you've entered seems unfamiliar, even frightening. The ability to dwell between two worlds is the art of making transitions. During your lifetime, you'll get many chances to master this art. You can start now.

Accept your feelings and move into action

Begin by telling yourself the unvarnished truth about how you feel. It's OK to feel anxious, isolated, homesick, or worried about making any transition. Such emotions are common among students as they enter higher education.

If you're basically mentally healthy, you always have the option to move into action—no matter how you feel. You can simply accept your feelings, whatever they are, and do something constructive. There's a saying: "Even when you feel depressed, you can still do the laundry." This idea applies to all the tasks of being a student.

Resisting or dwelling on unpleasant feelings tends to give them energy. Over time, accepting those feelings can defuse them. And because feelings are impermanent, they will naturally fade over time. In addition, being active distracts you—temporarily, and in a useful way—from feelings of fear, anxiety, or sadness. Action can even stimulate more positive feelings and change circumstances for the better.

Moving into action does not mean that you have to deny or repress your feelings. While doing something constructive, you can be aware of your feelings. Keeping a journal and sharing your feelings with trusted friends can make a huge difference in how you handle transitions.

If negative feelings persist and keep you from carrying on the tasks of daily life, then get professional help. Start with a counselor at the student health service on your campus. The mere act of seeking help can make a difference in how you feel.

Stay in the present moment

We all have a voice in our heads that hardly ever shuts up. If you don't believe it, conduct this experiment: Close your eyes for 10 seconds and pay attention to what is going on in your head. Please do this right now.

Perhaps your voice is saying, "Forget it. I'm in a hurry." Another might have said, "I wonder when 10 seconds is up." Another could have been saying, "What little voice? I don't hear any little voice." That's the voice.

This voice can take you anywhere into the past or future, at any time, especially when you are studying. When the voice takes you away, you might appear to be studying, but your brain is elsewhere in time and space.

Anxiety and fear arise when we allow this internal voice to dwell on past mistakes or imagine how

▶ sidebar

LEARN OPTIMISM

Martin Seligman, author of *Learned Optimism*, states that the key difference between optimists and pessimists is *explanatory style*—the way that they talk about events such as making transitions. Pessimists might describe the transition to higher education in ways that are:

- **Permanent:** "I'll never be able to handle college-level classes."
- **Pervasive:** "Whenever I get involved in a new situation, I always make a lot of mistakes."
- **Personal:** "I'm just no good at making transitions."

In contrast, optimists tend to make statements that can be described as:

- **Temporary:** "I'm feeling anxious about starting school, and that's normal at first."
- **Specific:** "This transition may be hard for me, but on the whole I can learn to handle change well."
- **External:** "My circumstances have changed a lot, so it's natural to find that I have a lot of new feelings."

The key point is that *over time you can learn to change your explanatory style.* Doing so can make a difference in how you think and feel about any event in your life. Notice occasions on which you talk about difficult events in terms that are permanent, pervasive, or personal. See if you can speak in ways that are more temporary, specific, and external, and then take constructive action.

events in the future could go wrong. When the voice is silent, we find that worries and regrets seem to fade. We fully experience the here and now. When we keep our focus on the present moment, we can handle almost any feeling and tackle any task that needs doing right now.

Create "zones" of stability

Not all the facets of our lives have to change at the same time. Balance transitions in one area with stability in another. While in school, keep in contact with family members and old friends. Maintain long-term relationships, including relationships with key places, such as your childhood home. Also postpone other major changes for now.

"Practice" the change

Before classes begin, get a map of your school and walk through your first day's schedule with a classmate or friend. Visit your classrooms. Locate your instructors' offices and note the hours that they're available to students. Even the simplest things you do to get familiar with a new academic routine can help.

▶ sidebar

RECALL HOW YOU MANAGED TRANSITIONS IN THE PAST

Complete the following sentences. Use the space below and continue on additional paper if needed.

Some major transitions I've experienced in my life are. . . .

During these transitions, I experienced the following feelings. . . .

I coped with these transitions by. . . .

The things that help me most in coping with transitions are. . . .

Make the Personal Transition to Higher Education

Even if you attended high school many years ago, you might find it useful to review some basic differences between high school and higher education. Higher education presents you with more choices: where to attend school, how to structure your time, where to live, and with whom to associate. In fact, it may help if you view higher education as a separate culture—a system based on a set of attitudes and behaviors that may be new to you.

Look for higher academic standards

You'll probably find that entering higher education marks a big change in academic standards. Often there are fewer tests in higher education than in high school, and the grading may be tougher. You'll probably

▶ sidebar

USEFUL SERVICES FOR STUDENTS IN HIGHER EDUCATION

The tuition and fees you pay include access to a range of resources that's hard to beat anywhere. Check your school's catalog for services such as the following. These are just a few examples. You help to pay for them, so use them.

Academic advisors can help you with selecting courses, choosing majors, career planning, and adjusting in general to the culture of higher education.

Alumni organizations can be good sources of information about the pitfalls and benefits of being a student at your school.

Arts organizations can include concert halls, museums, art galleries, observatories, and special libraries.

Athletic centers and gymnasiums often open weight rooms, swimming pools, indoor tracks, and athletic courts for students.

Chapels are usually open to students of many religions.

Child care is sometimes provided at a reasonable cost through the early-childhood education department.

Computer labs, where students can go 24 hours a day to work on projects and use the Internet, are often free.

Community resources—those located outside of the school—can range from credit counseling and chemical dependency treatment to public health clinics and churches. Check your local Yellow Pages or city Web site.

Counseling centers help students deal with the emotional pressures of school life, usually for free or at low cost.

Financial aid offices help students with loans, scholarships, grants, and work-study programs.

find that teachers expect you to study more than you did in high school. At the same time, your instructors may give you less guidance about what or how to study.

Also watch for differences in teaching styles. Teachers at colleges, universities, and vocational schools are often steeped in their subject matter. Many did not take courses in how to teach. They may not be as engaging as some of your high school teachers. And some professors are more interested in research than in teaching. Once you understand such differences, you can begin to accept and work with them.

Connect with people who can support you

To deal with the shock of entering any new culture, build support systems into your life. Cultivate new friendships, including those with members of other races and cultures. Use student services and study groups as ways to get support. Student services include career planning and placement, counseling services, financial aid, student ombudspersons, language clubs, and programs for minority students.

Job placement and career planning offices can help you find part-time employment while you are in school and a job after you graduate.

Registrars handle information about transcripts, grades, changing majors, transferring credits, and dropping or adding classes.

School media—including campus newspapers, radio stations, Web sites, and instructional television services—provide information about school policies and activities.

School security employees provide information about parking, bicycle regulations, and traffic rules. Some school security agencies will provide safe escort at night for students.

Student government can assist you to develop skills in leadership and teamwork. Many employers value this kind of experience.

Student health clinics often provide free or inexpensive treatment of minor problems. Many counseling and student health centers target certain services to people with disabilities.

Student organizations offer you an opportunity to explore fraternities, sororities, service clubs, veterans' organizations, religious groups, sports clubs, political groups, and programs for special populations. The latter include women's centers, multicultural student centers, and organizations for international students, disabled students, and gay and lesbian students.

Student unions are hubs for social activities, special programs, and free entertainment.

Tutoring programs can help even if you think you are hopelessly stuck in a course—usually for free. Student athletes and those who speak English as a second language can often get help here.

Promise yourself to meet one new person each week, and write a goal describing specific ways that you intend to do this. To begin, introduce yourself to classmates. Realize that most of the people in this new world of higher education are waiting to be welcomed. You can do that job.

Show up for class

In higher education, teachers generally don't take attendance. Yet you'll find that attending class is just as important as it's been at any time in your academic history— perhaps more important than before. The amount that you pay in tuition and fees makes a powerful argument for going to classes and getting your money's worth. And you'll probably find that the material you're tested on comes largely from events that take place in class.

"Showing up" for class means two things. The most visible is being physically present at class. Even more important, though, is showing up mentally. This mental presence includes taking detailed notes, asking questions, and contributing to class discussions.

☑ checklist

DISCOVER HOW MUCH YOU PAY TO ATTEND A CLASS

☐ Figure out how much you're paying to attend school this term. Include amounts for tuition, fees, books, child care, campus housing, food services, and transportation to and from school. In addition, estimate the amount you could earn if you were working full-time instead of attending school. Add this figure to your total costs.

☐ Figure out how many hours you're scheduled to spend in class each week. Multiply this figure by the number of weeks in your term. This is your total number of class hours for this term.

☐ Take the total cost from the first step and divide it by the total hours from the second step. The result is what you currently pay to attend one hour of class. Discovering this figure may give you financial incentive for regular attendance.

Study actively rather than passively

Some students view studying as a passive activity in which the only thing that's moving is the machinery of the mind. In reality, effective studying means expending energy—even consuming calories.

You can use simple, direct methods to infuse your learning with action. When you're at a desk, sit on the edge of your chair, as if you were about to spring out of it and sprint across the room. After reading a textbook chapter, write a summary of it. Pace back and forth and gesture as you recite material out loud. Use your hands. Get your whole body involved in studying.

Also experiment with standing up when you study. It's harder to fall asleep in this position. Your brain might work better when you alternate periods of sitting and standing.

Get involved in campus organizations and events

Many students in higher education are busier than they've ever been before. The reason is often the variety of extracurricular activities available to them: athletics, fraternities, sororities, student newspapers, debate teams, study groups, political action groups, and many more.

With this kind of involvement come potential benefits. People involved in extracurricular activities are often excellent students. Such activities help them bridge the worlds inside and outside the classroom. Through student organizations they develop new skills, explore possible careers, build contacts for jobs, and add experiences to their résumés. They make new friends among both students and faculty, work with people from other cultures, and sharpen their skills at conflict resolution.

▶ sidebar

SOME DIMENSIONS ON WHICH CULTURES DIFFER

DIFFERENCES IN WORD USAGE.
Words have different connotations across cultures—even when speakers are trying to communicate in English. Abstract terms, such as *family* and *love,* pose particular problems. So do slang terms and idioms, such as *Keep an eye out for me* or *I'm only pulling your leg.*

Dealing with such differences:
If you're speaking to someone who doesn't understand English well, keep the following ideas in mind:

- Use concrete, unambiguous terms whenever possible.
- Speak slowly and distinctly.
- To clarify your statement, restate your message in simple, direct language. Don't repeat the same words over and over again. Avoid slang.
- Because English courses for non-native speakers often emphasize written English, write down what you're saying.
- Stay calm and avoid conveying the nonverbal message that you're frustrated.

DIFFERENCES IN LEVEL OF SHARED DETAIL.
When negotiating contracts, people in the United States and many European cultures often discuss the terms in great detail. The idea is to avoid misunderstandings that come from "reading between the lines." In other cultures, the individuals involved in a negotiation may simply accept responsibility for the main outcomes without this level of discussion. They may see attempts to spell out all the details as condescending or even insulting.

Dealing with such differences:
Before you try to negotiate agreements or engage in sensitive discussions with members of another culture, find cultural "translators"—people from the minority culture who also function comfortably in the mainstream culture.

DIFFERENCES IN NONVERBAL LANGUAGE.
In many Western cultures, for example, moving the head from side to side signals disagreement. Yet to many people from India, the same gesture indicates agreement.

Dealing with such differences:
Observe the nonverbal language of people from other cultures. Do not make assumptions about what gestures mean. Be aware of your own posture, gestures, and tone of voice. When in doubt, adopt body language that is neutral.

Learn to thrive among diversity

Differing styles exist in every aspect of life—family structure, religion, relationships with authority, and more. For instance, Native Americans might avoid conflict and seek mediators. People from certain Asian cultures might feel it's rude to ask questions. Knowing about such differences can help you avoid misunderstandings.

Assume that differences in meanings exist, even if you don't know what they are. After first speaking to someone from another culture, don't assume that you've been understood or that you fully understand the other person. The same word or gesture can have different meanings at different times, even for members of the same culture. So check it out. Verify what you think you have heard. Listen to see if what you said is what the other person received.

In addition, practice looking for common ground. Some goals cross culture lines. Most people want health, physical safety, economic security, and education. Most students want to succeed in school and to prepare for a career. They often share the same teachers. They have access to many of the same resources at school. They meet in the classroom, on the athletic field, and at cultural events.

You can cultivate friends from other cultures through volunteering, serving on committees, or joining study groups—any activity in which people from other cultures are also involved. Then your understanding of other people can unfold in a natural, spontaneous way.

Thriving among diversity calls for holding two ideas in a delicate balance. One is to become aware of and celebrate our differences. The other is to remind ourselves of what we share.

Make the Financial Transition to Higher Education

Having a plan for paying for your entire education makes staying to the end a more realistic possibility. Create a master plan—a long-term budget listing how much money you need to complete your education and where you plan to get the money each year.

Financial aid includes money you don't pay back (grants and scholarships), money you do pay back (loans), and work-study programs that provide you a job while you're in school. Most students receive a package that includes several of these elements.

Once you receive financial aid, keep it flowing. Find out the requirements for keeping your loans, grants, and scholarships. Also get to know someone in the financial aid office at your school and chat with that person at least once each term. Ask about new programs and changes to existing programs. Remember that many financial aid packages are contingent on your making "satisfactory academic progress."

Monitor your income and expenses

Each month, review your checkbook, receipts, and other financial records. You could also write down each cash purchase you make on a 3x5 card or track your expenses with computer software.

▶ sidebar

TEN WAYS TO FUND YOUR HIGHER EDUCATION

Visit the financial aid office at your school to ask about the following sources of money:

1. **Federal grants** such as Pell Grants and Supplemental Educational Opportunity Grants (SEOG) do not have to be repaid. Also check with your state office of higher education for sources of grants.

2. **Work-study** programs arrange for jobs on or off campus. Your hours of work will be based on your class schedule and your academic progress.

3. **Loans** come in many forms. Perkins Loans are long-term loans based on financial need and have low interest rates. Federal loan programs offer low-interest loans from banks and credit unions. Ask about Stafford Loans, supplemental loans, consolidation loans, Ford Direct Student Loans, and the PLUS program (Parent Loans for Undergraduate Students).

4. **Scholarships** are available through most schools for outstanding performance in athletics, academics, or the arts. Some scholarships are based solely on financial need. Also inquire about scholarships from fraternal and community organizations, such as the Chamber of Commerce.

5. **Armed services offices,** such as the Veterans Administration, have money available for some veterans and their dependents. Active military personnel can take advantage of various financial aid programs by contacting their local personnel office.

6. **Tuition reimbursement programs** provided by employers offer financial aid for employees to attend school while working.

7. **Social Security payments** are available up to age 18 for unmarried students with a deceased parent or a parent who is disabled or drawing Social Security benefits.

8. **Relatives** will often provide financial help for a dedicated student.

9. **Personal savings** make up the bulk of money spent on higher education. To supplement savings, you can sell property or collect income from investments.

10. **Employment** is another way that students can get additional money. Working in a job related to your future career can supplement your education, as well as your finances.

Sort your expenses into major categories, such as groceries, eating out, entertainment, tuition, fees, transportation, and housing. Each month, total up how much you spend in these categories. You might be surprised at how much you spend on items such as fast-food and CDs. Once you know the actual amounts involved, you may find yourself decreasing these expenses automatically. That's the power of awareness.

Plan to reduce expenses

For many people, making more money is the most appealing way to fix a broken budget. However, when their income increases, most people continue to spend more than they make. You can avoid this dilemma by managing your expenses no matter how much money you make:

- **Look to the big-ticket items.** Your choices about which car to buy or where to live can save you tens of thousands of dollars.
- **Look to the small-ticket items.** Decreasing the money you spend on very small purchases can make the difference between a balanced budget and uncomfortable debt. That three-dollar cappuccino is tasty, but the amount that some people spend on them over the course of a year could give anyone the jitters.
- **Cook for yourself.** Instead of eating out, head to the grocery store. Shop for nutrition and value. Fresh fruits, vegetables, and whole grains not only are better for you than processed food, but they also cost less.
- **Keep your housing costs reasonable.** Sometimes a place a little farther from school or a little smaller will be much less expensive. You can keep your housing costs down by finding a roommate. Also look for opportunities to house-sit.
- **Notice what you spend on "fun."** Before you spend money on entertainment, ask yourself what the benefits will be and whether you could get the same benefits for less money. Free entertainment is everywhere.
- **Use public transportation or car pools.** A car can be the biggest financial burden in a student's budget.
- **Postpone purchases.** When you are ready to buy something, wait a week. What seems like a necessity today may not even cross your mind the day after tomorrow.

☑ checklist

USE CREDIT CARDS WITH CAUTION

Used wisely, credit cards can help us become conscious of what we spend. Used unwisely, they can leave us with a debt load that takes decades to pay down. The following three steps can help you take control of your credit card before it takes control of you. Write these steps on a 3x5 card, and don't leave home without it.

❏ **Tell the truth.** If you rely on credit cards to make ends meet every month, admit it. If you typically charge up the limit of your credit line and pay just the minimum balance each month, tell the truth about that, also. Discover what doesn't work—and what does work—about the way you use credit cards. Follow up by writing goals expressing how you plan to use your cards differently.

❏ **Scrutinize credit card offers.** Beware of cards offering low interest rates. These rates are often temporary. After a few months, they could double or triple. To simplify your financial life, consider using only one card.

❏ **Pay off the balance each month.** Keep track of how much you spend with credit cards each month. Then save an equal amount in cash. That way, you can pay off the card balance each month and avoid interest charges.

Handle the Health Demands of Transition

Healthy people meet the demands of daily life with energy to spare. Illness or stress may slow them down for a while, but then they bounce back. Preserving your health is one way to maintain the personal resources needed to succeed in higher education.

Eat for health and pleasure

By acting on three simple guidelines, you can eat to maintain energy, manage weight, and prevent disease:

- **Quantity.** The National Health and Nutrition Examination Surveys, a program from the Centers for Disease Control, confirm that Americans are eating too much. According to the 1999–2000 data, 65 percent of Americans are overweight; 31 percent are obese. To avoid becoming one of these statistics, begin by choosing *how much* you eat. Notice portion sizes. Pass on seconds and desserts.

- **Quality.** To prevent heart disease and cancer—major sources of premature death in developed countries—the United States Department of Agriculture now recommends a plant-based diet. Build most of your meals from plant foods—whole grains, fruits, and vegetables. You can get complete proteins from low-fat dairy products, lean meats, and soy foods. It's fine to enjoy fats and sweets, as long as you do so occasionally and in moderation. Also, keep in mind that your body is mostly water, so drink plenty of water each day.

- **Enjoyment.** Eating can be one of life's greatest pleasures. Take the time to enjoy your food. If you eat slowly and savor each bite, you can be satisfied with smaller portions— a way to reduce calories while increasing your enjoyment. Use mealtimes as chances to relax, reduce stress, and connect with people.

> ## sidebar
>
> ### TEN WAYS TO LOSE TEN POUNDS THIS YEAR
>
> According to a report from the U.S. Surgeon General, all of the following activities will burn an average of 150 calories per day, which translates into losing 10 pounds per year:
>
> - Climb stairs for 15 minutes.
> - Dance for 30 minutes.
> - Rake leaves for 30 minutes.
> - Run 1.5 miles in 15 minutes.
> - Shovel snow for 15 minutes.
> - Swim laps for 20 minutes.
> - Walk 2 miles in 30 minutes.
> - Bicycle 5 miles in 30 minutes.
> - Garden for 30 to 45 minutes.
> - Jump rope for 15 minutes.
>
> *These figures are based on the assumption that the number of calories you eat remains constant.* To double your potential weight loss, consume 150 calories less each day. As a point of reference, remember that a small chocolate chip cookie contains about 50 calories. A jelly-filled doughnut weighs in at 300 calories.

For more governmental guidelines on nutrition, visit the following Web site: http://www.health.gov/dietaryguidelines/dga2000/document/frontcover.htm.

Do exercise you enjoy

Regular exercise can improve your performance in school. Your brain usually functions better if the rest of your body is in shape, and exercise is one way to dissipate the tension that you build up while hunched over a keyboard hammering out a term paper.

Dieting alone doesn't create lean muscles and a strong heart. The only way to get lean is by moving. The formula for weight loss is simple: Eat better food, eat less food, and exercise.

Do something you enjoy. Start by walking briskly for at least 15 minutes every day. Increase that time gradually, and add a little running. Once you're in reasonable shape, you can stay there by doing aerobic activity on most days of the week. An hour of daily activity is ideal, but do whatever you can. Some activity is better than none.

Manage stress

Stress, at appropriate times and at manageable levels, is normal and useful. It can sharpen your awareness and boost your energy just when you need it the most. When stress persists or becomes excessive, however, it can be harmful.

Chances are that your stress level is too high if you consistently experience:

- Irritability
- Feelings of helplessness or persistent sadness
- Lowered productivity
- Strained relationships
- Health problems, such as upset stomach, frequent colds, and low energy level
- Difficulty falling asleep or staying asleep
- A persistent feeling of burnout

There are two things you can do as first aid for stress:

- **Learn to relax.** There are many types of relaxation exercises, ranging from yoga to guided visualization. One of the simplest is to close your eyes, sit in a relaxed yet upright position, and count your breaths. As thoughts and body sensations arise, just notice them and let them go. Over time, and with consistent practice, your mind will gradually clear.
- **Get aerobic exercise.** Vigorous movement is good for your heart, and it's also good for your mood. Exercise releases mood-altering chemicals in your brain and releases tensions.

If self-help techniques such as these don't work within a few weeks, get help. Check with the student health service on your campus.

Make the Transition from Education to Work

Many students view career planning as something to do during the last semester of the senior year. However, you're more likely to graduate to a

▶ sidebar

KNOW WHEN TO GET HELP FOR ALCOHOL OR OTHER DRUG ABUSE

In 2001, the College Alcohol Study from the Harvard School of Public Health found that 44 percent of college students classified themselves as binge drinkers. This finding was almost identical to results from companion surveys in 1993, 1997, and 1999. In these surveys, binge drinking was defined as consuming at least four alcoholic drinks in a row on a single occasion during the previous month.

Lectures giving reasons to avoid alcohol and other drug abuse can be pointless. Ultimately, we don't take care of our bodies because someone says we *should*. We might take care of ourselves when we see that use of chemicals is costing us more than we're getting. Following are signs that the costs are getting too high:

- Negative consequences due to alcohol or other drug use—falling grades, loss of interest in activities one used to value, or compromised relationships with friends or family.
- Regular drug use to relieve tension ("What a day! I need a drink.").
- Medical problems—stomach trouble, malnutrition, liver problems, anemia—that could be related to drinking or other drugs.
- Deciding to quit drugs or alcohol and then changing one's mind because it's too difficult.
- Having fights or accidents related to drinking or drugs.
- Getting in trouble with the police after or while drinking.
- Missing school or work due to a hangover.
- Having a blackout—a period of time one can't remember—after drinking.
- Financial stress due to the amounts of money spent on alcohol or other drugs.
- Needing increasing amounts of a drug to produce a desired effect.
- Experiencing withdrawal symptoms when trying to stop using a drug.
- Spending a great deal of time obtaining and using alcohol or other drugs.
- Using alcohol or another drug when it is physically dangerous to do so, such as when driving a car or working with machines.

When people continue to use alcohol or other drugs despite negative consequences, they're abusing chemicals. If they find it impossible to stop using on their own, they may be alcoholics or addicts.

Exhibiting any of the signs on the preceding list can indicate a need for help. The student health services at most schools can provide options. There are many—everything from confidential counseling and self-help groups to formal treatment programs. Taking charge of one's relationship to alcohol and other drugs can remove one of the greatest obstacles to success in higher education.

satisfying career if you start thinking about your career the moment that you enter higher education. You'll find suggestions for career planning in Chapter 8. But well before you plan a career or even choose a major, you can start forging connections between the world of education and the world of work.

Start a résumé now

Write a rough draft of your résumé now, even if you're not hunting for a job. Typically, a **résumé** is a fact sheet designed to help you land a job interview. However, drafting a rough résumé and continually updating it is one way to keep a record of your skills and achievements that might interest an employer in the future.

Keep in mind that a résumé is a piece of persuasive writing, not a dry recitation of facts. Write your résumé so that positive facts about you leap off the page. Describe your work experiences in short phrases that start with active verbs such as:

- *Supervised* three people.
- *Wrote* two annual reports.
- *Set up* sales calls.
- *Designed* a training program for new employees.

Show in your résumé that you understand the types of problems organizations face—and that you can offer your skills as solutions. Whenever you can, give evidence that you've used job skills to produce measurable results. For example: "Our program reduced the average training time for newly hired people by 25 percent." (For help in defining your job skills and career interests, see Chapter 8.)

Adding items to your résumé raises awareness of your strengths and helps you celebrate your accomplishments. Someday, when a job interviewer asks, "What can you offer my company?" you'll be ready with an answer.

Start a portfolio now

Although a **portfolio** might include the kinds of facts typically found in a résumé, it also includes tangible objects to verify those facts. These objects can be anything from transcripts of your grades to a video you produced. Résumés offer *facts*; portfolios provide *artifacts*.

Start building job contacts now

In addition to logging your skills and accomplishments, keep a list of key people you meet along the way. These include people who supervise you on jobs, internships, or volunteer projects. Also list teachers who know you well and can vouch for the quality of your work. Any of these people could serve as references, sources of recommendation letters, and even contacts for part-time or permanent jobs.

☑ checklist

WHAT TO INCLUDE IN YOUR RÉSUMÉ AND PORTFOLIO

The main headings to include in your **résumé** are:

❏ *Personal data*—your name, address, and contact information (phone number and e-mail address)

❏ *Desired job*, sometimes called an *objective* or *goal*

❏ *Skills*

❏ *Work experience*

❏ *Education*—a list of your degrees and the schools you've attended

The trick is to get all this information on one page. Hit the high points and keep sentences short. Make your résumé easy to skim by using bulleted lists under each heading.

To build the sections on skills and work experience, keep track of your accomplishments. Describe any rewards or citations you've received. List any special assignments you've completed for classes. Also, review the skills you developed during field experiences, internships, volunteer work, and previous jobs.

In addition, keep the following items on hand as possible artifacts for your **portfolio:**

❏ Brochures describing a product or service you created or provided

❏ Certificates, licenses, and awards

❏ Computer disks with sample publications, databases, or computer programs you've created

❏ Course descriptions and syllabi from classes you've taken or taught

❏ Formal evaluations of your work

❏ Job descriptions from positions you've held

❏ Letters of recommendation

❏ Lists of grants, scholarships, clients, customers, and organizations you've joined

❏ Newspaper and magazine articles about projects you participated in

❏ Objects you've created or received—anything from badges to jewelry

❏ Printouts of e-mail and Web pages (including your personal Web page)

❏ Programs from artistic performances or exhibitions

❏ Tapes (video or audio), compact discs, or CD-ROMs

❏ Transcripts of grades, test scores, vocational aptitude tests, or learning styles inventories

❏ Visual art, including drawings, photographs, collages, and computer graphics

❏ Writing samples, such as class reports, workplace memos, proposals, policy and mission statements, bids, manuscripts for articles and books, and published pieces or bibliographies of published writing

chapter

Using the Cycle of Learning

You've probably observed that people learn in different ways. Some like to think about facts and theories. Some learn better by direct experience, whereas others prefer to observe and reflect. And some people warm up to studying only when they see a direct connection between their interests and what they're asked to learn.

There's a term that points to such differences in people—*learning styles*. An understanding of learning styles offers direct benefits. You can create conditions under which you learn in ways that you prefer. You can absorb new ideas more efficiently and master new tasks in less time. In addition, you can choose more classes that you'll enjoy, declare a major that's in tune with your interests, and sort out your career options with more confidence.

Knowing about learning styles also allows you to work more effectively with other people. Understanding how people differ when they study in groups or tackle projects at work can help you get more done in teams. Understanding their learning styles can help you give better instructions, delegate tasks more appropriately, and resolve conflicts.

Look for Differences in Perception and Processing

When we learn, two things initially happen:

- We *perceive*. We notice events and use our senses to take in what we see, hear, and feel.
- We *process*. We mentally organize our perceptions in a way that helps us make sense of them.

The concept of *learning styles* acknowledges that people vary in how they prefer to perceive and process information.

Psychologists have created many theories about learning styles. One of the most well known is David Kolb's theory of experiential learning. According to Kolb, learning takes place in four modes:

1. **Concrete experience.** During this phase, you value tangible experiences that have a personal meaning for you. You could describe this mode as learning by *feeling*.
2. **Reflective observation.** Here you take time to notice what's going on around you and plan ways to respond. This mode involves learning by *watching*.
3. **Abstract conceptualization.** During this mode, you integrate your initial observations into more complex concepts and theories. This phase is also described as learning by *thinking*.
4. **Active experimentation.** During this phase, you apply ideas, test theories, and use new knowledge to influence other people. This phase involves learning by *doing*.

These four modes are elements of a complex theory. Even so, they describe *any* learning situation—from learning to drive a car to mastering the fine points of molecular biology. Say that you want to learn how to play rock guitar. You could use all four modes of learning to master this style of music:

1. You start with *concrete experiences*—listening to recordings that feature the guitar, placing a guitar in your hands and learning how to hold it, asking a guitar-playing friend to show you a few chords or melodic figures, and trying them out yourself.
2. You make *reflective observations* by going to see bands, watching what skilled guitar players do, and evaluating their techniques.
3. You engage in *abstract conceptualization* by taking lessons, studying instructional texts, and learning about music theory.
4. You *actively experiment* with concepts by forming a band of your own, conducting rehearsals, and scheduling some "gigs"—live performances. In turn, this provides you with concrete experiences to reflect on. From here you naturally cycle through the four modes of learning again.

Three points are especially important here. First, learning is the most natural thing you do. In fact, you are learning constantly from your day-to-day experiences, inside and outside the classroom. Second, none of the four modes is better than the others. Rather, they are all useful and worth exploring. Finally, the modes of learning create a cycle—not a

☑ checklist

EXPLORE YOUR LEARNING STYLES

Recall a recent learning experience—inside *or* outside the classroom—that you enjoyed. Then read through the following list and check off any statements that apply to you.

❐ I enjoy learning in ways that involve all my senses.

❐ When solving problems, I often rely on intuition as much as logical reasoning.

❐ I function well in unstructured learning situations in which I can take the initiative.

❐ Before taking action, I prefer to watch and ponder what's going on.

❐ I like to consider different points of view and generate many ideas about how things happen.

❐ When trying to understand information, I value patience, good judgment, and thoroughness.

❐ I enjoy intellectual analysis and like to view information from many perspectives.

❐ I value the scientific approach—using theories to make sense of experiences, creating predictions based on those theories, and testing those predictions.

❐ I usually excel in learning situations that are well defined and highly structured.

❐ Activity helps me learn, so I like to jump in and start doing things immediately.

❐ I like to use learning to produce new results in my life.

❐ I look for practical ways to apply what I learn.

In the preceding list, the first three items describe a preference for learning through concrete experience. The next three items illustrate learning through reflective observation. The following three describe conceptualization, and the final three refer to active experimentation.

This checklist is not a formal assessment of learning styles. Instead, it offers a way to start thinking about how you prefer to learn. For more information on learning style assessments, access the Master Student Guide to Academic Success Web site at masterstudent.college.hmco.com.

linear series of steps but a continuing process that you can use in many situations for the rest of your life.

Build the Complete Cycle of Learning into Your Courses

There's a saying: "Experience is the best teacher." Someone who thought critically about that statement said, "Beware the person with 20 years of experience. That's one year of experience followed by 19 years of repetition." The point is that we can learn from experience in many ways, and some are more powerful than others.

One way to learn more effectively is to see learning as a cycle that involves all four of the modes described previously. You can seek educational experiences that match your preferences, and you can expand your preferences so that you can learn in new ways. According to the theory of experiential learning, successful students:

- Involve themselves fully, openly, and without bias in new situations (learning through *concrete experience*).
- Make observations and think about them from many perspectives (learning through *reflective observation*).
- Create concepts that integrate their observations and initial ideas into logically sound theories (learning through *abstract conceptualization*).
- Test theories by making predictions and decisions, taking action, and solving problems (learning though *active experimentation*).

As you move through each of these modes, you complete the full cycle of learning and gain more from your educational experiences.

Approach any task with four questions

You might find that the way a teacher teaches is not always the way you prefer learning and that your teachers don't always promote all four phases of learning. To get more of what you need from your experiences in higher education, ask the following questions. Each one describes a different learning style; that is, a unique way of combining the four modes of learning described previously.

To capitalize on your preferred learning style, begin with the question that matters most to you. To explore other styles and increase the depth of your learning, ask and answer all four questions.

1. **Why?** Seek a rationale for your learning. Understand why it is important for you to learn about a specific topic or acquire a new skill. Find a purpose for acquiring new information and a personal connection with the content of a course. Ask how new information and ideas relate to what you already know.
2. **What?** Discover the key concepts and facts relating to a topic, the main steps in a procedure, or the key skills involved in a performance. Look for a theory or model to explain the key events you observe. Find out what experts have to say about the topic. Take thorough notes during lectures and complete all reading assignments.
3. **How?** Ask questions that help you understand how a process works and how you can test new ideas. Also look for opportunities to apply your learning through hands-on practice. You can conduct experiments, do projects, complete homework, create presentations, conduct research, tabulate findings, or even write a song that summarizes key concepts.

▶ sidebar

USE ALL FOUR MODES OF LEARNING

TO GAIN CONCRETE EXPERIENCE:

- See a live demonstration or performance related to your course content.
- Engage your emotions by reading a novel or seeing a film related to your course.
- Interview an expert in the subject you're learning or a master practitioner of a skill you want to gain.
- Conduct role-plays, exercises, or games based on your courses.
- Conduct an information interview with someone in your chosen career or "shadow" that person for a day on the job.
- Look for a part-time job, internship, or volunteer experience that complements what you do in class.
- Deepen your understanding of another culture and extend your foreign language skills by studying abroad.

TO PROMOTE REFLECTIVE OBSERVATION:

- Keep a personal journal and write about connections between your courses.
- Form a study group to discuss and debate topics related to your courses.
- Set up a Web site, computer bulletin board, e-mail list, or online chat room related to your major.
- Create analogies to make sense of concepts; for instance, see if you can find similarities between career planning and putting together a puzzle.
- Visit your course instructor during office hours to ask questions.
- During social events with friends and relatives, briefly explain what your courses are about.

TO PROMOTE ABSTRACT CONCEPTUALIZATION:

- Take notes on your reading in outline form; consider using word processing software with an outlining feature.
- Supplement assigned texts with other books, magazine and newspaper articles, and related Web sites.
- Attend lectures, by your current instructors and by others who teach the same subjects.
- Take ideas presented in text or lectures and translate them into visual form: tables, charts, diagrams, and maps (see Chapter 13).
- Take hand-drawn visuals and use computer software to recreate them with more complex graphics and animation.

TO PROMOTE ACTIVE EXPERIMENTATION:

- Conduct laboratory experiments or field observations.
- Go to settings in which theories are being applied or tested.
- Make predictions based on theories you learn and see if events in your daily life confirm your predictions.
- Try out a new behavior—such as a suggestion from this book—and observe its consequences in your life.

▶ sidebar

FOUR QUESTIONS THAT APPLY TO LEARNING ANYTHING

When we're learning well, we answer questions. According to David Kolb's theory of experiential learning, these four questions are especially important:

- **Why?** Discover a *purpose* for what you're learning.
- **What?** Master the *content*—the key ideas, information, and skills.
- **How?** Look for ways to *practice* what you learn.
- **What if?** Explore ways to *apply* new ideas and skills in several areas of your life.

4. **What if?** Test the implications of new ideas. Go beyond the classroom by adapting what you're learning to a different setting or another issue that you care about. Determine other areas in your life to which you can apply what you have just learned. If you enjoy keeping a journal for an English class, for example, then consider how keeping a journal can help you in a science or math class. Also seek opportunities to demonstrate your understanding. You could teach what you've learned to members of a study group, present findings from your research, report results from your experiments, or demonstrate how your project works.

Accept change and occasional discomfort

Your preferred learning styles can evolve and change over time. If your instructor asks you to form a group to complete an assignment, avoid joining a group in which everyone shares your learning style. Work on project teams with people who learn differently from you. Get together with people who both complement and challenge you.

Also look for situations in which you can safely practice new skills. If you enjoy reading, for example, look for ways to express what you learn by speaking, such as leading a study group on a textbook chapter.

Discomfort is a natural part of the learning process. Allow yourself to notice any struggle with a task or lack of interest in completing it. Remember that such feelings are temporary and that you are balancing your learning preferences. By choosing to move through discomfort, you consciously expand your ability to learn in new ways.

Learn from teachers—no matter what their style

When they experience difficulty in school, some students say:

- The instructor can't teach me.
- The classroom is not conducive to the way I learn.
- This teacher creates tests that are too hard for me.
- In class, we never have time for questions.
- The instructor doesn't teach to my learning style.

Such statements may be accurate. They can also prevent you from taking charge of your learning. As an alternative, you could make statements such as these:

- I will see my instructor outside of class to ask specific questions about what confuses me.
- To supplement this course, I will seek out-of-classroom experiences that match my learning style.
- I will discover whether my struggles with tests are due to gaps in my knowledge or to test-taking anxiety that makes it hard for me to remember what I already know.
- I can see this course as a chance to develop a new learning style.

Relate to People with Differing Learning Styles

As higher education and the workplace become more diverse and technology creates a global marketplace, you'll meet people who differ from you in profound ways. Your fellow students and coworkers will behave in ways that express a variety of preferences for perceiving information, processing ideas, and acting on what they learn. For example:

- A roommate who's continually moving while studying—reciting facts out loud, pacing, and gesturing—probably prefers concrete experience and learning by taking action.
- A coworker who talks continually on the phone about a project may prefer to learn by listening, talking, and forging key relationships.
- A supervisor who excels at abstract conceptualization may want to see detailed project plans and budgets submitted in writing well before a project swings into high gear.

Differences in learning style can be a stumbling block or an opportunity. When differences intersect, we have the potential for conflict and for creativity. Succeeding with peers often means seeing the classroom and workplace as a laboratory for learning from experience. Resolving conflict and learning from mistakes are all part of the learning cycle.

Discover the styles of people around you

You can learn a lot about other people's styles simply by observing them during the workday. Look for clues such as:

- **Approaches to a task that requires learning.** Some people process new information and ideas by sitting quietly and reading or writing. When learning to use a piece of equipment, such as a new computer, they'll read the instruction manual first. Others will skip the manual, unpack all the boxes, and start setting up equipment. And others might ask a more experienced colleague to guide them in person, step by step.

- **Word choice.** Some people like to process information visually. You might hear them say, "I'll look into that" or "Give me the big picture first." Others like to solve problems verbally: "Let's talk though this problem" or "I hear you!" In contrast, some people focus on body sensations ("This product feels great") or action ("Let's run with this idea and see what happens").
- **Body language.** Notice how often coworkers or classmates make eye contact with you and how close they sit or stand next to you. Observe their gestures, as well as the volume and tone of their voices.
- **Content preferences.** Notice what subjects they openly discuss and which topics they avoid. Some people talk freely about their feelings, their families, and even their personal finances. Others choose to remain silent on such topics and stick to work-related matters.
- **Process preferences.** Look for patterns in the ways that your coworkers and classmates meet goals. When attending meetings, for example, some might stick closely to the agenda and keep an eye on the clock. Other people might prefer to "go with the flow," even if it means working an extra hour or scrapping the agenda.

Accommodate differing styles

Once you've discovered differences in styles, look for ways to accommodate them. As you collaborate on projects with other students or coworkers, keep the following suggestions in mind:

- **Remember that some people want to reflect on the "big picture" first.** When introducing a project plan, you might say, "This process has four major steps." Before explaining the plan in detail, talk about the purpose of the project and the benefits of completing each step.
- **Allow time for active experimentation and concrete experience.** Offer people a chance to try out a new product or process for themselves—to literally "get the feel of it."
- **Allow for abstract conceptualization.** When leading a study group or conducting a training session, provide handouts that include plenty of visuals and step-by-step instructions. Visual learners and people who like to think abstractly will appreciate it. Also schedule periods for questions and answers.

- **When designing a project, encourage people to answer key questions.** Remember the four essential questions that guide learning. Answering *Why?* means defining the purpose and desired outcomes of the project. Answering *What?* means assigning major tasks, setting due dates for each task, and generating commitment to action. Answering *How?* means carrying out assigned tasks and meeting regularly to discuss what's working well and ways to improve the project. And answering *What if?* means discussing what the team has learned from the project and ways to apply that learning to the whole class or larger organization.
- **When working on teams, look for ways to complement each other's strengths.** If you're skilled at planning, find someone who excels at doing. Also seek people who can reflect on and interpret the team's experience. Pooling different styles allows you to draw on everyone's strengths.

Resolve conflict with respect for styles

When people's styles clash in educational or work settings, we have several options. One is to throw up our hands and resign ourselves to personality conflicts. Another option is to recognize differences, accept them, and respect them as complementary ways to meet common goals. From that perspective, you can:

- **Resolve conflict within yourself.** You might have mental pictures about classrooms and workplaces as places where people are all "supposed" to have the same style. Notice those pictures and gently let them go. If you *expect* to find differences in styles, you can more easily respect those differences.
- **Introduce a conversation about learning styles.** Attend a workshop on learning styles or bring such training directly to your classroom or office.
- **Let people take on tasks that fit their learning styles.** As you do, remember that style is both stable and dynamic. People gravitate toward the kinds of tasks they've succeeded at in the past. They can also broaden their styles by tackling new tasks to reinforce different modes of learning.
- **Rephrase complaints as requests.** "This class is a waste of my time" can be recast as "Please tell me what I'll gain if I participate actively in class." "The instructor talks too fast" can become "What strategies can I use for taking notes when the instructor covers the material rapidly?"

sidebar

RESOLVE CONFLICT WITH "I" MESSAGES

"You make me mad."
"You must be crazy."
"You don't love me anymore."
   "You" messages are hard to listen to. They label, judge, blame, and assume things that may or may not be true. They demand rebuttal.
   When communication is emotionally charged, replace "You" messages with "I" messages.

"You are rude" might become *"I feel upset."*
"You make me mad" could be *"I feel angry."*
"You must be crazy" can be *"I don't understand."*
   An "I" message can include any or all of the following five parts:

- **Observations.** Describe the facts—the indisputable, observable realities. Avoid judgments, interpretations, or opinions. Instead of saying, "You're a slob," say, "Last night's lasagna pan was still on the stove this morning."
- **Feelings.** Describe your own feelings. It is easier to listen to "I feel frustrated" than to "You never help me."
- **Wants.** You are far more likely to get what you want if you say what you want. Ask clearly. Instead of "Do the dishes when it's your turn, or else!" say, "I want to divide the housework fairly."
- **Thoughts.** Use caution here. Beginning your statement with an "I" doesn't always make it an "I" message. "I think you are a slob" is a "You" judgment in disguise. Instead, say, "I'd have more time to study if I didn't have to clean up so often."
- **Intentions.** State what you intend to do. Have a plan that doesn't depend on the other person. For example, instead of "From now on we're going to split the dishwashing evenly," you could say, "I intend to do my share of the housework and leave the rest undone."

Experiment with Learning Strategies

Psychologists often define learning as *an enduring change in behavior*. They create theories that predict the outcomes of particular behaviors. As scientists, psychologists also design experiments to test those predictions.

   This book presents a chance for you to become a working psychologist, with the main subject of study being yourself. In the chapters to come, you'll find dozens of suggestions for specific learning strategies that can promote your success in higher education and in your career.

Each chapter ends with an exercise designed to help you test these suggestions and change your own behavior over the long term. The steps in these exercises are based on the cycle of learning as explained in this chapter:

- **Ask *Why?* to discover possible benefits from chapter content.** When reading about note-taking strategies, for example, consider the positive differences that more effective notes could make. These might include better retention of key concepts, more efficient review for tests, and higher grades.

- **Ask *What?* to focus on a specific suggestion.** Review the suggestions in the chapter and list 5 or 10 that interest you. From this list, choose one that you'd be willing to start using in the next 24 hours and to use consistently for at least one week. Choose a behavior with the potential to make a tremendous impact on your life.

- **Ask How? to apply that suggestion during the coming week.** Think of a specific time and place to use your chosen suggestion, or schedule a time in your calendar to do it.

- **Ask *What if?* to reflect on your experience.** At the end of the week, evaluate how well the suggestion worked for you. If it worked well, consider making it habit. If the suggestion did not work well, ask why. Perhaps you can modify the suggestion so that it becomes a better fit for you. You may find that some suggestions simply don't work for you. If so, put them on the shelf for now and reconsider them later.

- **Repeat these steps with another suggestion.** Come back to your list of suggestions and choose another one to apply. Again, plan where and when you will act on that suggestion during the coming week. Then evaluate how well the suggestion worked for you. Repeating this cycle of choosing, applying, and evaluating suggestions can quickly increase your effectiveness in higher education and in any career that you choose.

THINKING CRITICALLY AND CREATIVELY

Quick Reference Guide to THINKING CRITICALLY AND CREATIVELY

3. EVALUATING IDEAS

Critical thinking is a path to freedom from half-truths and deception—one of the major goals of a liberal education.

1. **Start with attitudes (page 35)**
    The overall attitudes of critical thinkers are at least as important as their arsenal of skills. (See the sidebar on page 37).

2. **Look for assumptions (page 36)**
    A useful place to begin any exercise in critical thinking is looking for assumptions—the foundation of our opinions:
    ◆ Discover assumptions that are unstated and even held unconsciously. (See the examples on page 37.)
    ◆ Notice when speakers and writers are thorough enough to explicitly state their assumptions.

3. **Look for arguments (page 39)**
    Argument refers to series of assertions that are clear, coherent, and consistent. To discover them:
    ◆ "Come to terms" with a speaker or writer by finding definitions of their most important concepts.
    ◆ Understand the types of definitions. (See the sidebar on page 41).
    ◆ Also look for *assertions*—sentences that state the relationships between terms.

4. **Examine logic (page 42)**
    Use the tools of logic to discover assertions that contradict each other or rest on ambiguous terms:
    ◆ Recognize *deductive reasoning*, which starts with a general assertion and derives other assertions from it.
    ◆ Look for *inductive reasoning*, which starts with experiences and specific examples and moves to a general conclusion.
    ◆ Discover fallacies in logic by finding exceptions to implied assertions. (See the sidebar on page 44).

5. **Examine evidence (page 44)**
    Evidence for assertions comes in several forms, including facts, expert testimony, and examples.

Learn to evaluate evidence. (See the checklist on page 46).

4. CREATING NEW IDEAS

You can use thinking skills to create knowledge, as well as evaluate it.

1. **Brainstorm (page 48)**
    Use a set of techniques to generate as many ideas as possible in a short time. (See the sidebar on page 49).

2. **Play with ideas (page 50)**
    Use a variety of strategies to sustain creative thinking and refine your ideas:
    ◆ Read voraciously from many sources.
    ◆ Keep a journal to record your observations of the world around you, quotes from friends, important or offbeat ideas—anything.
    ◆ Keep your eyes open for an unmet need.
    ◆ Live with unanswered questions and let answers "simmer" in your subconscious mind.
    ◆ Remember that creativity often amounts to taking old ideas and combining them in new ways.
    ◆ Look for the obvious "truths" about a subject or the obvious solutions to a problem—then look for alternatives.
    ◆ Use a set of questions to generate new ideas. (See the checklist on page 55).

3. **Refine ideas (page 55)**
    Use the tools of critical thinking to follow up on your ideas and discover applications for them.

5. MAKING DECISIONS AND SOLVING PROBLEMS

Your skills in thinking culminate in your ability to make decisions and solve problems in daily life.

1. **Decisions create results, decrease options, and imply action (page 58)**
    Our lives are largely a result of the decisions we've made and the actions that flow from those decisions. When we truly make a decision, we give up actions that are inconsistent with it.

2. **Practice the art and science of decision making (page 59)**

Decision making involves both intellect and intuition, action and reflection. To make better decisions, remember the four *I*'s:

- Investigate
- Imagine
- Incubate
- Insight

(See the checklist on page 62).

3. **Problems present another layer of complexity (page 62)**

Decisions often boil down to answering a single question. Problem solving, on the other hand, calls for making a *series* of decisions and answering open-ended questions.

4. **Solve problems in four phases (page 63)**

Experiment with four *P*'s of problem solving:

1. State the **P**roblem.
2. Create **P**ossibilities for solutions.
3. Create a **P**lan to implement the most effective solution.
4. **P**erform your plan and evaluate the results. (See the checklist on page 65).

4. **Expand your skills by working in groups (page 65)**

Groups can often come up with more information, brainstorm more ideas, and generate more solutions than individuals working alone. To get the most benefits from working in groups:

- Draw up a list of ground rules or basic agreements about how the group will operate *before* considering a specific decision or problem.
- Consider operating by consensus on some issues—asking that all members agree to a decision or solution.
- Use the Decreasing Options Technique to sort and prioritize dozens of ideas, reducing them to a manageable number for discussion. (See the checklist on page 67).

Evaluating Ideas

C **ritical thinking underlies** reading, writing, speaking, and listening. These are the basic elements of communication—a process that defines much of what you do in higher education and occupies most of your waking hours.

Critical thinking is a skill that will never go out of style. History offers a continuing story of half-truths, faulty assumptions, and other nonsense once commonly accepted as true, such as the following statements:

- Illness results from an imbalance in the four vital fluids: blood, phlegm, water, and bile.
- Caucasians are inherently more intelligent than people of other races.
- Women are incapable of voting intelligently.

In response to such ideas rose the critical thinkers of history. Critical thinking is a path to freedom from half-truths and deception. This path rests on your right to question everything that you see, hear, and read. Acquiring the ability to evaluate ideas is one of the major goals of a liberal education.

Start with Attitudes

Critical thinking is an approach to the world, a way of life that goes beyond skill or technique. Critical thinkers have hearts as well as heads, and their overall attitudes or habits of mind are at least as important as their arsenal of skills.

The American Philosophical Association invited 46 scholars from the United States and Canada to agree on answers to two questions: What is college-level critical thinking? and What leads us to conclude that a person is an effective critical thinker? After 2 years of work, this panel concluded that critical thinkers are:

- **Truth seeking.** Critical thinkers want to know truth. In their quest, they are willing to consider and even accept ideas that undermine their assumptions or self-interest. These thinkers follow reason and evidence wherever they lead.
- **Open-minded.** A skilled critical thinker not only recognizes that people disagree–but also values this fact. She respects the right of others to express different views. Beyond seeking out a variety of viewpoints, critical thinkers check their own speaking and thinking for signs of bias.
- **Analytical.** The critical thinker recognizes statements that call for evidence. He is alert to potential problems. In addition, the critical thinker foresees possible consequences of adopting a point of view.
- **Systematic.** Staying organized and focused are two more qualities of a critical thinker. She's willing to patiently gather evidence, test ideas, and stay with a tough or complex question.
- **Self-confident.** Because he trusts his intellectual skills, the critical thinker is willing to seek truth, listen with an open mind, and do the hard and useful work of thinking.
- **Inquisitive.** The critical thinker wants to know. She is hungry for facts and concepts. She is willing to explore the universe of ideas even before she knows how to apply the insights she gains.
- **Mature.** As a mature person, the critical thinker possesses a wisdom born of experience. He understands that a problem can have several solutions—even solutions that seem to contradict each other. He resists the desire to reach quick, superficial answers, and he is willing to suspend judgment when evidence is incomplete. At the same time, he recognizes that human beings are often called to act before all the facts are in.*

Look for Assumptions

Assumptions are beliefs that guide our thinking and behavior. Assumptions can be simple and ordinary. For example, when you drive a car, you assume that other drivers know the meaning of traffic signals and stop signs.

In other cases, assumptions are more complex and have far-reaching implications. Scientists, for instance, assume that events in the world take place in a predictable way that can be accurately described in language and expressed in mathematical terms.

* Excerpt from Peter Facione, *Critical Thinking: What It Is and Why It Counts* (Millbrae, CA: California Academic Press, 1996). © 1996 California Academic Press. Used with permission.

A useful way to begin any exercise in critical thinking is to look for assumptions—the foundation of our opinions.

Look for unstated assumptions

Despite their power to influence our speaking and action, assumptions are often unstated—even held unconsciously. People can remain unaware of their most basic and far-reaching assumptions, the very ideas that shape their lives.

Heated conflict and hard feelings often result when people argue on the level of opinions, forgetting that the real conflict lies at the level of their assumptions. An example is the question about whether the government should fund public works programs that create jobs during a recession. People who argue in favor of such programs often assume that creating jobs is an appropriate task for the federal government. On the other hand, people who argue against such programs may assume that the government has no business interfering with the free workings of the economy.

There's little hope of resolving this conflict of opinion unless we discover and resolve the unstated assumptions about the proper role of government that underlie these two arguments.

Be alert for stated assumptions

Sometimes you will find speakers and writers who are thorough enough to explicitly state their assumptions. A famous example comes from the Declaration of Independence, adopted on July 4, 1776, by the 13 colonies that later developed into the United States:

> We hold these truths to be self-evident, that all men are created equal, that they are endowed by their Creator with certain unalienable Rights, that among these are Life, Liberty and the pursuit of Happiness. —That to secure these rights, Governments are instituted among Men, deriving their just powers from the consent of the governed, —That whenever any

---

> ## sidebar
>
> ### ATTITUDES OF CRITICAL THINKERS
>
> With some experience, you can learn to recognize the qualities of a critical thinker in yourself and the people around you. Listen for statements such as these:
>
> - "Let's follow this idea and see where it leads, even if we feel uncomfortable with what we find out." (TRUTH SEEKING)
> - "I have a point of view on this subject, and I'm anxious to hear yours as well." (OPEN-MINDED)
> - "Taking this stand on the issue commits me to take some new actions." (ANALYTICAL)
> - "The speaker made several interesting points, and I'd like to hear some more evidence to support each one." (SYSTEMATIC)
> - "After reading this book for the first time, I was confused. I'll be able to understand it after studying the book some more." (SELF-CONFIDENT)
> - "When I saw that painting for the first time, I wanted to know what was going on in the artist's life when she painted it." (INQUISITIVE)
> - "I'll wait to reach a conclusion on this issue until I gather some more facts." (MATURE)

◆ example

Read the following excerpt from a larger essay and see if you can list some of the author's assumptions.

It's Time to Turn the Last Page

By Steven Levy

No one is calling the 1900s the Century of the Book. But you could make a case for it. For most of those years, the heavy hitters in our culture landed their big punches between the covers of bound boards: Joyce, Freud, Proust, Salinger, Orwell ... even Bill Gates weighed in, twice. Sure, television eventually mesmerized the nation and the globe, but the number of books printed in the fading century surely dwarfed the production of all previous eras. And when e-commerce began, what did its flagship, Amazon.com, sell? Duh.

Still, when Y3K pundits look back on our time, they'll remember it as the Last Century of the Book. Why? As a common item of communication, artistic expression and celebrity anecdote, the physical object consisting of bound dead trees in shiny wrapper is headed for the antique heap. Its replacement will be a lightning-quick injection of digital bits into a handheld device with an ultrasharp display. Culture vultures and bookworms might cringe at the prospect, but it's as inevitable as page two's following page one. Books are goners, at least as far as being the dominant form of reading.

Most of the pieces are already in place: fast chips, long-lasting batteries, capacious disk drives and the Internet. Only two things, really, hold us back from having reading devices that are just as felicitous as the dust-jacketed packages we know and love. One is high-speed wireless bandwidth, so that the devices can be quickly loaded. Fixing that is a no-brainer. No one doubts that such a big digital transmission system will show up early in the millennium.

The second is a screen whose output is as sumptuous as the current books', which engage not only our minds but our sense of touch. Oh, and having it cost so little that we won't hesitate to drag the thing to the beach or grab it on the way to the loo. In other words, cheap enough to lose.

What are the odds of that happening? Let's see. In the last 50 years, we've made computers thousands of times more powerful, while shrinking them from the size of a basketball court to something you can cradle in your palm. All while dropping the price tag from millions of bucks to a few hundred. Does it really seem plausible that sometime next century we can't make a device that approximates the size and heft of a book or magazine, with a screen that's every bit as easy on the eyes as the Modern Library edition of *Sense and Sensibility*? Unless the world's computer scientists suddenly get struck stupid, we're going to get those devices, and they'll probably cost so little that we'll pay nothing for them—they'll be given away by content moguls so that we can buy more 21st-century news, pictures and literature. "The cards have been dealt," says Microsoft e-book czar Dick Brass. "The only difference is how fast people will play the hand."

This passage is based on at least two assumptions:

- The appeal of books rests on their size and price, as well as the fact that they are pleasing to touch.
- The trends currently shaping technology—the drive to make digital devices faster, smaller, and cheaper—will continue indefinitely.

You could disagree with these assumptions. For example, you might list other features of books that give them enduring appeal, even in an age of handheld digital devices. And you might argue that there is a limit to how cheap and fast digital devices can become.

Reread the excerpt to look for other assumptions and do some critical thinking about them.

Form of Government becomes destructive of these ends, it is the Right of the People to alter or to abolish it, and to institute new Government, laying its foundation on such principles and organizing its powers in such form, as to them shall seem most likely to effect their Safety and Happiness.

The "self-evident truths" listed in these passages are examples of assumptions:

- All men are created equal.
- Men are born with rights to life, liberty, and happiness.
- Governments exist to secure these rights and deserve to be overthrown if they fail.

In addition, this passage underlines a key feature of assumptions: They are literally a thinker's starting points. Careful thinkers will produce logical arguments and evidence to support most of their assertions. However, they are willing to take other assertions as "self-evident"—so obvious or fundamental that they do not need to be proved.

Over time, people can change their minds about which assumptions are worth accepting. Notice that in their list of assumptions, the men who framed the Declaration of Independence did not explicitly state that women or people of color are "endowed by their Creator with certain unalienable Rights." Later Americans passed amendments to the United States Constitution and a series of laws to widen the scope of the original "self-evident truths."

Look for Arguments

In popular usage, the word *argument* connotes disagreement, conflict, or even verbal violence. But for specialists in logic, this term has a different meaning. For them, *argument* refers to series of assertions that are clear, coherent, and consistent. Discovering arguments means looking for the key terms used by a writer or speaker and seeing how those terms are used to make assertions.

Look for key terms

A *term* is a word or phrase that denotes a clearly defined concept. Terms with several different meanings are ambiguous, and one common goal of critical thinking is to remove ambiguity.

This is an especially useful goal when we use terms to describe, justify, and motivate human behavior—words such as *wealth, happiness, peace, love, justice, charity, courage,* or *honor*. These terms can mean many things, and useful discussion about them can begin only when people share the same understanding of such words.

Remember that the word *communication* is closely linked to words such as *commune* and *common*. When people use terms in the same way, they reach a common ground. They commune—that is, create a genuine meeting of the minds. When that happens, the miracle of communication takes place—two minds operating with the same thought.

Before thinking critically about the ideas of others, make sure you understand their key terms. Your first task is to locate them. Skilled writers and speakers often take the time to list and define their key terms. Even when they don't, you can use clues to spot them:

- Look or listen for words that are new to you.
- Be alert for words or phrases that are frequently repeated—especially in prominent places in a text or in a speech, such as in an overview, an introduction, a summary, or a conclusion.
- When reading, check the index for words or phrases that have many page references. Also see if the text includes a glossary. And look for words that are printed in *italics* or **boldface**.

As you look for clues, remember that several different words or phrases can stand for the same term. In this chapter, for example, *self-evident truth* and *assumption* are different words that refer to the same concept.

Look for assertions

A speaker's or writer's key terms occur in a larger context, called an assertion. An *assertion* is a complete sentence that contains one or more key terms. The function of an assertion is to define a term or to state relationships between terms. Finding such relationships gets to the essence of what we mean by the term *knowledge*.

To find a speaker's or writer's assertions, listen or look for key sentences. These are sentences that make an important point or state a general conclusion. In the following paragraph (taken from Steven

▶ sidebar

TYPES OF DEFINITIONS

A powerful step in critical thinking is "coming to terms"—defining the key words in your speaking and writing and decoding the definitions given by others. Look for the following kinds of definitions:

- **Aristotelian definition.** Aristotle, an ancient Greek philosopher who wrote extensively on logic, suggested a pattern for effective definitions. First, present the thing you want to define as a member of a larger class. Then state how that thing differs from other members of its class.
  Example: A guitar (the term to be defined) is a musical instrument (a larger class) with six or twelve strings (characteristics that distinguish the guitar from other musical instruments).
- **Operational definition.** You may sometimes find it useful to define a term by describing it as the result of an action or series of actions.
  Example: To tell time (the term to be defined), you check the positions of the hands on an analog watch (an action) or read the hours and minutes displayed on a digital clock (another possible action).
- **Stipulative definition.** Sometimes thinkers acknowledge that a term can legitimately be defined in many ways and choose to use that term with single definition in mind.
  Example: "When I use the word *love*, I mean the ability to see that the needs and desires of another person are as important as my own needs and desires."

Levy's essay excerpted on pages 38–39), the first two sentences make an assertion. The following sentences then offer supporting details:

> No one is calling the 1900s the Century of the Book. But you could make a case for it. For most of those years, the heavy hitters in our culture landed their big punches between the covers of bound boards: Joyce, Freud, Proust, Salinger, Orwell . . . even Bill Gates weighed in, twice. Sure, television eventually mesmerized the nation and the globe, but the number of books printed in the fading century surely dwarfed the production of all previous eras. And when e-commerce began, what did its flagship, Amazon.com, sell? Duh.

Often speakers and writers will give you clues to their key sentences. Speakers will pause to emphasize these sentences or precede them with phrases such as, "My point is that. . . ." Writers may present key sentences in italics or boldface or include them in summaries.

Spotting assertions can be tricky for several reasons. For one, a single key sentence can express several assertions. Also, several different sentences can express the same assertion. In the paragraph quoted, for instance, Levy's assertion could also be stated this way: "During the twentieth century, the book was a key element in mass communication." To make sure you understand an assertion, see if you can state it in your own words.

Examine Logic

Author Steven Covey summarizes one of the habits of highly effective people as, "First seek to understand, then to be understood." Once you define key terms and discover assertions, you can truly say that you've taken the time to understand the ideas of another person. Now you're in a position to make yourself understood—to offer an evaluation of that person's ideas based on your own critical thinking.

A primary tool for evaluating ideas is logic. As you list a speaker's or writer's assertions, you may find gaps between them—assertions that contradict each other or rest on ambiguous terms. Finding and avoiding such gaps is the aim of people who study logic. These people often distinguish two ways of making arguments: deductive and inductive reasoning. Errors in logic can occur with either type of reasoning.

Look for deductive reasoning

Deductive reasoning starts with a general assertion and derives other assertions from it. The steps in deductive reasoning can often be listed as a sequence of assertions, starting with the most general one and arriving at a more specific conclusion. For example:

1. Most corporate lawyers are politically conservative (general assertion).
2. My mother is a corporate lawyer.
3. Therefore, my mother is politically conservative (specific conclusion).

In this type of reasoning, each assertion is like a link in a chain. A weakness in any link can break the chain of logic.

The argument given here may have several weak links. Before accepting assertion 1, for example, you could demand evidence—perhaps well-conducted surveys given to representative groups of corporate lawyers to determine their political views. Or you could find examples of corporate lawyers who are not politically conservative. Going even further, you could press for a definition of the term *politically conservative*, which has many potential meanings.

Look for inductive reasoning

With inductive reasoning, the chain of logic proceeds in the opposite "direction," from specific to general.

Suppose that you apply for a job and the interviewer says, "We've hired three people from your school and they've worked out well for us. When we found out where you're taking classes, our management team was immediately interested."

In this case, the interviewer began with specific examples: *We've hired three people from your school and they worked out well for us.* From there the interviewer proceeded to a more general (though unstated) conclusion: *Students from your school make good employees.* This is a simple example of inductive reasoning.

Inductive reasoning is heavily used in the natural and social sciences—for example, in testing the safety and usefulness of new medications. Medical researchers might design an experiment involving two groups of women, all with similar medical histories and a certain type of breast cancer. Researchers could then give the new medication to one group of women and give the other group a placebo (a simple sugar pill with no known therapeutic effects). If the women who took the actual medication show improvements in health while the placebo group does not, this would be evidence for the medication's effectiveness.

In this case, the researchers would be using inductive reasoning, starting with the experiences of specific women and moving to a general conclusion about the medication.

Test logic by looking for implied assertions

You can follow a two-step method for thinking critically about any viewpoint, no matter whether it results from deductive or inductive reasoning. First, look for assertions, both assumed and explicitly stated. Second, see if you can find any exceptions to these assertions. This technique helps detect many errors in logic.

Consider this viewpoint: "My mother and father have a good marriage. After all, they're still together after 35 years." Underlying these two sentences is an assumption: *Good marriages are those that last a long time.* Yet there are possible exceptions to this assumption. For example, you may know of married couples who stay together for decades even though they confess to being unhappy in the relationship.

Suppose that you see this newspaper headline: "Student tries to commit suicide after failing to pass bar exam." Seeing this headline, you might conclude that the student's failure to pass the exam led to a depression that caused his suicide attempt. However, this is simply an assumption that can be stated in the following way: *When two events occur closely together in time, the first event is the cause of the second event.* Perhaps the student's depression was in fact caused by another traumatic event not mentioned in the headline, such as breaking up with a longtime girlfriend.

▶ sidebar

COMMON FALLACIES IN LOGIC

A proper test for logic can sometimes reveal fallacies in an argument. Here are some common fallacies to look for whenever you are considering a viewpoint.

1. **Jumping to conclusions.** Jumping to conclusions is the only exercise that some lazy thinkers get. This fallacy involves drawing conclusions without sufficient evidence. Take the bank officer who hears about a student failing to pay back an education loan. After that, the officer turns down all loan applications from students. This person has jumped to a conclusion about all students based on one negative example.

2. **Attacking the person.** This mistake is common at election time. An example is the candidate who claims that her opponent has failed to attend church regularly during the campaign. This may be true—and it can also be irrelevant to the true issues in the campaign.

3. **Appealing to an "authority."** A professional athlete endorses a brand of breakfast cereal. A soft drink company pays a famous musician to feature its product in a rock video. The promotional brochure for an advertising agency lists all the large companies that have used its services. In each case, the companies involved are trying to win your confidence—and your dollars—by citing authorities. The underlying assumption is: *Famous people and organizations buy our product. Therefore, you should buy it, too.* Problems arise when the authority is simply a celebrity with no true expertise in the topic at hand.

4. **Pointing to a false cause.** The fact that one event follows another does not mean that the two events have a cause-and-effect relationship. All we can really say is that the events may be correlated. As children's vocabularies improve, for example, they can get more cavities. This does not mean that increasing your vocabulary causes cavities. Instead, the increase in cavities is due to other factors, such as physical maturation and changes in diet.

5. **Thinking in "all-or-nothing" terms.** Consider these statements: *Doctors are greedy. . . . You can't trust politicians. . . . Students these days are just in school to get high-paying jobs; they lack idealism. . . . Homeless people don't want to work.* Such opinions gloss over individual differences, claiming that all members of a group are exactly alike. They also ignore key facts—for instance, that some doctors volunteer their time at free medical clinics and that many homeless people are children who are too young to work.

Examine Evidence

In addition to testing arguments with the tools of logic, you can think critically by assessing the evidence used to support those arguments. Evidence comes in several forms, including facts, expert testimony, and examples.

Consider the following passage from Sven Birkert's book, *The Gutenberg Elegies: The Fate of Reading in an Electronic Age*. In this passage, Birkerts argues that most Americans get their news about current events from televised images instead of newspapers. He also asserts that television news is controlled by large corporations competing for greater shares of a global audience :

> Think of it. Fifty to a hundred million people (maybe a conservative estimate) form their ideas about what is going on in America and in the world from the same basic package of edited images—to the extent that the image itself has lost much of its once-fearsome power. Daily newspapers, with their long columns of print, struggle against declining sales. Fewer and fewer people under the age of fifty read them; computers will soon make packaged information a custom product. But if the printed sheet is heading for obsolescence, people are tuning in to the signals. The screen is where the information and entertainment wars will be fought. The communications conglomerates are waging bitter takeover battles in their zeal to establish global empires. As Jonathan Crary has written in "The Eclipse of the Spectacle," "Telecommunications is the new arterial network, analogous in part to what railroads were for capitalism in the nineteenth century. And it is this electronic substitute for geography that corporate and national entities are now carving up."*

Here Birkerts offers several types of evidence:

- **Fact**—a "conservative estimate" that "fifty to a hundred million people" in America base their ideas about the world on televised images. Statistics and other numerical data such as this can be presented as facts to back an assertion.
- **Examples** of the declining power of the printed word: "Daily newspapers, with their long columns of print, struggle against declining sales. Fewer and fewer people under the age of fifty read them. . . ."
- **Expert opinion.** To support his assertion about the power of "communications conglomerates," Birkerts quotes a passage from another writer named Jonathan Crary. Here Crary is presented as an expert who agrees with Birkerts.
- **Emotional appeal.** Birkerts uses words and phrases with an emotional charge, referring to companies waging "bitter takeover battles" in their "zeal" to establish "global empires."

The last element in this list is not always seen as a type of evidence. According to one viewpoint, the job of a critical thinker is keep emotions in check. It is true that emotional bias can lead to errors in thinking. However, human beings are not purely rational creatures of thought, and tasteful appeals to emotion can play a powerful role in critical thinking.

---

* Sven Birkerts, *The Gutenberg Elegies: The Fate of Reading in an Electronic Age.* Copyright © 1994 Sven Birkerts. Reprinted by permission of Faber and Faber, Inc., an affiliate of Farrar Straus & Giroux, LLC.

One example of effective emotional appeal comes from a famous speech by Dr. Martin Luther King, Jr., delivered on August 28, 1963, on the steps of the Lincoln Memorial in Washington, D.C. :

> I have a dream that one day this nation will rise up and live out the true meaning of its creed: "We hold these truths to be self-evident: that all men are created equal."
>
> I have a dream that one day on the red hills of Georgia the sons of former slaves and the sons of former slaveowners will be able to sit down together at a table of brotherhood.
>
> I have a dream that one day even the state of Mississippi, a desert state, sweltering with the heat of injustice and oppression, will be transformed into an oasis of freedom and justice.
>
> I have a dream that my four children will one day live in a nation where they will not be judged by the color of their skin but by the content of their character.*

☑ checklist

TEN WAYS TO EVALUATE EVIDENCE

As you think critically about facts, examples, expert opinions, and emotional appeals, ask the following questions:

❒ Are all or most of the relevant facts presented?
❒ Are the facts consistent with each other?
❒ Are facts presented accurately or in a misleading way?
❒ Are enough examples included to make a solid case for the assertion?
❒ Do the examples truly support the assertion?
❒ Are the examples typical? That is, could the author or speaker support the assertion with other examples that are similar?
❒ Is the expert credible—truly knowledgeable about the topic?
❒ Is the expert biased? For example, is the expert paid to represent the views of a corporation that is promoting a product or service?
❒ Is the expert quoted accurately?
❒ Is emotional appeal used in a way that is consistent with sound logic and other forms of evidence?

*Martin Luther King, Jr., "I Have a Dream" excerpt. Reprinted by arrangement with the Estate of Martin Luther King, Jr., c/o Writers House as agent for the proprietor. New York, NY. Copyright © 1963 Dr. Martin Luther King, Jr., copyright renewed 1991 Coretta Scott King.

⊳ experiment WITH A STRATEGY FROM THIS CHAPTER

Describe a time in your life when you felt stuck in your thinking, unable to choose among several viewpoints on a key issue in your life. In the space below, list the specific time, place, and circumstances involved:

Now scan this chapter for any suggestions for critical thinking that could help you in situations similar to the one you just described. Summarize each suggestion in one sentence and list them:

chapter 4

Creating New Ideas

The point of education is not just to gain knowledge. The point is to use original thinking to create new knowledge—not in mechanical or programmed ways, like a computer, but in imaginative and innovative ways.

Most of us think of creativity as the province of the poet, the novelist, the painter, or the musician. But creativity is also the domain of the theoretical physicist, such as Albert Einstein, who formulated his theories of relativity after imagining what it might be like to ride on a beam of light at 186,000 miles per second. Creativity is practiced by the accountant who finds a new tax deduction for a client, the doctor who diagnoses a rare illness, and the mechanic who identifies an intermittent noise in your car engine. The creative process—long regarded as mysterious and unteachable—is actually one used by many people in many professions. And it is a process that you consciously cultivate.

Brainstorm

Alex Osborn introduced the concept of brainstorming in his 1953 book *Applied Imagination.* Osborn's book presented brainstorming as a technique for creating as many ideas as possible in a short period of time.

Brainstorming is still a popular creativity technique. When you are stuck on a problem, brainstorming can break the logjam. If you run out of money two days before payday every week, you could brainstorm ways to make your money last longer. You can brainstorm ways to pay for your education. You can brainstorm ways to find a job or topics for your master's thesis. The following checklist offers guidelines for tapping this method for unearthing new ideas.

▶ sidebar

GUIDELINES FOR BRAINSTORMING

Despite the popularity of brainstorming, the technique is not always used effectively. Keep the following guidelines in mind:

- *Focus on a single problem or issue*. State your focus as a question. Open-ended questions that start with the words *what, how, who, where*, and *when* often make effective focusing questions.
- *Relax*. Creativity is enhanced by a state of relaxed alertness. If you are tense or anxious, use relaxation techniques such as those described in Chapter 18 for test anxiety.
- *Set a quota or goal for the number of solutions you want to generate*. Goals give your subconscious mind something to aim for.
- *Set a time limit*. Use a clock to time it to the minute. Digital sports watches with built-in stopwatches work well. Experiment with various lengths of time. Both short and long brainstorms can be powerful.
- *Allow all answers*. The basis of brainstorming is attitudes of permissiveness and patience. One of Alex Osborn's original slogans for brainstorming was "all input, no putdown." Accept every idea. If it pops into your head, put it down on paper. Quantity, not quality, is the goal. Avoid making judgments and evaluations during the brainstorming session. If you get stuck, think of an outlandish idea and write it down. One crazy idea can unleash a flood of other, more workable solutions.
- *Brainstorm with others*. This is a powerful technique. Group brainstorms take on lives of their own. Assign one member of the group to write down solutions. Feed off the ideas of others, and remember to avoid evaluating or judging anyone's idea during the brainstorm.

Also keep in mind some brainstorming techniques to avoid, as they tend to squelch rather than spur ideas:

- Allowing the person with the most perceived power—such as a teacher or supervisor—to speak first. Other group members may hesitate to pursue a new line of thinking or offer contradictory ideas.
- Requiring each member of the brainstorming group to speak in turn. This puts people on the spot and introduces unnecessary tension. Let people speak voluntarily and spontaneously.
- Failing to write down suggested ideas, or expecting everyone in the group to take notes. People will stop thinking in order to keep writing. Instead, designate one person in the group to take notes.

Play with Ideas

Even people who describe themselves as "uncreative" can come up with hundreds of new ideas during the course of a lifetime. The main difference between them and the people we call "creative" may be that creative people record all their ideas—good, bad, and indifferent—and refine them over time. Use the following suggestions for the proper care and feeding of your ideas.

Expose yourself to many sources of ideas

To fuel your creativity, read voraciously, including newspapers and magazines. Keep a clip file of interesting articles. Explore beyond mainstream journalism. There are hundreds of small-circulation specialty magazines and Internet sites. They cover almost any subject you can imagine. Take time to browse and skim through them at random, with no specific aim in mind.

Keep letter-sized files of important correspondence, magazine and news articles, and other material. You can also create idea files on a personal computer using word processing, outlining, or database software.

Keep a journal

One way to care for your ideas is to take a cue from Leonardo da Vinci and Virginia Woolf: Start keeping a journal. Journals don't have to be exclusively about your thoughts and feelings. You can include your observations of the world around you, quotes from friends, important or offbeat ideas—anything.

In your journal, include random insights, notes on your reading, and useful ideas you encounter in class. Collect jokes, also.

One thing that stops people from keeping a journal is writer's block. To get past this problem, do a free writing exercise: Set a timer and write for five minutes without stopping to revise. Just keep your hand moving and write anything that pops into your head. Put yourself on automatic pilot until the words start happening on their own.

There are many other ways to get started:

- **Write letters—including those you don't plan to send.** The person you're "sending" the letter to can be famous or obscure, near or far, dead or alive. This can be a useful way to deal with anger or grief. (For a fictional description of this technique, see the novel *Herzog* by Saul Bellow.)
- **Use leading phrases and incomplete sentences to jump-start your writing.** For example, many journal entries can start with "I discovered that I. . . ." or "I intend to. . . ." Invent your own lead-ins.

- **Dream wildly.** Create a compelling future. Include the details—what you want to have, do, and be 5, 10, or 50 years from now. Write as if you've already attained your long-term goals. After this kind of brainstorm, focus on one goal and write an action plan to meet it.

- **Make lists.** Write down the five most influential people in your life and what they taught you. If you're a parent, list the three most important skills you want to teach your children. Keep a list of your favorite quotations. Record notable things that you and your friends say. List new words and their definitions. Writing them down helps make these words part of your working vocabulary.

- **Reflect on the significance of your courses.** Mine your own experiences for examples of the ideas you're learning about. Speculate about how you might apply what you're learning in class.

- **Imagine that you're sitting face to face with the author of a textbook.** Write what you would say to this person. Argue. Debate. Note questions you'd want to ask this person and then pose them in class.

- **Remember that journals don't have to be limited to words on paper.** Draw. Paint. Create a collage or sculpture. Visualizing through art is a powerful way to remember our experiences. Write a piece of music. Dictate your journal entries into a tape recorder or key them into a computer. Use a journal to take risks and explore new learning styles.

If you're shy about doing any of this, remember that no one else has to see your work. Your journal is in safe hands—your own.

Safeguard your ideas even if you're pressed for time. Jotting down four or five words is enough to capture the essence of an idea. You can write down one quote in a minute or two. And if you carry 3x5 cards in a pocket or purse, you can record ideas while standing in a line or waiting for appointments to begin.

Review your journal regularly. Some amusing thought that came to you in November might be the perfect solution to a problem the following March.

Keep your eyes open for an unmet need

Edward Land started to work on the concept of Polaroid photography after vacationing with his daughter, who asked: "Daddy, why do we have to wait for pictures to be developed?" Laptop computers were created for people who found it hard to part with their desktop computers while traveling. Cellular phones, fax machines, and MP3 players were created to meet similar needs.

Sometimes needs are met as a result of serendipity—a happy and creative coincidence of ideas. Spence Silver, a research scientist at 3M, invented a new chemical by accident while looking for ways to improve tape adhesives. This chemical did not stick strongly when coated onto tape backings. Even so, Silver believed it had potential uses.

His invention languished for years until Art Fry, who worked in new product development at 3M, attended a seminar by Silver. Fry had long been frustrated with the scrap-paper bookmarks he used to mark his place in his church hymnal during choir practice. One day it suddenly occurred to Fry that Silver's adhesive could be used to make a perfect bookmark—one that could be fastened temporarily to a page and then easily but securely refastened on another page. That "aha!" yielded the Post-it® note in 1980, and billions have been sold since then.

Let ideas percolate

Living with the problem invites a solution. Write down data, possible solutions, or an unanswered question on index cards and carry them with you. Look at the cards before you go to bed at night. Review them when you are waiting for the bus. Make them part of your life and think about them frequently.

A part of our mind works as we sleep. You've experienced this directly if you've ever fallen asleep with a problem on your mind and awakened the next morning with a solution. For some people, the solution appears in a dream or in the twilight consciousness just before falling asleep or waking.

You can experiment with this process. Ask yourself a question as you fall asleep. Keep pencil and paper or a tape recorder near your bed. The moment you wake up, begin writing or speaking and see if an answer to your question emerges.

Sometimes the best ideas bubble up out of silence, when the mind comes to a still point and you fully enter the present moment. After posing a question to yourself, cultivate periods of silence. Do not push for a result. Simply let answers emerge on their own. Learn to trust your creative process, even when no answers are in sight.

If you allow time for the creative process, it will work. In his book about writing, *The Spooky Art,* Norman Mailer wrote: "If you tell yourself you are going to be at your desk tomorrow, you are by that declaration asking your unconscious to prepare the material." Trust that a solution will show up. It may happen at times when you least expect it: while shaving, standing in the shower, or waiting in line at the grocery store. Frustration and a feeling of being stuck are often signals that a solution is imminent.

Juxtapose different ideas and look for relationships

It has been said that there are no new ideas, only new ways to combine old ideas. Creativity is the ability to discover those new combinations.

Creative people can put unrelated facts next to each other and invent a relationship, even if it seems absurd at first. In *The Act of Creation*, novelist Arthur Koestler explains creativity as finding a new context in which to combine opposites. Koestler invented a word for this process—*bisociation*—which he defines as perceiving an idea in "two self-consistent but habitually incompatible frames of reference."

Art, science, and technology abound with examples of bisociation. Architect Paolo Soleri called for the design of large structures to obey the laws of ecology. Prior to him, architecture and ecology were seen as separate disciplines. But he envisioned a field that included the basic principles of both—*arcology*. Other fields, such as medical economics, were formed by a similar creative process.

Many writers have used bisociation to create new ways of structuring language. Jack Kerouac, a poet and novelist associated with the Beat Movement of the 1950s, often wrote to imitate the rhythms used by jazz musicians when they improvise. Most people see little common ground between writing and jazz. But in his essay *Essentials of Spontaneous Prose*, Kerouac called for flowing sentences freed from needless punctuation that had the momentum of a long musical phrase: "No periods separating sentence-structures already arbitrarily riddled by false colons and timid usually needless commas—but the vigorous space dash separating rhetorical breathing (as jazz musician drawing breath between outblown phrases)."

Bisociation can help you succeed in higher education. Look for ways to combine the strategies explained throughout this book—even strategies that you see as unrelated. Techniques that you use to manage time may also help you manage stress. (See the checklist "Use Two-Week Planning to Reduce Stress" in Chapter 7.) A strategy you use to reduce test anxiety might also help you reduce your fear of public speaking. Changing one behavior can create a cascade of benefits that touches many aspects of your life.

Take an "obvious" truth and challenge it

Look for the obvious "truths" about a subject or the obvious solutions to a problem. Then dump them. Ask yourself: Well, I think that X is true, but if X were not true, what would happen next? This creativity technique can yield many ideas for speeches and papers. It begins with taking an assertion you're certain about and looking for as many ways as possible to challenge it.

Many Americans, for example, speak of the 1950s as a time of social conformity but remember the 1960s as an era in which a spirit of creative dissent flourished. This "truth," which may appear obvious at first, presents a perfect subject for creative tinkering. You can challenge this assertion in several ways:

State the opposite and make a case for it. For example, reverse the preceding assertion so that it becomes this: "The 1950s was a time of creative dissent, whereas the 1960s was an era of social conformity." To support this new assertion, you can point to daring experiments in the arts during the 1950s, including the "pop art" paintings of Jasper Johns and the jazz-infused musical *West Side Story*. And as evidence that the 1960s was a conservative era, you could point to the Republican presidency of Richard Nixon and the revival of traditional folk music that took place early in the decade.

Move from general to specific. To assert that the 1950s was a time of social conformity but that the 1960s was an era of dissent is to make a general statement, one that may be too broad to say anything meaningful about these periods of American history. It's more likely that there were a variety of factors at work during *both* of these decades—social forces that promoted conformity on the one hand and dissent on the other.

With this idea in mind, you could change the original, general assertion to mention specific cultural trends: "The 1950s was a time of political conservatism paired with bold experiments in the arts, whereas the 1960s ushered in a broad antiwar movement paired with a resurgence in traditional folk music."

Question assumptions. The statement that the 1950s was a time of social conformity whereas the 1960s was an era of creative dissent is based on several assumptions. One is that trends based on creative dissent, such as the "hippie movement" of the 1960s, can appear seemingly out of nowhere, without historical precedent.

This is a good assumption to question. Social movements can take many years to develop. It's possible that the seeds of the hippie movement were planted in the 1950s—perhaps even earlier. In fact, you could argue that the "hippies" of the 1960s were the ideological children of the "beatniks" of the 1950s—a group of writers and other artists deeply influenced by the poetry of Allen Ginsberg and the novels of Jack Kerouac. Thinking along such lines, you could create a new assertion: "Despite the social conformity that marked many aspects of the 1950s, the artists of this decade created a spirit of social dissent that flowered into a flourishing counterculture and antiwar movement during the 1960s."

☑ checklist

ASK QUESTIONS TO GENERATE NEW IDEAS

Questions promote curiosity, create new distinctions, and multiply possibilities. Start from the assumption that you are brilliant and that asking questions can help you unlock that brilliance.

☐ *Write something you're sure of and put a question mark after it.* Perhaps one of the things you know about your educational plans is that you would never take a course in philosophy. In that case, you could write, "I don't take philosophy courses?" That suggests another question: "Is there ever a circumstance when I could serve my success in school by taking a philosophy course?" Taking such a course could promote your skills in both critical thinking and writing. Powerful questions sometimes take tried-and-true "facts" and lead us to doubt them.

☐ *Ask about what's missing.* Another way to invent a useful question is to notice what's missing from your life and then ask a question about how to supply it. For example, if you want to take better notes, you can write, "What's missing for me is skill in taking notes. How can I gain more skill in taking notes?" Or "What's missing is time. How do I create time in my day to actually do the things that I say I want to do?"

☐ *Begin a general question, then brainstorm endings.* Beginning a general question and brainstorming a long list of endings can help you invent a question that you've never asked before. For instance:

WHAT CAN I DO WHEN . . . ? What can I do when an instructor calls on me in class and I have no idea what to say? What can I do when an instructor doesn't show up for class on time? What can I do when I feel overwhelmed with assignments?

HOW CAN I . . . ? How can I get just the kinds of courses that I want? How can I expand my career options? How can I choose a major? How can I become much more effective as a student, starting today?

WHEN DO I . . . ? When do I drop a class? When do I meet with an instructor about changing one of my grades?

Refine Ideas

Many people overlook the follow-up to creative thinking: critical thinking as described in the previous chapter of this book. This step involves molding and shaping a rough-cut idea into a polished creation. The necessary skills include the ability to spot assumptions, apply the rules of logic, weigh evidence, separate fact from opinion, organize thoughts, and avoid careless errors. Write about your ideas in more detail and ask other people for input. All this can be demanding work. Just as often, it can be energizing and fun.

After a brainstorming session or creative frenzy of writing in your journal, take a break to clear your head. Then come back to your newfound and unrefined ideas. Sift, review, evaluate, and edit. Toss out any truly nutty ideas, but not before you give them a chance.

Sometimes the craziest, most outlandish solutions, although un-workable in themselves, lead to new ways to solve problems. Say that you held a brainstorming session about ways to finance your education. One of the suggestions was to ask everyone you know—even strangers you meet on the street—for money. That may sound crazy. But it does suggest a more practical idea: Ask all the people in your extended family for a no-interest loan. You might get a favorable response from an uncle and aunt who do not have college-bound children of their own but are happy to help fund a relative's education.

▶ experiment WITH A STRATEGY FROM THIS CHAPTER

Think of a significant problem that you face at home, at work, or in school right now. If that problem has been around for a number of weeks, months (or even years), that's all the better. Use the following space to describe that problem in writing:

Next, scan this chapter for a suggestion that you can use to solve this problem, such as:

- Brainstorming
- Exposing yourself to many sources of ideas
- Keeping a journal
- Looking for an unmet need
- Letting ideas percolate
- Juxtaposing different ideas and looking for new relationships
- Taking an obvious truth and challenging it
- Asking open-ended questions to generate new ideas

From this list, choose one strategy. In the space below, describe a way to use it, prefer-ably within the next 24 hours:

After using the strategy and observing the results, describe how well the strategy worked for you:

If the strategy worked well, consider making it habit. If it did *not* work well, list some ways to modify the strategy so that it becomes a better fit for you:

5

Making Decisions and Solving Problems

Your skills in thinking culminate in your ability to make decisions and solve problems in daily life. The stakes are high. Consider how you respond when you're faced with key decisions—the need to choose a college, a major, a career, or even a spouse. Also reflect on how you solve daily problems—everything from balancing your budget to resolving conflict with family, friends, coworkers, and teachers. Your responses in each of these situations can affect the quality of your life for decades to come. And each is a situation to which you can bring your thinking skills.

Decisions Create Results, Decrease Options, and Imply Action

Our lives are largely a result of the decisions we've made and the actions that flow from those decisions. By making new decisions, we can create new results. An old saying sums it up: "If you always do what you've always done, you'll always get what you've always gotten." By taking charge of our decisions, we take charge of our lives.

We are making decisions all the time, whether we realize it or not. Even avoiding decisions is a form of decision making. The student who puts off studying for a test until the last minute may really be saying, "I've decided this course is not important" or "I've decided not to give this course much time."

Decisions are more than wishes or desires. There's a world of difference between "I wish I could be a better student" and "I will take more powerful notes, read with greater retention, and review my class notes daily." Decisions are specific and lead to focused action.

When we decide, we narrow down. We give up actions that are inconsistent with our decision. We exclude options. We decrease the range of our behaviors. Deciding to lose weight rules out eating bigger portions of food. Deciding to enter medical school after you graduate rules out attending law school, at least for the near future.

There comes a time to move from the realm of reflection and commitment to the arena of action. Once we actually make a decision, we usually follow it with action, the clue to a true decision. By moving into action, we gain valuable feedback about the results of our decisions and the opportunity to make even more decisions.

Practice the Art and Science of Decision Making

Herodotus, an ancient Greek and author of one of the first histories of Western culture, wrote about a tribe with a three-step method for making decisions. First, they made a preliminary decision during an afternoon council meeting. Second, they met again in the evening for several rounds of drinks and made another preliminary decision. Finally, they met again the following morning, reviewed both the previous day's decisions with sober minds, and issued their final, binding decision.

This anecdote from Herodotus is not a recommendation to use alcohol as an aid to decision making. However, the story does make a point: When making decisions, you may benefit by looking at the problem from at least two points of view—one coldly rational and one that's more instinctive and spontaneous, the product of your intuition or "gut wisdom."

Decision making is both science and art. Decisions present you with a chance to create many options and then narrow them down to a few that you'll actually implement. It provides you the opportunity to generate many possibilities for action and the need to eventually focus on one. This process involves intellect and intuition, action and reflection. Some aspects of this process can be explained and even reduced to step-by-step procedures. Other aspects transcend rational explanation and depend on flashes of insight from your subconscious mind.

The essence of skill in decision making is balancing these dynamics so that you do justice to the canons of critical thinking while letting your mind soar to new creative peaks. The next time you face a decision, consider the following process, explained by Isa Engleberg and Dianna Wynn, authors of *Working in Groups: Communication Principles and Strategies*. Each step in the process can be described by a word that begins with the letter *I*.

1. Investigate

Powerful decisions flow from the quality of the information we have on hand. Many times failure results from not having the facts we need to make a decision. When you're faced with decisions about what courses to take next term, you need information on class times, locations, and instructors. When you're faced with a decision about which job offer to take, you need information about salary, benefits, and working conditions. Think of the multiple levels of information needed when you decide whether to get married, whether to raise children, or whether to change careers.

Often your initial task is to gather facts by using the research skills described in Chapters 20 and 21 of this book. You can turn to published sources of information, both print and online. You can also search out experts with special knowledge of a subject related to your decision. Each of these strategies is a tool for investigating sources of information in the outside world.

In addition, many decisions call for investigating your internal world—the invisible but compelling world of your values, life purpose, and goals. When we know specifically what we want from life, making decisions becomes easier. The value of having a long-term plan for our lives is that it provides a basis for many of our year-to-year and week-to-week decisions. When we're clear about what we want to accomplish in 5 years, 10 years, or even 50 years, it's easier to make a meaningful decision today.

2. Imagine

This phase of decision making is about generating as many options as possible, no matter how outlandish those options may seem at first. During this phase of decision making, the guidelines for brainstorming given in Chapter 4 will prove useful.

Alex Osborn, who first described brainstorming, compared the process of creating ideas to using the gas pedal on a car floorboard and of evaluating ideas to using the brake pedal. If you drive with one foot on the brake pedal and the other foot on the gas pedal at the same time, you can damage your car. Likewise, trying to evaluate ideas at the same time that you create them compromises your ability to make innovative decisions.

Certain comments can put the brakes on new ideas and squelch creativity in record time. For example, when considering a new policy or procedure, people can speak from a mindset of inertia: "We've never done it that way before." They can also speak from a sense of resignation: "We'll never get this idea past the boss." Or they can use the weight of tradition to smother new ideas: "We've been using this procedure for years, and it's too late to change now." When you notice such voices and consciously choose to put them on hold, you start to unleash your imagination.

To further promote imagination, ask questions that start with *what if?* To expand your career options, for example, ask yourself: What if I won a lottery that provided me with tax-free income of $100,000 per year for the rest of my life? What would I do with my life then? Or: What if a foundation granted me $5 million to create a project that would make a lasting contribution to the world? What project would I undertake?

Of course, you can evaluate your brainstormed ideas at a later time. This step has been described as the application of perspiration to inspiration. Here is your opportunity to apply the key skills of critical thinkers—spotting assumptions, weighing evidence, separating fact from opinion, organizing thoughts, and avoiding errors in logic. This is the time to do the hard and rewarding work of throwing out truly unworkable ideas and refining rough ideas into reasonable courses of action.

3. Incubate

Incubation is based on the idea that you can use time as an ally. During this phase, you take a break from gathering facts and inventing imaginative solutions. The key to this phase is watchful waiting—allowing time to let ideas combine, simmer, and percolate outside the confines of the conscious mind before you take decisive action.

Some decisions seem to make themselves. A solution pops into our minds and we gain newfound clarity. Suddenly we realize what we've truly wanted all along. Intuitive decisions usually arrive after we've gathered the relevant facts and faced a problem for some time. (Remember that using intuition is not the same as forgetting about the decision or refusing to make it.)

Sometimes you will face dilemmas—situations in which any course of action seems to lead to undesirable consequences. In such cases, consider putting a decision on hold. Wait it out. Do nothing until the circumstances change, making one alternative clearly preferable to another, or until an effective solution announces itself.

Incubation allows for intuition, times when a logical decision seems to emerge from a place beyond your logical mind. Logic alone will not enable you to decide whether to raise children, whether to follow a spiritual path, or whether to accept a job that pays less but offers greater fulfillment. When faced with decisions such as these, the processes of critical thinking can take you only so far. Incubation and intuition can complete the circle.

4. Insight!

Aha! is the burst of creative energy heralded by the arrival of a new, original idea. It is the sudden emergence of a new pattern, a previously undetected relationship, or an unusual combination of familiar elements. *Aha!* is the moment when your fact gathering, imagination, and incubation finally pay off—the moment when you know your decision is made, when your next step becomes clear. *Aha!* is an exhilarating experience.

Nineteenth-century poet Emily Dickinson described the *aha!* this way: "If I feel physically as if the top of my head were taken off, I know that is poetry." Yet *aha!* does not always result in a timeless poem or other work of art. *Aha!* can describe the moment when you declare your major, choose your career, or make any other decision that shapes the course of your life. Skill with *aha!* consists largely in recognizing such moments when they appear and following up the insight with appropriate action.

Action is key. Action reveals the consequences of your decision. After making an appropriate and powerful decision, the circumstances of your life fall into place. You approach each day with less effort and more ease. And if your decision was not appropriate, you'll get immediate feedback: Your choice of major will not feel right, your choice of career won't ring true, or a key relationship in your life will go off track. New problems will arise, and new decisions will cry out to be made. Instead of taking this situation as a sign of failure, you can view it as another chance to gain skill at decision making.

Problems Present Another Layer of Complexity

Many people use the terms *decision making* and *problem solving* interchangeably, as if the two processes are the same. Of course, there are many overlaps. Both processes hinge on your ability to think critically and creatively. Yet when actually trying your hand at these processes, you'll discover that problem solving exists at an even higher level of complexity than decision making.

To understand this point, start by considering the nature of decision making. When faced with a decision, you're asked to make a judgment call. Often the decision boils down to a single question that can be answered yes or no, or a choice between two major options: Is the defendant guilty or not guilty? Do we hire this person or keep looking for another? Do I cast my vote for this candidate or someone else?

☑ checklist

USE THE "FOUR I'S" OF DECISION MAKING

When faced with a decision, take the time to complete the cycle of creative and critical thinking:
- ❏ **Investigate.** Gather the facts needed to make your decision.
- ❏ **Imagine.** Create as many options or possible solutions as you can, then list the pros and cons of each one.
- ❏ **Incubate.** Allow time for information and ideas to simmer in your subconscious mind.
- ❏ **Insight!** Recognize and respect the moment of insight—the moment when your next step of action becomes clear.

Problem solving, on the other hand, calls for making a *series* of decisions and answering questions that are more open-ended: How can I raise enough money to fund my education? How can I manage my time so that I finish projects by the due date? How can I resolve conflicts with my partner?

Solve Problems in Four Phases

There is a vast literature on problem-solving techniques. Much of this published work can be traced to the book *How We Think* by John Dewey, an influential American philosopher. Dewey listed five steps that demonstrate sound critical thinking in moving from problem to solution:

1. Perceive a "felt difficulty"—the sense that an important question needs to be answered or that a circumstance in your life needs to be changed.
2. Define the problem by stating it clearly and concisely.
3. Suggest possible solutions.
4. Rationally test each solution by anticipating its possible consequences.
5. Act on the preferred solution, evaluate the consequences, and determine whether a new solution is needed.

Much of what you'll read and hear about problem solving represents variations and elaborations on Dewey's five steps. This section explains one variation. To assist yourself in remembering this method, reduce Dewey's five steps to four and begin each step with a "P" word: *Problem, Possibilities, Plan,* and *Performance*.

Experiment with these four steps, but remember that the order is not absolute. You could reverse that order, for example, by reflecting on a new behavior you'd like to develop, viewing it as a solution, and seeing what problems in your life that behavior might solve.

Phase 1: The Problem

To define a problem effectively, understand what a problem is: a mismatch between what you want and what you have. Problem solving is all about reducing the gap between these two factors.

Start with what you have. Tell the truth about what you do in your life right now, without shame or blame. For example: "I often get sleepy while reading my physics assignments, and after closing the book I often cannot remember what I just read."

Next, describe in detail what you want. Go for specifics: "I want to remain alert as I read about physics. I also want to accurately summarize each chapter I read."

One key point: When we define a problem in limiting ways, our solutions merely generate new problems. Remember that the problem you define dictates the solution you get. As Einstein said, "The world we have made is a result of the level of thinking we have done thus far. We cannot solve problems at the same level at which we created them."

This idea has many applications to success in school. An example is the student who struggles with note-taking. The problem, he thinks, is that his notes are too sketchy. The logical "solution" is to take more notes, and his new goal is to write down almost everything his instructors say. No matter how fast and furiously he writes, the student cannot capture all the instructors' comments.

Consider what happens when this student defines the problem in a new way. After more thought, he decides that his dilemma is not the quantity of his notes but their quality. He adopts a new format for taking notes, dividing his paper into two columns. In the right-hand column he writes down only the main points of each lecture. And in the left-hand column he notes two or three supporting details for each point.

While doing so, he makes the joyous discovery that there are usually just three or four core ideas to remember from each lecture. He originally thought the solution was to take more notes. What really worked was taking notes in a new way.

For added clarity, see if you can state the problem as a single question. This focuses your thinking and makes it easier to isolate and analyze the underlying issues.

You might find it tempting to gloss over this first step in problem solving, especially if your learning style favors moving into action quickly. However, consider the advantages of delaying action until you've taken time to define a problem precisely. The definition phase paves the way for the remaining three phases. Once you define a problem, you're well on the way to no longer having a problem. A clear definition of the problem can immediately suggest appropriate ways to solve it.

Phase 2: The Possibilities

Now put on your creative-thinking hat. Open up. Brainstorm as many possible solutions to the problem as you can. To get started, review the suggestions for creative thinking given in Chapter 4. Then use your critical thinking skills to weigh the pros and cons of each solution and settle on one. To complete this step, you may need to do research and gather information about the possible consequences of each solution.

Phase 3: The Plan

After rereading your problem definition and list of possibilities, choose the solution that seems most workable and plan to implement it. Think about what specific actions will reduce the gap between what you have and what you want. To create a powerful plan, list those actions in sequence and give yourself a due date to complete each one.

If you're working in a group, ask participants to visualize what the solution will look like and how it will operate when it's fully implemented in the future. With that image in mind, ask participants to list the steps they'll take to make the solution a reality and arrange those steps in chronological order.

Phase 4: The Performance

The final step gets you off your chair and out into the world. Now you actually *do* what you planned. Though this step doesn't take long to explain, it's as significant as the others. Ultimately, our skill in solving problems lies in what we do. Through the quality of our actions, we become the architect of our success.

Be sure to evaluate the results of your actions. The messy complexity of life and the fact that people and circumstances are constantly changing mean that solutions seldom "stay put." In fact, any solution has the potential to create new problems. If that happens, cycle through the four steps of problem solving again.

Expand Your Skills by Working in Groups

Many of the ideas in this chapter will help you make decisions and solve problems on your own. But to realize the full potential of these ideas, experiment with them in the context of a group.

It is true that groups can wander off the topic, waste time, or get derailed by personal conflicts. Yet groups can often come up with more information, brainstorm more ideas, and generate more solutions than individuals working alone. Making decisions and solving problems in the company of people you respect is one of the most exhilarating experiences you can have in higher education, in your career, and in your family life.

☑ checklist

USE THE FOUR "P's" OF PROBLEM SOLVING

- ❏ State the *Problem*. Whenever possible, state the problem as a single question that you want to answer.
- ❏ Create *Possibilities*. Use creative thinking to generate many possible answers to your question and critical thinking to eventually focus on one.
- ❏ *Plan* to implement the preferred solution. Create a clear list of steps that you can take to make your solution a reality.
- ❏ *Perform* your plan and evaluate the results. After acting on your plan, consider whether your solution worked or created additional problems that you need to solve.

Build a cohesive group

When meeting with other people to make decisions or solve problems, schedule some time at the beginning to establish constructive guidelines for working together. Before considering a specific decision or problem, draw up a list of ground rules or basic agreements about how the group will operate. For example:

- We will consider all points of view.
- We will focus on decisions and solutions, not on the personalities or private agendas of any group member.
- We promise to review our group's effectiveness from time to time and consider the need to change our procedures.

Consider voting

Voting presents a simple and straightforward way to make decisions in a group. Voting may be the preferred option under circumstances such as the following:

- The issue is not controversial.
- Group members must make a quick decision.
- The group is so large that discussion becomes awkward or time-consuming.
- The group is deadlocked and has exhausted other options for arriving at a decision or solution.

Although voting has the advantage of simplicity, it presents a possible disadvantage: undermining group cohesion over a controversial issue. This can happen whenever a decision or solution wins by only a slight majority—say, 55 percent in favor and 45 percent against. To prevent this outcome, you can require that at least two-thirds of the group members vote in favor of a decision or solution before it is considered passed.

Consider going for consensus

Groups that operate by consensus ask that all members agree to a decision or solution. Operating by consensus preserves group cohesion by assuring that each member fully supports the group's choice. However, going for consensus can be time-consuming. Also, it may not work well when a particular member dominates the group discussion or when an issue is so controversial that it generates emotionally charged discussion.

To promote your group's chances of reaching consensus, remember to:

- Allow all members to speak.
- Permit disagreements and make sure they are fully explored.
- Agree only to decisions and solutions that you can fully support.
- Avoid changing your mind simply to avoid conflict or save time.

Experiment with the Decreasing Options Technique

The Decreasing Options Technique (DOT) offers an efficient way to sort and rank a large pool of ideas created by groups of people in meetings. With DOT, you can sort and prioritize dozens of ideas, reducing them to a manageable number for discussion. This technique is especially useful for large groups that are asked to arrive at a decision in a short time.

Before you put DOT in action, go to an office supply store and get several hundred adhesive dots—small stickers that come in several colors and can be attached to a sheet of paper. Meeting participants will post the ideas they generate and place the dots next to their ideas, as explained in the checklist below.

In essence, the DOT method provides a visual and kinesthetic way to reduce, sort, and rank large numbers of ideas. The method is especially useful for groups with diverse viewpoints that generate competing ideas on controversial issues. This method also allows for contribution from all participants, not just those who are most vocal.

You can also use the DOT method online with bulletin boards or "virtual" meetings. Participants can use e-mail or networking software to post their ideas and manipulate computer graphics that look like sticker dots.

☑ checklist

USE THE DECREASING OPTIONS TECHNIQUE TO SORT AND RANK IDEAS

❏ **Ask meeting participants to brainstorm ideas**. Permit all ideas to be expressed. Don't censor or edit them at this stage.

❏ **Summarize each idea in a single word, phrase, or sentence on a large sheet of paper**. Write letters that are big enough to be seen across the meeting room. Place only one idea on each sheet of paper.

❏ **Post the sheets where all meeting participants can see them**. To save time, ask participants to submit ideas before the meeting takes place. That way you can summarize and post ideas ahead of time.

❏ **Do an initial "edit" of the ideas**. Ask participants if they can eliminate some ideas as obviously unworkable. Also, group similar ideas together and eliminate duplications.

❏ **"Dot" ideas**. Give each participant a handful of sticker dots. Then ask participants to go around the room and place a dot next to the ideas that they consider most important. A variation on this process is to give each participant a limited number of dots. You can also assign different levels of priority to each color of sticker.

❏ **Discuss the most important ideas.** Stand back and review the ideas. The group's favored ideas will stand out clearly as the sheets with the most dots. Now you can bring these high-priority ideas to the discussion table.

experiment WITH A STRATEGY FROM THIS CHAPTER

Think of a decision that you face right now or a problem that you want to solve. To gain the most benefit from this experiment, focus on a major decision or a persistent problem that creates negative consequences in your life. Describe that decision or problem in writing in the space below:

Now briefly review the major ideas of this chapter, looking for a suggestion that you can apply to making this decision or solving this problem. These ideas include:

- The four *I*'s of decision making
- The four *P*'s of problem solving
- Working in groups
  - Building group cohesion
  - Making decisions by voting
  - Making decisions by consensus
  - Using the Decreasing Options Technique to sort and rank ideas

In the following space, describe the suggestion that you will use. Include a specific description of how, when, and where you will apply the suggestion.

After applying this suggestion in your daily life, reflect on how well it worked for you. If it worked well, consider making this new behavior a habit. If it did not work well, write about how you can modify the suggestion or apply it in a new way so that it does promote your success:

PLANNING TO SUCCEED

Quick Reference Guide to PLANNING TO SUCCEED

6. CHOOSING YOUR LIFE PURPOSE AND GOALS

Life planning means thinking first about your life purpose and then translating it into specific goals for the long and short range.

1. **Write a statement of your life purpose (page 71)**
   Your life purpose is an umbrella, something that's big enough to include all that you want in life—everything that you want to be, do, and have. To create one:
   - Brainstorm some tentative statements of purpose—each in a single sentence. (See the examples listed on page 72.)
   - Edit your purpose statement, remembering that small shifts in wording can have major implications for the way that you manage your time and conduct your daily life.
   - Besides writing a purpose for your life, write a purpose for any key aspect of your life—your education, your family, your career, or anything else.

2. **Write long-term goals (page 73)**
   Long-term goals represent major targets in your life—precise, written descriptions of things that you want to accomplish at least one year into the future. To create such goals:
   - Create a lifeline to get a picture of what you want to accomplish decades into the future. (See the example on page 75.)
   - Use your lifeline to create long-term goals.
   - Check for characteristics of effective goal statements. (See the checklist on page 76.)

3. **Plan for the mid-term (page 75)**
   Take your long-term goals and break each of them down into more immediate milestones:
   - List any actions you could take in the next 12 months or academic year to bring yourself closer to that goal.
   - Use a yearly planner to record mid-term goals.

4. **Plan for the short term (page 77)**
   Short-term goals are those you intend to accomplish within the next month, based on your purpose statement, long-term goals, and mid-term goals. To record short-term goals:
   - Use a calendar to schedule commitments that will take place at a certain date and time.
   - Use a to-do list to record specific tasks to accomplish today or within the next week.
   - Use strategies to set priorities. (See the sidebar on page 80.)

7. MANAGING YOUR TIME

Every human being gets the same allotment of hours: 24 per day, 168 per week. Effective and efficient people simply manage these hours with exceptional skill.

1. **Use a time monitor to track your activity (page 82)**
   Begin by discovering what works—and what doesn't work—about the way you use time right now:
   - Choose a specific period during which to monitor your time—at least one week.
   - Record the times that you start and stop each daily activity using index cards, a calendar, or computer software.
   - At the end of each day, compute the total hours you devoted to each activity.
   - After you've monitored your time for at least one week, group your activities together into broader categories, listing the number of hours you spend in each category.
   - Based on your data, create a visual image of the way you spend your life. (See the example of a Time Monitor on page 85.)

2. **Plan to create balance in your life (page [XX])**
   Armed with the data you gained by monitoring your time, plan ways to reduce your work hours, increase your study hours, or make other adjustments as you choose:
   - Allow some extra space in your calendar to deal with unexpected delays.

- ◆ Realistically estimate the number of hours you'll need to complete tasks.
- ◆ Learn to say no to low-priority tasks and requests.
- ◆ Look for specific ways to balance home, work, and study commitments. (See the sidebar on page 88.)
- ◆ Delegate some tasks to other people.
- ◆ Take advantage of your circadian rhythms—the times of day when you have the greatest energy.
- ◆ Create a regular study space.
- ◆ Use two-week planning to reduce stress. (See the checklist on page 89.)

3. **Get past procrastination (page 90)**
Procrastination can undermine any schedule, no matter how carefully constructed. However, the problem is unnecessary. To solve it:
- ◆ Notice the specific ways in which you procrastinate.
- ◆ Check for attitudes that promote procrastination.
- ◆ Instead of waiting to feel "motivated" before you take action, apply the principle that action *creates* motivation.

8. CHOOSING YOUR MAJOR AND PLANNING YOUR CAREER

A satisfying and lucrative career is often the goal of education.

1. **Explore your skills (page 93)**
Talking the language of skills provides a key to planning your career, which in turn can help you choose your major:
- ◆ *Content* skills reflect how much you know about a specific subject or how well you can perform a particular procedure.
- ◆ *Transferable* skills are general abilities that apply across many different content areas.
- ◆ Use a journal to list your current activities, along with the content and transferable skills you're developing through each activity.
- ◆ Use the SCANS Reports to assess your skills. (See the sidebar on pages 96–97.)
- ◆ Look for experiences both inside and outside the classroom to help you gain new skills.

2. **Choose your major (page 95)**
Ask yourself what choices of major are compatible with your life purpose and goals:
- ◆ Resist pressure to choose too early, before you fully research your options and assess your interests.
- ◆ Remember that most of the majors offered in higher education can help you prepare for several different careers or for further study in graduate school.
- ◆ Consider creating your own major.
- ◆ Make a trial choice based on eliminating all the majors that do *not* interest you.
- ◆ As you perform the more intellectual task of researching various majors and courses, respect your intuition or "gut wisdom" in making choices.
- ◆ Look for workplace experiences, such as internships, that can help you test your choice of major—and perhaps change it.
- ◆ Add flexibility to your academic program by choosing a minor that expands your career options.

3. **Choose your career (page 99)**
The processes of choosing a major and choosing a career have many parallels:
- ◆ Start from the premise that you already know a lot about your career preferences.
- ◆ Start by ruling out careers that do *not* interest you.
- ◆ Make a trial career choice.
- ◆ Do an internship, summer job, or volunteer position in a field that interests you.
- ◆ Consult sources of information on career planning. (See the sidebar on page 101.)

4. **Create a career plan (page 101)**
Begin planning your career now, remembering that you can change your plan at any time:
- ◆ Brainstorm goals based on your trial choice of career and put them on a timeline. (See the example on page 102.)
- ◆ Refine your goals by adding specifics, such as the names of organizations you'd like to work with and names of people who can hire you.
- ◆ Do career planning tasks throughout your entire stay in higher education. (See the checklist on pages 104–105.)

chapter 6

Choosing Your Life Purpose and Goals

When people talk about getting organized, they often say, "I've just got to use my time better." Time management skills are useful, especially when you're involved in higher education. But there's a helpful step to take *before* you get down to the gritty details of scheduling the next day, week, or month. That step is choosing what you want to be and do over the course of your entire life.

"Plan life, not time," writes Ralph Keyes in his book *Timelock: How Life Got So Hectic and What You Can Do about It.* "Reflect regularly on your life as a whole. Evaluate all activities, even the most trivial, by whether they add to that life." Keyes suggests using this question as the acid test: "Does what I'm doing contribute to the life I want to lead?"

You can answer this with conviction by thinking first about your life purpose. Translating that purpose into long-term, mid-term, and short-term goals will make your life planning even more powerful.

Write a Statement of Your Life Purpose

Having a succinct statement of your overall purpose in life can be a huge help in determining what you want, planning your time, and achieving balance in your life.

Your purpose is an umbrella, something that's big enough to include all that you want in life—everything that you want to be, do, and have. An effective purpose statement tells you when goals or behaviors are off track. With your purpose firmly in mind, you can plan more effectively. You can make moment-to-moment choices about how to use your time with clarity and integrity.

A life purpose differs from a goal. A purpose represents an overall direction and statement of your core values. A purpose—for example, a desire to become more wise, loving, or accomplished at your career—is never fully accomplished. Instead, it becomes the journey of a lifetime. In contrast, goals are items that you can put on a list and cross off as you accomplish them. A single purpose statement can generate many related goals.

Brainstorm some statements of purpose

Following are some guidelines for getting started in writing your purpose statement:

- Prompt yourself with questions: What am I striving for? What is the aim or goal of my life? What is the main result I want in my life? What am I determined or resolved to achieve with my life?
- If you have no idea what to write, then just make up a purpose for now. You can change it later.
- Write several different versions of your life purpose. Later you can select one statement or combine several statements.

Refine your purpose statement

When you have several versions of your life purpose in writing, take the time to edit and refine the statements. Remember that small shifts in wording can have major implications for the way that you manage your time and conduct your daily life.

Remember that effective purpose statements are:

- **Brief.** Keep your purpose statement down to one sentence. Make your purpose statement short enough to recall in a flash as you make split-second decisions about using your time each day.
- **Memorable.** Rewrite your purpose statement until it excites your passion, creates enthusiasm, and wins your commitment. An effective purpose statement engages your heart, as well as your mind.
- **Inclusive.** See if your purpose can serve as an umbrella for everything you desire. If you find that your purpose statement excludes some of the important things you want, then you can revise your purpose statement to create a bigger "umbrella."
- **Directive.** A powerful statement of purpose implies a clear direction for your daily activities. It excludes activities that are not consistent with your core values. Your purpose statement also prompts you to add certain activities to your life or to make more time for them. To illustrate this idea, take your purpose statement and compare it with the data you collected while monitoring your time. See if all your daily activities align with your purpose statement. For example, your purpose might state that you want to be healthy—even though you seldom schedule time for exercise.

When you become aware of this contradiction, you can decrease the time you spend at other activities so that you have more time for exercise.

Live on purpose

Besides writing a purpose for your life, you can write a purpose for each aspect of your life—your education, your family, your career, individual projects at work, volunteer work, your vacation, or anything else. Ask: What do I want from this relationship? Why is this project important to me? Experiment with living with a purpose, on purpose, moment to moment.

Write Long-term Goals

Your purpose might include wonderful sentiments such as: *I want to be a good person. I want to be financially secure.* Or *I want to be happy.* But left in a general form, these statements may have little connection to your daily life. To get the most benefit from your statement of purpose, translate it into specific goals.

◆ examples

STATEMENTS OF LIFE PURPOSE

Following are examples of life purposes:

My purpose is to live, learn, love, and laugh.

My purpose is to have a wonderful life and to dramatically contribute to the quality of life on earth.

I intend to become financially independent and raise happy, healthy children.

I intend to live in harmony with all creation.

My purpose is to be a healing presence in the world.

My purpose is to promote the well-being of my family.

I intend to seek to relieve suffering and serve others.

My purpose is to become a famous, accomplished pianist.

My purpose is to serve.

My purpose is to be loved and be loving.

I intend to promote evolutionary change and be a catalyst for growth.

My purpose is to have a great time and laugh a lot.

Long-term goals are a first step toward getting your head out of the clouds. These goals clearly represent major targets in your life—precise, written descriptions of things that you want to accomplish at least one year into the future. Long-term goals can even take years or decades to achieve. They can include goals for your education, career, personal relationships, travel, financial security—whatever is important to you.

Some examples of long-term goals are:

- *Complete my college education in four years.*
- *Work as a kindergarten teacher.*
- *Create a part-time consulting business that generates a full-time income—enough money to support me and my family.*

- *Eliminate all debt from my life by age 40.*
- *Start my own business by age 30.*
- *Retire by age 50 and then start a nonprofit organization devoted to alleviating poverty.*
- *Learn to play the guitar well enough so that I could make a living in music after I graduate.*

Writing long-term goals offers a chance for you to use some essential thinking skills—for example, the ability to generate ideas with creative thinking techniques and the ability to evaluate them with critical thinking. After creating many possibilities for long-term goals, you can narrow your list down to the goals that create the most value for you. Later in this chapter, you can also read about translating long-term goals into mid-term and short-term goals, making the leap in thinking from abstract concepts to more immediate and concrete activities. (See pages 75-80.)

One benefit of long-term goal setting is that you can connect your education to something that you truly care about. Knowing that your courses will help you to accomplish a long-term goal is one way to justify all the money, time, and effort it takes to succeed in higher education.

Create a lifeline

One powerful way to create long-term goals that go decades into the future is to create a lifeline. Experiment with the following instructions:

1. Begin by taking a blank sheet of paper and orienting it horizontally. For ease in writing, you might want to use a sheet larger than notebook size, such as 11x17 inches. Using larger paper also adds significance to what you're about to create.
2. Draw a horizontal line across the middle of your paper. This is your lifeline. It represents the approximate number of years you'll be alive.
3. On the far left end of the line, draw a dot and label it with your date of birth.
4. Estimate how long you might live. Then place a dot about three-fourths of the way to the right and label it with your projected date of death. Remember that this step simply serves a useful function for this exercise and has no connection to reality. You're under no obligation to die on the date you write! The purpose of projecting a death date is just to remind you that you're mortal.
5. Next, place a dot on your lifeline that represents the present. Label it with today's date.

6. At appropriate points to the left of today's date, plot some significant events in your life. Examples are graduations, marriages, career changes, childrens' birth dates, deaths of relatives, and the dates when you landed a new job or started a business. Take at least 10 minutes for this part of the exercise.

7. Now set goals for the time between today and when you might die. Do this by adding dots to the right of today's date. Label these dots with goals that represent what you'd like to be, do, or have in the future. Add a target date to meet each goal.

◆ **example**

EXCERPT FROM A LIFELINE

Following is one section of a sample lifeline:

2005 — Declare my major in graphic design

2006 — Complete an internship with a local design firm

2007 — Graduate with a B.A. and travel in Europe for three months

2008 — Begin a full-time job in graphic design

2012 — Finish repaying student loans and begin saving for a sabbatical

2015 — Take a six-month sabbatical from work

2018 — Start my own small business focusing on magazine design

2023 — Delegate enough tasks so that I can run my business while working only 20 hours per week

You can repeat this exercise many times, ranging from once a month to once a decade. Each time you create a lifeline, you can gain new insights into the past and create a new vision for your future. Look at your lifeline as a living document—one that changes as you learn and grow. Be sure to place your lifeline in a visible place and look at it often.

Use your lifeline to create long-term goals

Creating a lifeline can yield a compelling vision of your future for years or even decades to come. Now take your lifeline to another level of power: Use it to create effective long-term goals. Take any entry on your lifeline and see if you can state it in a more precise way—one that paves the way for more immediate action. Use the following checklist as a guide.

Plan for the Mid-term

One way to make long-term goals more effective is to examine them up close. Do this by taking each long-term goal that matters to you and breaking it down into more immediate milestones: mid-term goals. Taking this step greatly increases the odds that you will meet your long-term goals and enjoy their potential benefits.

☑ checklist

CHARACTERISTICS OF AN EFFECTIVE GOAL STATEMENT

Statements of goals vary widely. Yet the most effective goals share three characteristics. These goals are:

❒ **Concrete.** Goals describe specific changes you'd like to make in yourself or your environment. Think in detail about how things would be different if your goal were attained. List the specific changes in what you'd see, feel, touch, taste, hear, be, do, or have. A financial goal probably would include an exact dollar amount. Concrete goals make clear what actions are needed and what results are expected. For example: *My career goal is to get a degree in journalism with double minors in earth sciences and Portuguese so that I can work as a reporter covering the environment in Brazil.*

❒ **Concise.** Like an effective purpose statement, an effective goal statement is short and memorable. Keep each goal statement to one sentence—25 words or less, as the old saying goes.

❒ **Congruent.** Check each goal you write to make sure that it is consistent with your statement of life purpose. Also ensure that goals are consistent with each other. For example, you might have a goal to spend more time with your family. But if you also have a financial goal that requires you to work 14-hour days, there's a contradiction that calls for your attention.

Flesh out your long-term goals

Take a few minutes to review your lifeline or other lists of long-term goals. Then focus on one of those goals. List any actions you could take in the next 12 months or academic year to bring yourself closer to that goal.

Say that your long-term goal is to start your own business by age 30. Some mid-term goals that could move you closer to this goal are:

- Take a community education course in how to start a small business.
- Brainstorm a list of products and services that I could sell.
- Brainstorm a list of potential clients for my business.
- Brainstorm a list of potential competitors for my business.
- Interview three small business owners in my community.
- Determine a possible location for my business.

Another technique for creating mid-term goals is to create a "mini-lifeline" for each long-term goal. (See the instructions for creating a lifeline on pages 74–75.) On a sheet of paper, draw a horizontal line. Place a dot on the far right end of this line, label the dot with your long-term goal, and assign a due date for that goal. Then place dots on the left side of the line to represent the goals that you'll meet in order to accomplish your long-term goal. Assign each of those interim goals a due date as well.

Use a yearly planner to record mid-term goals

Many office supply stores carry planners that include a two-page spread showing an entire academic year or calendar year at a glance. These are ideal tools for recording your mid-term goals.

As you record mid-term goals, include *any* key dates for the upcoming quarter, semester, or calendar year. These can relate to any area of life—academic, career, or family events. Examples include:

- Test dates
- Lab sessions
- Due dates for assignments
- Days classes will be canceled
- Interim due dates, such as when you plan to complete the first draft of a term paper
- Birthdays, anniversaries, and other special occasions
- Medical and dental checkups
- Car maintenance schedules
- Concerts and plays
- Due dates for major bills—insurance, taxes, car registration, credit card and installment loan payments, medical expenses, interest charges, and charitable contributions
- Trips, vacations, and holidays

You can also be creative and make your own materials. A big roll of newsprint pinned to a bulletin board or taped to a wall can serve nicely as a way to display your lifeline and mid-term goals. To make your goals more vivid, become an artist. Record your goals in colored markers and accompany them with illustrations.

Plan for the Short Term

Short-term goals are those you intend to accomplish within the next month, based on your purpose statement, long-term goals, and mid-term goals. To record short-term goals, you can use two tools:

- A calendar or planner that shows a month, week, or day at a glance
- A to-do list with items ranked by priority

Use a calendar

Using your planner, schedule any commitments that will take place at a certain date and time over the next seven days—meetings, appointments, and the like. You can also schedule due dates for assignments, review sessions for tests, and any other key events you want to remember. Carry your planner with you during the school or work day so that you can jot down commitments as they occur to you.

Some calendars and planners show only one day at a time. These can be useful, especially for people who need to schedule appointments hour by hour. But keep in mind the power of planning a whole week at a time. Weekly planning can give you a wider perspective on your activity, help you spot different options for scheduling events, and free you from feeling that you have to accomplish everything in one day.

As you use your weekly planner to record short-term goals, keep the following suggestions in mind:

- **Schedule fixed blocks of time first.** Start with class time and work time, for instance. These time periods are usually determined in advance. Other activities must be scheduled around them. As an alternative to entering your class schedule in your calendar each week, you can simply print out your class schedule, store it in your weekly planner, and consult it as needed.
- **Study two hours for every hour in class.** In higher education, it's standard advice to allow two hours of study time for every hour spent in class. If you are taking 15 credit hours, plan to spend 30 hours a week studying. The benefits of following the above advice will be apparent at exam time.

  Note: This guideline is just that—a guideline, not an absolute rule. Note how many hours you actually spend studying for each hour of class. Then ask how your schedule is working. You may want to allow more study time for some subjects.
- **Avoid scheduling marathon study sessions.** When possible, study in shorter sessions. Three 3-hour sessions are usually far more productive than one 9-hour session. When you do study in long sessions, stop and rest for a few minutes every hour. Give your brain a chance to take a break.
- **Include time for errands and travel.** The time we spend buying toothpaste, paying bills, and doing laundry is easy to overlook. These little errands can destroy a tight schedule and make us feel rushed and harried all week. Plan for them and remember to allow for travel time between locations.
- **Schedule time for fun.** Fun is important. Brains that are constantly stimulated by new ideas and new challenges need time off to digest them. Take time to browse aimlessly through the library, stroll with no destination, ride a bike, listen to music, socialize, or do other things you enjoy.

- **Allow flexibility in your schedule.** Recognize that unexpected things will happen and allow for them. Leave some holes in your schedule. Build in blocks of unplanned time. Consider setting aside time each week marked "flex time" or "open time." These are hours to use for emergencies, spontaneous activities, catching up, or seizing new opportunities.

- **Set clear starting and stopping times.** Tasks often expand to fill the time we allot for them. An alternative is to plan a certain amount of time for that reading assignment, set a timer, and stick to it. Feeling rushed or sacrificing quality is not the aim here. The point is to push yourself a little and discover what your time requirements really are.

- **Plan beyond the week.** After you gain experience with weekly planning, experiment with scheduling two weeks at a time. Planning in this way can make it easier to put activities in context—to see how your daily goals relate to longer range goals.

Use a to-do list

Your to-do list is a specific list of tasks you want to accomplish today or within the next week. These goals are not tied to a certain date and time; you can do them at any time of the day or on any day of the week. Keep this list with you, cross out items when you complete them, and add new items when you think of them.

You can record your to-do items for the day or the week on one sheet of paper. Another option is to put each to-do item on its own index card. This allows for easy sorting of jobs by priority or time. You can shuffle and rearrange cards at will. Also, you'll never have to recopy an entire to-do list. When you complete a to-do item, simply throw away or recycle the card.

Cards work well because you can slip them into your pocket, carry them with you, and record items on the run. Store all your to-do cards near the place you usually study. Every evening, pull the cards that list items you want to do the following day. If you have to-do items that extend beyond the current week, then put those items in a separate pile.

Play with arranging your cards into different categories; for example, all the cards that pertain to a single class or project can go into a single pile. To keep your piles of cards organized, store them in a file box made for this purpose, an item you can find at any office supply store.

You can also turn to cards when you feel overwhelmed by all the things you intend to do. Simply list each to-do item on a separate card and estimate the time you'll need to complete each item. If you're overbooked, then move cards to another day or week, or keep rearranging them until you come up with a solution. Group similar items together. For example, gather together all the cards that list phone calls for you to make. Plan to make all those calls at the same time. Also, put cards that list errands in the same pile. Grouping similar items together and doing them all in a single session can save you time.

Computer technology offers other options for recording to-do items. Just open up a word processing file on your desktop or laptop computer and key in all your to-do items. On a single computer screen you'll be able to see at least a couple of dozen to-do items. As with index cards, you can delete and rearrange to-do items to your heart's content.

Keep some possible disadvantages of technology in mind, however: the cost of technology along with the time it takes to boot up these devices and key in your to-do items. For planning, it's tough to beat good old-fashioned pencil and index cards—clean, quick, and cheap.

▶ sidebar

WAYS TO SET PRIORITIES

To make sure that you stay focused on what's important and avoid overscheduling, rank each to-do item by priority. One option is to simply label each item as *A*, *B*, or *C*. Items that are most important to get done today become your *A*'s. *B*'s are less important, and *C*'s can be moved to another day or week if you run short of time.

Use your to-do list to keep yourself on task, working on your *A*'s. Don't panic or berate yourself when you realize that in the last six hours, you have completed 11 *C*'s and not a single *A*. Calmly return to the *A*'s.

The *ABC* system is not the only way to rank items on your to-do list. Some people prefer the "80-20" system. This is based on the idea that 80 percent of the value from any to-do list comes from only 20 percent of the tasks on that list. So on a daily to-do list of 10 items, find the two items that will contribute most to your life. Complete those tasks without fail.

Another option is to rank items as "yes," "no," or "maybe." Do all of the tasks marked "yes." Ignore those marked "no." And put all the "maybes" on the shelf for later. You can come back to the "maybes" and mark them "yes" or "no."

As you complete tasks, cross them off your list, throw away cards, or delete them from your computer file. Letting go of to-do items can be satisfying and fun, yielding a visible reward and sense of accomplishment.

experiment WITH A STRATEGY FROM THIS CHAPTER

To get the most value from this chapter, apply the cycle of learning explained in Chapter 2 (pages 24–28).

First, review the major strategies explained in this chapter:

- Write a one-sentence statement of your life purpose.
- Based on your lifeline, create long-term goals.
- Create mid-term goals and record them in a yearly calendar.
- Create short-term goals and record them in a calendar and to-do list.

From this list, choose one strategy. In the space below, describe a way to use it, preferably within the next 24 hours:

After using the strategy and observing the results, use the space below to describe how well the strategy worked for you:

If the strategy worked well, consider making it habit. If it did *not* work well, list some ways to modify the strategy so that it becomes a better fit for you:

7

Managing Your Time

When you entered higher education, your life took on a sudden complexity. A typical day for you may be full of separate, unrelated tasks—reading; attending lectures; reviewing notes; working at a paid job; writing papers; doing special projects, research, and errands; interacting with friends and family members. Maintaining your focus and balancing your commitments in the midst of all this activity can be a continuous challenge.

A solution is time management. That phrase can call forth images of restriction and control. However, managing your time does not mean that you have to become a hyperefficient robot, chained to your to-do list and a slave to your calendar book. Instead, the idea behind time management is to impose just the amount of structure on your life that's needed to promote your success—no less and no more.

Every human being gets the same allotment of hours: 24 per day, 168 per week. You may know people who seem busy and accomplished, yet efficient and relaxed. None of these people have more hours in the day or week than you do. They simply manage their time and use their allotted hours with exceptional skill.

Use a Time Monitor to Track Your Activity

Begin time management by discovering what works and what doesn't work about the way you use time right now. The first step is to discover exactly how many hours you devote to each of your typical daily activities. This is called *time monitoring*.

Most of us have little idea where our time really goes. But with some heightened awareness and minimal record keeping, you can discover exactly how you spend your time. With this knowledge you can diagnose time-related problems with pinpoint accuracy. You can delete the time wasters and the life drainers—the activities that consume the most hours yet deliver the least in results or satisfaction. You can plan to expand or contract certain activities so that the hours of your lifetime add up in the way that you choose.

Learning to monitor your use of time will deliver benefits for the rest of your life. What you learn becomes more than a technique. It's transformed into a habit, a constant awareness of how you spend your lifetime.

To get the most benefit from this chapter, proceed like a scientist. Adopt the hypothesis that you can manage your time in more optimal ways. Then see if you can confirm or refute that hypothesis by collecting precise data in the laboratory—the laboratory in this case being your life.

Choose a specific period in which to monitor your time

To get the most benefit from monitoring your time, do it for at least one week. You can extend this practice over two weeks or even one month. Monitoring your time over greater intervals can reveal broader patterns in your behavior and yield greater insights into the way that you spend your most precious resource: you.

Track your activity

Record the times that you start and stop each daily activity over a period of 24 hours: sleeping, eating, studying, traveling to and from class, working, watching television, listening to music, sitting in lectures, taking care of the kids, running errands. To promote accuracy and accumulate useful data, track your activity in 15-minute intervals.

Choose how to record your data

One option is to carry a 3x5 index card with you each day for recording your activities. (See the example given on the following page.) Or you can use a daily calendar that includes slots for scheduling appointments at each hour of the day. Instead of scheduling events ahead of time, simply note how you actually spend each hour. You may even develop your own form for monitoring your time or learn to use computer software for this purpose. (Database programs are especially suited to time monitoring.) With practice, you'll able to record your data in a few minutes each day, no matter what method you use.

Summarize your daily data

At the end of the day, compute the total hours you devoted to each activity. Examples might include eight hours for sleeping, two hours for watching a movie, three hours of class, and six hours for studying.

If you think you already have a good idea of how you manage time, then predict how many hours you spend right now in activities such as

▶ figure 7.1 **AN EXAMPLE OF A 3 X 5 CARD**

Activity	Start	Stop
Sleeping	11:00 pm	6:00 am
Jog/Stretch	6:00 am	7:00 am
Shower/Dress	7:00 am	7:30 am
Breakfast	7:30 am	8:00 am
Travel to Campus	8:30 am	9:00 am
History	9:00 am	10:20 am
Check Email	10:30 am	11:00 am
English Lit	11:00 am	12:00 pm
Lunch/Review for Psych test	12:00 pm	1:00 pm
Work Study Job	1:00 pm	4:00 pm
Run Errands	4:00 pm	5:00 pm
Travel Home	5:00 pm	5:30 pm
Watch TV/Relax	5:30 pm	6:30 pm
Dinner/Socialize	6:30 pm	8:00 pm
Read Chapter 4/English	8:00 pm	9:00 pm
Make Flashcards for Psych test	9:00 pm	10:00 pm
Review notes from today's History/English Lectures	10:00 pm	11:00 pm

- -

Sleeping: 7 hours   Eating: 3 hours   Travel: 1 hour

Work: 3 hours   Study: 4 hours   In Class: 2 1/2 hours

Social/Relax: 2 1/2 hours   Grooming/Exercise: 1 1/2 hours

Errands/Email: 1 1/2 hours

sleeping, studying, working, or socializing. After you monitor your time for one week, see how accurate your predictions were. You'll quickly see why time management begins with acquiring a solid body of baseline data about your current use of time.

Note: As you read and apply these suggestions for monitoring your time, keep them in perspective. No one says that you have to keep track of the rest of your life in 15-minute intervals. Eventually you can monitor selected activities in your life and keep track of them only for as long as it is useful to you.

Group your activities into major categories

After you've monitored your time for at least one week, group your activities together into broader categories. Examples are *sleep, class, study,* and *meals.* Another category, *grooming,* might include showering, putting on makeup, brushing teeth, getting dressed. *Travel* can include walking, driving, taking the bus, and riding your bike. Other categories could be *exercise, entertainment, work, television, domestic,* and *children.*

List the number of hours you spend in each category

Write in the categories that work for you, and then add up how much time you spent in each of your categories. Make sure the grand total of all categories is 168 hours per week.

Reflect on your time monitor

Next, take this data and play with it. Create a visual image of the way you spend your life. Computer software can be especially useful for this purpose. A simple chart with a list of categories will do nicely.

 example

EXCERPT FROM A TIME MONITOR

One way to track your activities over a week is to put them into a chart, such as this one:

Task	Estimated Time for Completion (in hours)
Class	15
Study/Reading for Classes	45
Meals (including cooking)	21
Free Time	10
Exercise	4
Clean Apartment	3
Laundry	2
Call Family	2
Work	10
Personal Maintenance	7
Sleep	49
Total	*168*

Another option for visualizing your activity is to create a pie chart such as the one below:

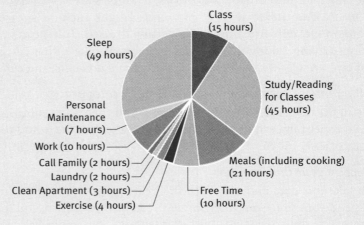

A pie chart can work powerfully for two reasons. First, a circle is a fixed shape, reinforcing the idea that you have only have a fixed amount of time to work with: 24 hours per day, 168 hours per week. Second, seeing your life represented on a pie chart tempts you to adjust the sizes of the slices—each slice being a category of activity. You make this adjustment by consciously choosing to devote more or less time to each category.

Plan to Create Balance in Your Life

After reviewing the results of your time monitoring, take a minute to let the numbers sink in. Compare your total hours for each category of activity to your predicted hours for each category. Then notice your reactions. You might be surprised. You might feel disappointed or even angry about where your time goes.

Use those feelings as fuel for planning. Plan how much time you want to spend on each category of daily activity that you monitored. To do this, you can take the same form you used to monitor your time and use it to plan instead. On this form, block out the number of hours you'd ideally like to spend on each of your daily activities.

The ultimate benefit of monitoring and planning your time is *balance*. You might discover that you're working far more hours than you want or spending far fewer hours at a hobby that's important to you. Armed with the data you gained by monitoring your time, you can plan ways to reduce your work hours, increase your hobby hours, or make other adjustments as you choose.

As you plan, allow yourself to have fun. Approach planning in the spirit of adventure. Think of yourself as an artist who's creating a new life, one that's characterized by symmetry, balance, and proportion.

The simple act of monitoring your time may give you immediate insights into ways to adjust your activities for greater balance. Also consider the following suggestions.

Place "buffer zones" in your schedule

Set due dates with care. If you estimate that you can get a paper done in five days, build some cushion into your schedule. Start the writing project a day or two earlier. Allow some extra space in your calendar to deal with unexpected delays.

Estimate hours for tasks

Exercise the same kind of care when estimating the number of hours you'll need to complete tasks. When building contractors schedule the number of hours needed to complete a construction project, they often take their first estimate and double it. This is an especially useful guideline for scheduling any large task, especially when you are inexperienced at estimating hours. Over time, as you gain practice at monitoring your time and planning, you'll be able to estimate with more confidence.

Learn to say no

This is a time-saver and a valuable life skill for everyone. Many people think that it is rude to refuse a request. But saying no can be done effectively and courteously. When you tell people that you can't do what they ask because you are busy educating yourself, most of them will understand.

Delegate tasks

Instead of doing all the housework or cooking by yourself, for example, assign some of the tasks to family members or roommates. Rather than making a trip to the library to look up a simple fact, call and ask a library assistant to do it. Instead of driving across town to deliver a package, hire a delivery service to do it. All these tactics can free up extra hours for studying.

It's not practical to delegate certain study tasks, such as writing term papers or completing reading assignments. However, you can still draw on the ideas of other people in completing such tasks. For instance, form a writing group to edit and critique papers, brainstorm topics or titles, and develop lists of sources.

Take advantage of your circadian rhythms

Many people learn best in daylight hours. If this is true for you, then schedule study time for your most difficult subjects when the sun is up.

▶ **sidebar**

BALANCE HOME, WORK, AND SCHOOL

Using a time monitor gives you the foundation for creating balance: awareness of exactly how much time you currently devote to activities at home, work, and school. With that awareness, you can make conscious adjustments in the number of hours you devote to each domain of activity. For example:

- If your responsibilities at work or home will be heavy in the near future, then register for fewer classes next term.
- Look for a better-paying job—one that allows you to maintain your income while working fewer hours.
- Make an appointment with someone at the financial aid office to ask about grants and scholarships—another way to maintain income if you choose to reduce work hours.
- Use the suggestions for money management in Chapter 1 to reduce your spending, which can give you the option to work less.
- Ask if there are any household chores you can do less frequently, delegate to family members, or simply let go while you're in school.
- Choose recreational activities carefully, focusing on those that relax and "recharge" you the most.
- Be prepared for small blocks of free time during the day: Plan study or work tasks that you can complete in 15 minutes or less.
- As you experiment with strategies from this book, notice which ones allow you to reduce the quantity of study time without sacrificing the quality of your academic performance.
- Don't load your schedule with classes that require unusually heavy amounts of reading or writing.
- Schedule blocks of study time throughout the entire week, none longer than three hours at a time.
- Also schedule blocks of time to spend with family members and close friends.

When you're in a time crunch, get up early or stay up late. Experiment with getting up 15 minutes earlier or going to bed 15 minutes later each day on a more long-term basis. Over the course of one year, either choice will yield 91 extra hours of waking activity.

Create a regular study space

Use a regular study area. Your body and your mind know where you are. They become trained when you use the same place to study, day after day. When you arrive at that particular place, you can focus your attention more quickly. Libraries are designed for learning and are particularly good places to study. As a general guideline, don't study where you sleep.

☑ checklist

USE TWO-WEEK PLANNING TO REDUCE STRESS

It's easy to know when your life is filled with too many commitments that take too much time. Often the message will come directly from your gut—a part of the human body that often sends signals of stress.

Time management can help you heal that knot in your stomach. If you're used to planning one day or one week in advance, then try your hand at planning two weeks ahead. This allows enough time for you to spot potential "crunches" in your schedule and then take preventive action. Experiment with the following steps:

❐ **List upcoming tasks**. Write down all the significant tasks you want to complete in the next 14 days. List each task on a separate index card, or use a word processing program on your computer.

❐ **Estimate the time you *need* for these tasks**. Take the tasks you listed in the previous step and estimate the number of hours needed to complete each one. Write your estimate on each card or next to each item listed on your computer. *Be realistic*. When in doubt, take your first estimate and double it. To complete this step, add up all your estimates to get a total number of hours.

❐ **Sort tasks into categories and choose how much time you *want* to spend on each category**. Common categories are *work, school*, and *family*. Sort your index cards into separate stacks based on these categories, or create separate lists on your computer. Next, figure out the number of hours you want to spend on each category. If you're employed full-time, for instance, you might want to limit yourself to 80 hours at work (40 hours per week for the next two weeks).

❐ **Assign task priorities**. Rate each task based on your commitment to completing it. Tasks that you're *absolutely* committed to getting done in the next two weeks get an *A* priority. Tasks that you *could* get done but that are less urgent or important get a *C* priority. *Note*: This is a twist on the *ABC* priority system recommended in Chapter 6. See if using just two levels of priority rather than three helps you to get a clearer sense of your commitments.

❐ **Use the "three-*D*" system to create balance.** Add up the number of hours for all your *A*-priority tasks. This step could be revealing. For example, you might discover that you *need* 100 hours to complete work tasks over the next two weeks, even though you only *want* to work 80 hours. If something like this happens, use the "three *D*'s" to reduce your *A*-priority tasks: *downgrade* some of them to *C*-priority, *delay* some tasks to the following two-week period, or *delegate* tasks to someone else. Keep adjusting tasks until you reduce the number of hours you *need* for tasks to fit the number of hours you *want* to spend.

❐ **Schedule *A*-priority tasks**. Finally, take your calendar and block out an appropriate number of hours for *A*-priority tasks. Scheduling specific dates and times for these tasks and making them visible on your calendar can increase the odds that you'll get them done.

Get Past Procrastination

Students consistently report that procrastination is one of their biggest problems. Procrastination can undermine any schedule, no matter how carefully constructed. However, the problem is unnecessary. It is also surprisingly simple to solve (though not always easy). Consider the following suggestions.

Notice how you procrastinate

Start by recording the facts. Everyone has an individual style of procrastination. Some people procrastinate at the beginning of a project, taking a long time to get started. Others start out with gusto and fizzle out before the end, failing to finish what they begin. Discover the details of your particular style and describe them in writing.

Taking this step will help you precisely diagnose your problems with procrastination. It will also point out some potential solutions.

Note: Don't judge yourself for procrastinating. Making judgments can sap your energy and make it harder to observe yourself.

Check for attitudes that promote procrastination

Certain attitudes fuel procrastination and keep you from experiencing the rewards in life that you deserve. In their book, *Procrastination: Why You Do It and What to Do about It*, psychologists Jane Burka and Lenora Yuen list these examples:

> *I must be perfect.*
> *Everything I do should go easily and without effort.*
> *It's safer to do nothing than to take a risk and fail.*
> *If it's not done right, it's not worth doing at all.*
> *If I do well this time, I must always do well.*
> *If I succeed, someone will get hurt.** *

If you find such beliefs running through your mind, write them down. Getting a belief out of your head and onto paper can rob that belief of its power. Also write a more effective belief that you want to adopt. For example: "Even if I don't complete this task perfectly, it's good enough for now and I can still learn from my mistakes."

Accept your feelings of resistance, then move into action

If you wait to exercise until you feel energetic, you might wait for months. Instead, get moving now and watch your feelings change. After five minutes of brisk walking, you might be in the mood for a 20-

---

*Excerpt from Jane Burka and Lenora Yuen, *Procrastination: Why You Do It and What to Do About It.* Copyright © 1984 Perseus Books Group. Used with permission.

minute run. Don't wait to feel "motivated" before you take action. Instead, apply the principle that action *creates* motivation.

This principle can apply to any task you've been putting off. You can move into action no matter how you feel about a task. Simply notice your feelings of resistance, accept them, and then do one task related to your goal. Then do one more task, and another. Keep at it, one task at a time, and watch procrastination disappear.

experiment WITH A STRATEGY FROM THIS CHAPTER

To get the most value from this chapter, apply the cycle of learning explained in Chapter 2 (pages 24–28).

First, review the major strategies explained in this chapter:

- Use a time monitor to track your daily activity.
- Plan to create balance in your life
  - Place "buffer zones" in your schedule
  - Learn to say no
  - Delegate tasks
  - Take advantage of your circadian rhythms
  - Take advantage of waiting time
  - Estimate hours for tasks
  - Create a regular study space
- Get past procrastination
  - Notice when you procrastinate
  - Check for attitudes that promote procrastination
  - Accept feelings of resistance
  - Move into action

From this list, choose one strategy. In the space below, describe a way to use it, preferably within the next 24 hours:

After using the strategy and observing the results, use the space below to describe how well the strategy worked for you:

If the strategy worked well, consider making it habit. If it did *not* work well, list some ways to modify the strategy so that it becomes a better fit for you:

Choosing Your Major and Planning Your Career

A satisfying and lucrative career is often the goal of education. It pays to clearly define your career goals and your strategy for reaching them. Then you can plan your education effectively.

Explore Your Skills

The word *job* brings to mind many other terms. Among them are *tasks, roles, duties, chores, responsibilities,* and *functions.* But one word comes closest to the heart of what we do in our jobs. That word is *skill.*

Skills are the core content—the "skeleton"— of any job. A career consists of the skills you use across several jobs in a related field. Talking the language of skills provides a key to planning your career, which in turn can help you choose your major.

Look for two kinds of skills

Begin from the perspective that you have many skills. One dictionary defines *skill* as "the ability coming from one's knowledge, practice, aptitude, etc., to do something well."

You gain skills from taking advanced degrees or spending years in the work force. But there are ways to gain skills other than through formal education or professional experience. In fact, *any* activity that you improve with practice can be called a skill. Just by going to school, running a household, relating to people, and pursuing your interests, you're constantly developing skills. If you can run a meeting, organize your study area, plant a garden, comfort a troubled friend, or draw interesting doodles, you've got skills that are worth money.

Keep in mind that there are at least two types of skills: content skills and transferable skills. Recognizing all your skills, content and transferable, can help you assess the full range of your current abilities and choose new skills to develop.

Content skills reflect how much you know about a specific subject or how well you can perform a particular procedure. The ability to speak Spanish is a content skill. So are the abilities to program a computer, repair a car transmission, fix a broken television, or play the piano in a jazz band. In each case, these activities call for specialized knowledge and activity.

Transferable skills are general abilities that apply across many different content areas. For example, if you do well at writing term papers in history, you could probably write well about English literature, computers, or just about anything else. You may need to acquire some new content knowledge, but you already have the ability to write—that is, to compare, analyze, and combine ideas and express them in words.

Following are more examples of transferable skills:

- Attending to detail
- Budgeting
- Calculating
- Coaching
- Consulting
- Counseling
- Drawing
- Editing
- Estimating costs
- Keeping records
- Leading meetings
- Listening
- Managing projects
- Managing time
- Negotiating
- Note taking
- Planning
- Public speaking
- Reading
- Scheduling
- Selling
- Supervising
- Teaching
- Training
- Writing

This is only a partial list. You can learn to recognize more. In fact, most of the topics covered in this book are examples of transferable skills.

Use a journal to assess your current skills

One useful tool in planning your academic experience and career is a skill journal. You can create this journal on paper or computer using a simple two-column format.

In one column, list any of your current activities—both in and out of class—that lead to skill development. Examples of these activities are studying, volunteering, doing internships, working part-time or full-time, taking part in study groups, caring for children, and performing household duties.

In the second column, list the skills you use to perform each activity. Also note any accomplishments, rewards, or other forms of recognition related to the use of those skills.

Your skill journal is far more than an academic exercise. It can furnish the raw material for résumés, letters of application, and other crucial documents related to your major and career. To create the most value from this journal, update it continually.

Plan to develop new skills

The courses you take in higher education—both to fulfill general education requirements and to complete a major or minor—offer continual opportunities to develop skills. So do part-time or full-time jobs, internships, volunteer programs, and service learning programs.

As you choose your courses and participate in extracurricular experiences, return to your skill journal. Look for experiences both inside and outside the classroom that will help you gain new skills.

Choose Your Major

The prospect of choosing a major can seem daunting, even intimidating. To reduce the stress that's sometimes associated with this choice, back up to the big picture. Ask yourself what choices of major are compatible with your life purpose and goals (see Chapter 6). Also keep the following suggestions in mind.

Resist pressure to choose early

For many people in higher education, freshman year is too early to settle on the final choice of a major. If you're undecided about your major when you enter higher education, you're probably in the majority of people on your campus. And if you change your major several times, you will not be unusual.

▶ sidebar

USE THE SCANS REPORTS TO ASSESS YOUR SKILLS

In the early 1990s, the U.S. Department of Labor began issuing reports created by the Secretary's Commission on Achieving Necessary Skills (SCANS). This series of documents, called the *SCANS reports,* lists skills that can promote success for workers as they enter the next century. You can use these influential documents to develop your résumé, plan your career, and link your school experiences to the world of work.

The SCANS reports identify three foundations (basic skills, thinking skills, and personal qualities) and five core competencies (abilities to work with resources, interpersonal skills, information, systems, and technology). More details about each of these follow.

BASIC SKILLS

- Reading to locate, understand, and interpret written information.
- Writing to communicate ideas and information.
- Using arithmetic to perform basic computations and solve problems.
- Listening to interpret and respond to verbal messages and other cues.

THINKING SKILLS

- Speaking to inform and persuade others.
- Creative thinking to generate new ideas.
- Decision making to set and meet goals.
- Problem solving to identify challenges and implement action plans.
- Seeing things in the mind's eye to interpret and create symbols, pictures, graphs, and other visual tools.
- Knowing how to learn.

PERSONAL QUALITIES

- Responsibility to exert high effort and persist in meeting goals.
- Self-esteem to maintain a positive view of your abilities.
- Social skills that demonstrate adaptability and empathy.
- Self-management to assess yourself accurately, set personal goals, and monitor personal progress.

Keep this choice in perspective

Choosing your major and choosing your career can be intimately related activities. However, your choice of a major does not bind you to a certain job or career. Most of the majors offered in higher education can help you prepare for several different careers or for further study in graduate school.

Remember that many people work in careers unrelated to their majors. In addition, the odds are that you'll change careers several times during

RESOURCES
- Allocating time for goal-relevant activities.
- Allocating money to prepare budgets and meet them.
- Allocating materials and facilities.
- Allocating human resources to assign tasks effectively and provide others with feedback.

INTERPERSONAL SKILLS
- Participating as a member of a team.
- Teaching others.
- Serving clients and customers.
- Exercising leadership.
- Negotiating to reach agreements.
- Working with diversity.

INFORMATION
- Acquiring and evaluating information.
- Organizing and maintaining information.
- Interpreting and communicating information in oral, written, and visual forms.
- Using computers to process information.

SYSTEMS
- Understanding how social and technological systems operate.
- Monitoring and correcting performance.
- Improving or designing systems.

TECHNOLOGY
- Selecting appropriate technology.
- Applying technology to tasks.
- Maintaining and troubleshooting technology.

Adapted from U.S. Department of Labor, Skills and Tasks for Jobs: A SCANS Report for America 2000. *1992. Online: wdr.doleta.gov/SCANS/whatwork/whatwork.html*

your life. One benefit of higher education is mobility—gaining transferable skills that can help you move into a new job or career at any time.

Design your own major

When choosing a major, you may not need to limit yourself to those listed in your course catalog. Many schools now have flexible programs that allow for independent study. Through such programs you might be able to combine two existing majors or even invent one. Some people graduate without a conventional major, creating a one-of-a-kind degree of their own design.

Make a trial choice

Chances are you already know a lot about what your major's going to be. To verify this, do a short experiment.

First, search your school's catalog, online or in print, for a list of available majors. Now cross out all those majors you already know are not right for you. You will probably eliminate well over half the list.

Next, scan the remaining majors. Sort this list into two categories: *yes* and *maybe*. Focusing on your "yes" choices will reduce the list even more and perhaps even give you a trial choice of major.

You can repeat this experiment at any point during your time in higher education. As you do, be willing to move items from the "maybe" category to the "yes" category. Also feel free to increase your list of "no's."

Use your intellect and your intuition

Pretend that you have to choose a major today. Write down the first ideas that come to mind, and don't stop to censor any choices. Hold on to this list, which reflects your intuition or "gut wisdom," as you perform the more intellectual task of researching various majors and courses. Your research may lead to a major that's not on the list, or it may confirm one of your original ideas.

Test your choice and be willing to change

When you've made a trial choice of major, take on the role of a scientist. Treat your choice as a hypothesis and then design a series of experiences to test it. For example:

- Study your school's list of required courses for this major and ask yourself whether these classes offer a good fit for your interests and long-term goals.
- Discuss your trial choice with a teacher, academic advisor, or career counselor.
- Enroll in a course related to your possible major.
- Find a volunteer experience, internship, part-time job, or service learning experience related to your trial choice.
- Meet informally with students who have declared the same major.
- Interview someone who works in a field related to the major.
- Ask other people—friends, family members, teachers—to suggest a major based on their knowledge of you.

If these experiences confirm your major, you can celebrate the fact that you're making an informed choice. If they result in choosing a new major, celebrate that outcome as well. Changing majors is often a natural result of getting to know yourself and your educational program better.

Choose a minor to expand your options
You can add flexibility to your academic program through your choice of a minor. This course of study can complement your choice of a major. The student who wants to be a minister could opt for a minor in English; all those courses in composition can help in writing sermons. Or the student with a major in psychology might choose a minor in business administration with the idea of managing a counseling service some day.

Choose Your Career
Note that the processes of choosing a major and choosing a career have many parallels. The suggestions given here mirror several of the ideas presented earlier in this chapter about choosing your major.

Consider that you already know a lot about your career choices
You've already made many decisions about your career. This is true for young people who say, "I don't have any idea what I want to be when I grow up." It's also true for mid-life career changers.

Take, for example, the student who can't decide if she wants to be a cost accountant or a tax accountant and then jumps to the conclusion that she is totally lost when it comes to career planning. It's the same with the student who doesn't know if he wants to be a veterinary assistant or a nurse.

These people forget that they already know a lot about their career choices. The person who couldn't decide between veterinary assistance and nursing had already ruled out becoming a lawyer, computer programmer, or teacher. He just didn't know yet whether he had the right bedside manner for horses or for people. The person who was debating tax accounting versus cost accounting already knew she didn't want to be a doctor, playwright, or taxicab driver. She did know she liked working with numbers and balancing books.

In each case, these people have already narrowed their list of career choices to a number of jobs in the same field—jobs that draw on the same core skills. In general, they already know what they want to be when they grow up.

Start by ruling out careers
Find a long list of occupations. (One source is *The Occupational Outlook Handbook,* a government publication available at many libraries.) Using a stack of index cards, write down 50 randomly selected job titles, one title per card. Sort through the cards and divide them into two piles.

Label one pile "Careers I've Definitely Ruled Out for Now." Label the other pile "Possibilities I'm Willing to Consider."

It's common for people to go through a stack of such cards and end up with 45 in the "definitely ruled out" pile and five in the "possibilities" pile. This demonstrates that they already have a career in mind.

Make a trial choice

Many people approach career planning as if they were panning for gold. They keep sifting through the dirt, clearing the dust, and throwing out the rocks. They are hoping to strike it rich and discover the perfect career.

Other people believe they'll wake up one morning, see the heavens part, and suddenly know what they're supposed to do. Many of them are still waiting for that magical day to dawn.

We can approach career planning in a different way. Career planning can be the bridge between our dreams and the reality of our future. Instead of seeing a career as something we discover, we can see it as something we choose. We don't find the right career. We create it.

There's a big difference between these two approaches. Thinking that there's only one "correct" choice for your career can lead to a lot of anxiety: "Did I choose the right one? What if I made a mistake?"

Viewing your career as your creation helps you relax. Instead of anguishing over finding the right career, you stay open to possibilities. You choose one career today, knowing that you can choose again later.

Suppose that you've narrowed your list of possible careers to five, and you still can't decide. Then just choose one. Any one. Many people will have five careers in a lifetime anyway. You may be able to do all your careers, and you can do any one of them first. The important thing is to choose.

Test Your Choice and Be Willing to Change

Choosing your career is not something to do in an information vacuum. Rather, choose after you've done a lot of research. That includes research into yourself—your skills and interests—and a thorough knowledge of what careers are available.

Career-planning materials and counselors can help you on both counts. You can take skills assessments to find out more about what you like doing. You can take career-planning courses and read books about careers. You can contact people who are actually doing the job you're researching and ask them what it's like. You can also choose an internship, summer job, or volunteer position in a field that interests you. What's more, the people you meet through these experiences are possible sources of recommendations, referrals, and employment in the future.

Career planning is not a once-and-for-all proposition. Rather, career plans are made to be changed and refined as you gain new information about yourself and the world. Career planning never ends. If your present career no longer feels right, you can choose again—no matter what stage of life you're in. The process is the same, whether you're choosing your first career or your fifth.

Create a Career Plan

You can create a career plan at any time—right now, even before you assess your skills, research jobs, or complete any of the other tasks mentioned in this chapter. Keep in mind that any career plan you create can be revised later. In fact, powerful career plans are often reviewed and

▶ sidebar

SOURCES OF INFORMATION FOR CAREER PLANNING

Vocational assessments are resources for discovering your skills and interests. These assessments are also called *vocational aptitude tests, skill inventories,* and *interest assessments.* You can learn more about them through your school's career center or library.

Before you take an assessment, find out whether there is a cost involved and whether anyone will go over the results with you. Also remember that these are not tests. There are no right or wrong answers to the questions they ask. Rather, they are sources of information about your interests and skills. Some examples of vocational assessments are:

- *California Psychological Inventory*
- *Career Ability Placement Survey*
- *Career Thoughts Inventory*
- *Hall Occupational Orientation Inventory*
- *Myers-Briggs Type Indicator Instrument*
- *Strong Interest Inventory*

In addition to taking assessments, take the time to research jobs and careers related to your skills and goals. Again, your campus library and career center or a job placement center can guide you to published sources of information, both online and in print. Examples include:

- *The Occupational Outlook Handbook,* published by the U.S. government, both in print and online at www.bls.gov/oco/home.htm.
- *O*NET* at www.doleta.gov/programs.onet/glance.asp, an online job encyclopedia.
- *What Color Is Your Parachute?* by Richard Bolles, a best-selling book on career planning and job hunting, updated yearly.
- *The Ultimate Job Hunter's Guidebook* by Susan D. Greene and Melanie C. L. Martel.
- *The Job Hunter's Bible* at www.JobHuntersBible.com, created by Richard Bolles.
- *Career Resource Center* at www.careers.org.
- *America's Job Bank* at www.ajb.dni.us.

updated. The point is to jump into the process, have fun, and start making choices about your future. The following suggestions offer ways to get started:

Brainstorm your career goals

To begin, write down any career-related ideas—the very first thoughts that come to mind. Use the following tips to spur your creativity:

- Remember that your career plan can be lengthy and detailed or as short as one sentence or one paragraph.
- Experiment with several different formats for recording your career plan. One option is to simply describe the next job you want to find and list the steps you will take to get it. Another is to create a list of career goals that extends years into the future and encompasses several different jobs. An alternative to making lists is to create visuals such as a lifeline (see Chapter 6, pages 74–75).
- Speak about your career plan. Simply talk about where you'd like to work and what you'd like to do. Speak into a tape recorder, or ask a friend to listen and take notes.

No matter what format or process you choose to create your career plan, put it in writing at some point. The process of writing allows you to revise your plan, and revision can make it clearer.

◆ **example**

EXCERPT FROM A CAREER PLAN

- May 2007—Graduate with a teaching degree
- August 2008—Begin teaching high-school physics
- September 2015—Begin saving 5 percent of my income to fund a personal sabbatical
- September 2019—Return to school for a graduate degree in school administration
- September 2021—Begin my career as a high school principal
- September 2025—Take a one-year sabbatical to live and work part-time in New Zealand
- September 2026—Return to job as high school principal
- January 2029—Begin a home-based business consulting with teachers and principals about ways to avoid job burnout

Refine your goals by adding specifics

One key to making your career plan real and ensuring that you can act on it is naming. Go back over your plan to see if you can include specific names whenever they're appropriate.

Name your job. Take the skills you enjoy using and find out which jobs use them. What are those jobs called? List them. Note that the same job may have several different names.

Name the organizations you want to work for. You may already know that you want to seek employment at a specific business or nonprofit organization. On the other hand, if you want to be self-employed or start your own business, then name the product or service you'd sell. Also list some possible names for your business and potential clients or customers.

Name your contacts. Take the list of organizations you just compiled. What people in these organizations are responsible for hiring? List those people and contact them directly. If you choose self-employment, list the names of possible customers or clients. All these people are job contacts.

Expand your list of contacts by brainstorming with your family and friends. Come up with a list of names—anyone who can help you with career planning and job hunting. Write each of these names on a 3x5 card or Rolodex card. You can also use a spiral-bound notebook or computer.

Next, call the key people on your list. After you speak with them, make brief notes about what you discussed. Also, jot down any actions you agreed to take, such as a follow-up call.

Consider everyone you meet a potential member of your job network, and be prepared to talk about what you do. Develop a "pitch"—a short statement of your career goal that you can easily share with your contacts. For example: "After I graduate, I plan to work in the travel business. I'm looking for an internship in a travel agency for next summer. Do you know of any that take interns?"

Name your location. Ask if your career choices are consistent with your preferences about where to live and work. For example, someone who wants to make a living as a studio musician might consider living in a large city such as New York or Toronto. This contrasts with the freelance graphic artist who conducts her business mainly by phone, fax, and mail. She may be able to live just about anywhere and still pursue her career.

☑ checklist

A FOUR-YEAR PLAN FOR CAREER PLANNING

The following guide to career planning is adapted from *Career Development from First Year to Senior Year*, a publication of the career center at Colorado State University. If your schooling does not follow a traditional four-year plan, then adapt this checklist. Also note that one suggestion applies to all four years: Keep your grades up.

First Year: Awareness
Identify your interests, values, skills, and achievements and use this knowledge to gather information about possible majors and careers:
❒ Visit your school's career center and learn about its services.
❒ Make an appointment with a career counselor.
❒ Get involved in student organizations, volunteer programs, and service learning.
❒ Talk to your parents, relatives, teachers, and friends about the process of career planning.
❒ Explore majors by browsing your school catalog.
❒ Meet with academic and department advisors to identify courses that can help you explore your interests.
❒ Investigate part-time jobs and internship opportunities related to possible choices of major or career.

Sophomore Year: Exploration
Explore how your choice of major fits with possible career goals:
❒ Meet with academic advisors and choose a major.
❒ Learn specifics about occupations related to your major—employment outlook, salary ranges, job responsibilities, and education requirements.
❒ Register for specific services from your school's career center, such as career counseling, career fairs, online job searches, and campus recruiting.
❒ Develop a résumé and write cover letters for part-time jobs or internships.
❒ Schedule a videotaped practice interview.
❒ Consider a leadership role with student organizations, volunteer programs, or service learning programs.
❒ Keep talking with parents, relatives, faculty, and friends about career goals.

Junior Year: Experience

While continuing to research careers, gain hands-on experience:

- ❐ Continue to take part in internships, volunteerism, and part-time jobs related to your chosen major and career.
- ❐ Begin information interviewing with people working in careers related to your major.
- ❐ If you're considering graduate or professional schools, learn about requirements for admission.
- ❐ Schedule regular meetings with your career counselor and continue to visit your school's career center.
- ❐ Connect with people working in your chosen field and "shadow" them on the job.
- ❐ Update your résumé, have it critiqued at the career center, and schedule a videotaped practice interview.
- ❐ Attend career fairs to network with employers, find out about industries and companies, and discuss internships.
- ❐ Check with your faculty advisor to ensure you are on track for graduation.
- ❐ Take electives that are relevant to your career goals.
- ❐ Join professional organizations in your field to network with employers and learn more about the industry.

Senior Year: Job Search

Make specific decisions about career goals and begin job searching:

- ❐ Develop a network of contacts for your job search—people you met during internships, service learning, volunteering, information interviews, job shadowing, and career fairs.
- ❐ If you plan to attend graduate or professional school, complete the application process.
- ❐ Use career center services to identify, research, and contact potential employers.
- ❐ Update your résumé and schedule another videotaped practice interview.
- ❐ Meet with faculty, employers, or advisors to ask them to write letters of recommendation.
- ❐ Stay active in professional organizations related to your career.

Source: "Career Development from First Year to Senior Year," taken from http://career.stuser.colostate.edu/seminar1/freshman.html.

▶experiment WITH A STRATEGY FROM THIS CHAPTER

To get the most value from this chapter, apply the cycle of learning explained in Chapter 2 (pages 24–28).

First, review the major strategies explained in this chapter:

- Explore your skills
  - Assess your current skills
  - Choose skills you want to gain and plan to develop them
- Choose your major
  - Resist the pressure to choose early
  - Keep this choice in perspective
  - Make a trial choice
  - Test your choice and be willing to change
  - Choose a minor to expand your options
- Choose your career
  - Start by ruling out careers
  - Make a trial choice
  - Test your choice and be willing to change
- Create a career plan
  - Brainstorm your career goals
  - Refine your goals

From this list, choose one strategy. In the space below, describe a way to use it, preferably within the next 24 hours:

After using the strategy and observing the results, use the space below to describe how well the strategy worked for you:

If the strategy worked well, consider making it habit. If it did *not* work well, list some ways to modify the strategy so that it becomes a better fit for you:

READING AND NOTE-TAKING WITH A PURPOSE

Quick Reference Guide to READING AND NOTE-TAKING WITH A PURPOSE

9. USING THREE STEPS TO ACTIVE READING

The strategies used by skilled readers fall into three main categories.

1. **Ask questions about what you read (page 111)**
   To frame questions about your reading:
   - Preview by scanning key elements of the text. (See the checklist on page 112).
   - Create an informal outline to understand the structure of the reading. (See the example on page 113).
   - List the questions you want to answer as you read. (See the sidebar on page 114.)

2. **Read to answer your questions (page 114)**
   After previewing, outlining, and framing questions:
   - Read with focused attention; plan to expend energy.
   - Make several "passes" through the text at varying levels of speed and depth of understanding.
   - Consider underlining or annotating your text in other ways. (See the sidebar on page 116.)

3. **Reflect on the answers (page 116)**
   After extracting key points and significant details from a text, burn them into your memory and practice critical thinking:
   - From the text, get the answers to the questions you raised earlier and write those answers down.
   - Use recitation to rehearse the ideas and facts you want to remember.
   - Evaluate the author's ideas and use them to create insights of your own.

10. BECOMING A FLEXIBLE READER

Learn to absorb information and ideas published in many media—both print and electronic.

1. **Make choices about what to read (page 121)**
   Books about time management often mention the "80/20" principle: 80 percent of the value created by any group derives from only 20 percent of its members. You can apply this idea to reading:
   - Focus on the content that creates the most value for you.
   - Remember that in order to find the "top 20" items in any group, you must attend to 100 percent of the items.
   - Estimate the total number of hours you'll need to complete your entire reading load for the current term; then schedule blocks of time in your calendar for reading.
   - As you read, constantly ask: *What's most important here?*

2. **Adjust your reading pace (page 124)**
   You can often read faster simply by making a conscious effort to do so:
   - Set goals to read a certain amount of material in a limited period of time; keep track of your progress.
   - As you read, release tension simply by noticing it.
   - Notice and release *regression*—the habit of instantly going back to text that you've already read.
   - Notice and release *vocalizing*—reading word by word, silently or out loud.
   - To build your skills, practice the above techniques with simpler reading materials.
   - Remember that speed reading isn't everything; staying *flexible* with your speed is more important.
   - Use strategies to overcome confusion. (See the sidebar on page 126.)

3. **Read across the curriculum (page 125)**
   Vary your reading strategies as needed for texts in different disciplines:

- Find the *animating questions*—the fundamental inquiries raised in each discipline.
- Ask different questions as you read to *understand* theories, to *solve* problems, and to *interpret* events and gain *insight*. (For examples, see pages 126–129.)

4. **Build your vocabulary (page 130)**

A large vocabulary increases the range of materials you can read and gives you more options for self-expression when speaking or writing. To build your vocabulary:

- Keep a dictionary handy as you read.
- Use a computer to create a personalized list of key words and definitions. (See the checklist on page 130.)
- Distinguish between the major parts of words: prefixes, roots, and suffixes.
- Learn common prefixes, roots, and suffixes. (See the checklist on pages 131–133.)
- While reading, deduce the meaning of words by paying attention to their context—for example, their position in lists, comparisons, and contrasts.

11. USING SEVEN TOOLS FOR POWERFUL NOTES

While you are participating in higher education, you may spend hundreds of hours taking notes. Experimenting with ways to make those notes more effective is a direct investment in your success.

1. **Set the stage for note-taking (page 135)**

You can promote your success at the task by "psyching up"—setting the physical and mental stage to receive what your teachers have to offer:

- Complete required reading before you go to class.
- Arrive early to put your brain in gear by reviewing reading, rereading notes, or working problems.
- Sit in the front of the classroom—a signal that you're ready to fully participate in class.
- Develop the habit of labeling and dating your notes at the beginning of each class.

2. **Choose your technology for note-taking (page 137)**

More technology is available for taking notes than ever before. To choose wisely:

- Consider the pros and cons of recorders (see page 137).
- Consider the pros and cons of using laptop computers in class (see page 138).
- Consider the reliability of the simplest technology for note-taking: paper and pen.
- Give your eyes a break by leaving plenty of space in your notes; no matter what technology or note-taking format you use.
- Take effective notes on online material. (See the sidebar on page 139.)

3. **Sharpen your listening skills (page 140)**

Your ability to take notes in any course—from American history to zoology—can improve when you master a core set of listening skills:

- Look for ways to overcome external distractions.
- Give the speaker feedback; make eye contact and ask questions. Remember that you can listen fully and take accurate notes even when you disagree with a lecturer.
- Don't let your attitude about an instructor's lecture style, habits, or appearance get in the way of taking notes.
- Be prepared for lecturers who talk fast. (See the sidebar on page 141.)

4. **Use abbreviations carefully (page 142)**

Use standard abbreviations; if you make up your own, write a key explaining them in your notes. (See the sidebar on page 143.)

5. **Use key words (page 142)**

Taking effective notes calls for split-second decisions about which words are essential to record and which are extraneous:

- Reduce a speaker's material to key words— usually nouns, verbs, and technical terms. (See the example on page 144.)

6. **Listen for levels of ideas (page 144)**

Listen for signals from the speaker that reveal the organization of her material:

- Notice transitional words and phrases that signal a new major topic.
- In your notes, reveal levels of ideas through visual devices such as lists and charts; underline or otherwise emphasize main topics and key points. (See the example on page 146.)
- Put brackets around extra material, such as your own thoughts and major digressions from the stated topic.

7. **Predict test questions (page 147)**

Predicting test questions can keep you focused on key content and help you choose your learning strategies:

- Start a separate section in your notebook labeled *Test Questions*.
- Create a signal to flag possible test items in your notes.
- Notice what topics your teacher emphasizes verbally and look for nonverbal cues that material is important—for example, material written on the board.
- Ask your instructor to describe the tests she plans to give: how long they will be and what kind of questions to expect.
- Brainstorm possible test questions and answer them.

- Remember the obvious—the teacher who introduces a topic and says: *This will be on the test.*

12. NOTES: EXPERIMENTING WITH THE CORNELL FORMAT

Think of your notes as a textbook that *you* create—one that's more current and more in tune with your learning preferences than any book you could ever buy.

1. **Create your Cornell notes (page 151)**
   The cornerstone of this system is simple: a wide margin on the left-hand side of the page called the *cue column*. You can also leave a two-inch space at the bottom of the page—the *summary area*. (See the example on page 153.)

2. **Study from your Cornell notes (page 152)**
   - Edit your notes by proofreading and rewriting illegible or unclear passages.
   - Fill in the cue column with key words, questions, or headings.
   - Use the cue column to recite the main points from your notes.
   - Use the summary area to reflect on the "big picture." (See the example on page 155.)

13. NOTES: EXPERIMENTING WITH MAPS

Maps quickly, vividly, and accurately show the relationships between ideas in visual form.

1. **Create mind maps (page 157)**
   See the sample mind map on page 159. Then play with the following steps for creating your own mind maps:
   - Write the main topic in the center of the page.
   - Add minor topics.
   - Use key words only.
   - Add visuals and color.
   - Allow space.
   - Link maps together.
   - Study from mind maps by revising them, recreating them from memory, and reciting the main points from them.
   - Combine mind maps with other types of notes.

2. **Create concept maps (page 161)**
   See the sample concept map on page 162 and then create your own concept maps:
   - Choose one concept as a focus.
   - List related concepts.
   - Arrange concepts in a hierarchy from general to specific.
   - Add links—key words that describe the relationship between concepts.
   - Revise your map for accurate links and hierarchy of concepts.
   - Study from concept maps by revising them, recreating them from memory, and reciting the main points from them.

- Supplement maps with other graphic organizers. (See the checklist on page 164.)

14. NOTES: EXPERIMENTING WITH OUTLINES

Outlines don't have to be rigid, dull affairs. In fact, they can help you reveal the structure of an entire subject matter.

1. **Create outlines (page 165)**
   Outlines consist of *headings*—words, phrases, or sentences arranged in a hierarchy that ranges from general to specific. To get the most from outlining:
   - Distinguish between levels of headings.
   - Choose your heading styles—the visual differences between the various levels of headings.
   - Create topic outlines.
   - Create outlines that use full sentences as headings.

   See the sample outlines on pages 166–168.

2. **Create outlines with a computer (page 168)**
   With computer software, outlining becomes a flexible and intuitive tool for sharpening your thinking.
   - Create headings at various levels.
   - Alternately hide and reveal various levels of headings and text.
   - Edit headings with ease.
   - Use outlines to promote critical thinking: By reflecting on the wording and sequence of headings, you can spot gaps in logic, missing topics, and topics that need to be deleted or rearranged.
   - Use outlines to collaborate with other writers: Create major headings as a group; then print out copies of the outline and ask each person in the group, working alone, to fill in another level or two of headings below each major heading.

3. **Study from outlines (page 170)**
   Revise and recite from your outlines; also recreate them from memory.

15. CREATING MORE VALUE FROM YOUR NOTES

Add value to your notes by continuously updating, condensing, reorganizing, reviewing, and refining them.

1. **Revise your notes (page 172)**
   Approach your notes as works in progress—documents that can almost always be improved:
   - Stage 1: Evaluate your notes and then clean them up. (See the sidebar on page 173.)
   - Stage 2: Recreate your notes in a new format.

2. **Review your notes (page 174)**
   - Review notes within 24 hours; review them again each week and as a whole before a major test.
   - Use rehearsal to reinforce memory of your notes. (See the sidebar on page 175.)

3. **Expand on your notes with a personal journal (page 176)**
   Reflect on the significance of your courses and mine

your own experiences for examples of the ideas you're learning about:

- Use a journal to record personal insights and plan changes in behavior.
- Use a journal to manage stress by recording and refuting disempowering thoughts.
- Create a powerful journal simply by creating lists. (See the checklist on page 178.)

4. **Take notes on reading (page 178)**

Sometimes you will want more extensive notes on your reading than you can write in a margin of your text:

- Use a variety of formats—Cornell notes, maps, outlines, or a format of your own creation. Or write quickly about what you intend to remember from the text, and don't worry about following any format.
- Copy a few key passages from your text word for word.
- Test your understanding by capturing the main point of an entire chapter in a single paragraph or a single sentence.
- Pretend that you're taking an essay exam: Create an open-ended question on a topic from your reading and then write your answer.
- Single out a particularly difficult section of a text and make separate notes.

For examples of ways to take notes on reading, see pages 180–181.

chapter 9

Using Three Steps to Active Reading

Picture yourself sitting at a desk, an open book in your hands. Your eyes are open, and it looks as though you're reading. Suddenly your head jerks up. You blink. You realize your eyes have been scanning the page for 10 minutes. Even so, you can't remember a single thing you have read.

Contrast this scenario with the image of an active reader. This is a person who:

- Stays alert, poses questions about what she reads, and searches for the answers.
- Recognizes levels of information within the text, separating the main points and general principles from supporting details.
- Quizzes herself about the material, makes written notes, and lists unanswered questions.
- Instantly spots key terms and takes the time to find the definitions of unfamiliar words.
- Thinks critically about the ideas in text and looks for ways to apply them.

That sounds like a lot to do. Yet skilled readers routinely accomplish all this and more while enjoying their reading. One way to experience their kind of success is to approach reading with a system in mind. Using the following three steps can turn you into an active reader by the time you finish this chapter.

Ask Questions About What You Read

Learning is born of questions. Questions open up inquiries. Questions focus your attention and prompt you to become an active learner. Questions help you get your money's worth from your textbooks.

Powerful reading starts with powerful questions. To frame questions about your reading, first do a preview. Also create an informal outline to discover how the material is organized.

Preview

Previewing can significantly increase your comprehension of reading material. It's also an easy way to get started when an assignment looks too big to handle.

If you are starting a new book, look over the table of contents and flip through the text page by page. If you're going to read one chapter, flip through the pages of that chapter. Pay special attention to material located at the beginning and end of each chapter. You'll often find summaries and other useful cues there. Even if your assignment is merely a few pages in a book, you can benefit from a brief preview of the table of contents.

Keep the preview short. If the entire reading assignment will take less than an hour, your preview might take five minutes.

When previewing, look for familiar concepts, facts, or ideas. These items can help link new information to previously learned material. Also look for ideas that spark your imagination or curiosity. Ask yourself how the material can relate to your long-term goals.

Outline

With complex material, take time to understand the structure of what you are about to read. Outlining actively organizes your thoughts about the assignment, and it can make complex information easier to understand. If your textbook provides chapter outlines, spend some time studying them.

Eventually you can make a formal outline of your reading (see Chapter 14). But to get started, stick with a simple, informal outline. Capture each topic in a single word or phrase. List topics in the order in which

☑ checklist

WHAT TO LOOK FOR WHEN YOU PREVIEW

❑ **"Front matter,"** such as the copyright page, preface, dedication, introduction, and table of contents; also look for sectional or chapter tables of contents, chapter previews, and abstracts.

❑ **Graphically highlighted material**—anything underlined or printed in large, bold, or italic type.

❑ **Visuals,** including boxes, charts, tables, diagrams, illustrations, and photographs.

❑ **"Back matter,"** such as a glossary, bibliography, list of references or works cited, and index; in books, look for chapter summaries and lists of review questions.

they're mentioned in the text. You can create this outline in pencil in the margins of a book or article. For added precision, copy your outline on separate paper and edit it after reading. Or open up a computer file and create your outline there.

The amount of time you spend on this step will vary. For some assignments (fiction and poetry, for example), skip it. For other assignments, a 10-second mental outline is all you need.

List questions

Before you begin a careful reading, determine what you want from an assignment. Write a list of questions.

Have fun with this technique. Make the questions playful or creative. You don't need an answer to every question that you ask. The purpose of making up questions is to get your brain involved in the assignment.

Questions can come from the previous steps, previewing and outlining. For example:

- **Brainstorm a list of topics covered in a chapter**. Then write a question about each topic.
- **Turn chapter headings and subheadings into questions**. For example, if a heading is "Transference and Suggestion," ask yourself: *What are transference and suggestion? How does transference relate to suggestion?* Make up a quiz as if you were teaching this subject to your classmates.
- **Have an imaginary dialogue with your teacher or with the author of the book**. List the questions you would ask.
- **If you do not understand a concept, write specific questions about it**. The more detailed your questions, the more powerful this technique becomes.

 example

A HEADING-BASED OUTLINE

Headings in the text can serve as major and minor entries in your outline. For added clarity, distinguish major headings from minor headings.

Using the headings in this chapter, you could create the following outline:

1. ASK QUESTIONS ABOUT WHAT YOU READ [major heading]
   Preview [minor heading]
   Outline [minor heading]
   Question [minor heading]

2. READ TO ANSWER YOUR QUESTIONS [major heading]
   Read with focused attention [minor heading]
   Make several passes through the text [minor heading]

3. REFLECT ON WHAT YOU READ [major heading]
   Answer your questions [minor heading]
   Reflect by reciting [minor heading]
   Think critically about your reading [minor heading]
   Note: Feel free to rewrite headings so that they are more meaningful to you. Substitute complete sentences for headings that consist of just a single word or phrase. In addition, you can write a sentence or two after each heading to include some more details about the topic.

▶ sidebar

SIX KINDS OF QUESTIONS TO ASK BEFORE READING

You've probably heard of the six "journalist questions": *Who? What? When? Where? Why? How?* Journalism students learn to ask these questions about any event and to answer some or all of them in the first paragraph of a news article.

You can use the same list as springboards for questions about your reading. Some examples follow.

- Ask *who?* Who wrote this, and what qualifications or special experience does this author bring to bear on the subject? Who is the publisher? Has this organization published other useful texts on the same subject?
- Ask *what?* What are the key terms in this material, and what is a definition for each one? What are the major topics covered in this text? What do I already know about these topics? What are the main points the author makes about each topic? Can I give an example of each major concept? What points will the author make next?
- Ask *when?* When was this material published, and does it matter? (For scientific and technical topics, you may want the most current information that's available.)
- Ask *where?* Where can I use the ideas and information contained in this text? Where can I find out more about the topics covered?
- Ask *why?* Why did my teacher make this reading assignment? Why does this material matter to me?
- Ask *how?* How could I explain this material to someone else? How can I organize or visualize this information to make it more vivid? How can I remember these ideas? How can I relate this material to something I already know? How will I be tested or otherwise evaluated on this material? How can learning this material benefit me in this course, in another course, or in my life outside the classroom?

Note: These six kinds of questions will lead you to common test items.

Keep track of your questions. Write them on index cards, one question per card. Or open up a word processing file on your computer and key in your questions. Take your unanswered questions to class, where they can be springboards for class discussion.

Read to Answer Your Questions

Previewing, outlining, and questioning set the stage for incoming information by warming up a space in your mental storage area. Now you're ready to inspect the text in greater detail.

Read with focused attention

It's easy to fool yourself about reading. Just having an open book in your hand and moving your eyes across a page doesn't mean you are reading effectively. Reading textbooks takes energy, even if you do it sitting down.

As you read, be conscious of where you are and what you are doing. When you notice your attention wandering, gently bring it back to the present.

One way to stay focused is to avoid marathon reading sessions. Schedule breaks and set a reasonable goal for the entire session. Then reward yourself with an enjoyable activity for 5 or 10 minutes every hour or two.

For difficult reading, set shorter goals. Read for a half-hour and then take a break. Most students find that shorter periods of reading distributed throughout the day and week can be more effective than long sessions.

You can use the following techniques to stay focused during these sessions:

- **Visualize the material.** Form mental pictures of the concepts as they are presented. Get a "feel" for the subject. If you read that a voucher system can help control cash disbursements, picture a voucher handing out dollar bills. If you are reading about the microorganism called a paramecium, imagine what it would feel like to run your finger around the long, cigar-shaped body of the organism.

- **Read it out loud.** This is especially useful for complicated material. Some of us remember better and understand more quickly when we hear an idea.

- **Get off the couch.** Read at a desk or table and sit up, on the edge of your chair, with your feet flat on the floor. If you're feeling adventurous, read standing up.

- **Get moving.** Make reading a physical as well as intellectual experience. As you read out loud, get up and pace around the room. Read important passages slowly and emphatically, and add appropriate gestures.

Make several passes through the text

Somehow, students get the idea that reading means opening a book and dutifully slogging through the text—line by line, page by page—moving in a straight line from the first word to the last. Actually, this can be an inflexible and ineffective way to interact with published material.

Feel free to shake up your routine. Make several "passes" through any reading material. During a preview, for example, just scan the text to look for key words and highlighted material.

Next, skim the entire chapter or article again, spending a little more time and taking in more than you did during your preview.

▶ sidebar

WAYS TO ANNOTATE A BOOK

One way to read actively is to mark up the material. Something happens when you annotate a book—that is, mark it with a pencil or pen. When you make notes in the margin, you can hear yourself talking with the author. When you doodle and underline, you can see the author's ideas take shape. You can even argue with an author or create your own ideas.

Of course, you can only annotate books that you own, and that means you must buy them. The payoff is that you get to mark up the material in a way that truly makes it your own. For example:

- *Underline* the main points—phrases or sentences that answer your questions about the text.
- *Place asterisks (*)* in the margin next to an especially important sentence or term.
- *Circle* key terms and words to look up later in a dictionary.
- *Write short definitions* of key terms in the margin.
- *Write a "Q"* in the margin to highlight possible test questions or questions to ask in class.
- *Write personal comments* in the margin—points of agreement or disagreement with the author.
- *Write mini-indexes* in the margin—the numbers of other pages in the book on which the same topic is discussed.
- *Draw* diagrams, pictures, tables, or maps to translate straight text into visual terms.
- *Number* each step in a series of related points.

Note: Avoid annotating too soon. Wait until you complete a chapter or section to make sure you know what is important. Then annotate.

Also, underline sparingly, usually less than 10 percent of the text. If you mark up too much on a page, you defeat the purpose: to flag the most important material for review.

Finally, read in more depth, proceeding word by word through some or all of the text. Save this type of close reading for the most important material—usually the sections that directly answer the questions you raised while previewing.

Reflect on the Answers

Reflecting on your reading completes the cycle you began by previewing, outlining, and asking questions. The idea is to extract the key points and significant details that answer your questions and to burn those answers into your memory so that you can retrieve them at will. In addition, you can think critically about all this material and create a view-point of your own.

Answer your questions

From the text, get the answers to the questions you raised earlier and write those answers down. Note when you don't get the answers you wanted to find, and write down new questions. Bring these questions to class or see your instructor personally.

If you listed your questions on index cards, write an answer on the back of each card. If you entered your questions in a computer file, then open it up again and add answers. Either way, you'll instantly have use-ful review materials on hand.

When you read, create an image of yourself as a person in search of the answers. You are a detective, watching for every clue, sitting erect in your straight-backed chair, demanding that your textbook give you what you want: the answers.

Reflect by reciting

To understand the reasons for reflection, briefly review the way that your memory works:

- The process starts with sense perception, such as words and images printed on a page or displayed on a screen.
- Your brain translates these perceptions into ideas and places them in your short-term memory.
- However, the content of short-term memory will quickly fade un-less you actively rehearse it.

Reciting offers one means of rehearsal. The benefits are enormous. Reciting helps to move information into your long-term memory. What's more, reciting instantly focuses your attention and turns you into an active learner. If you recite the key points from a chapter by ex-plaining them to someone, you engage your sense of hearing as well as seeing. If you recite by writing a summary of what you've read, you move your fingers and engage all your kinesthetic senses. In each way, your reading experience becomes more vivid.

When you recite, you get important feedback about your learning. If there are any gaps in your understanding of the material, they'll become obvious as you speak or write. Also, reciting forces you to put ideas in your own words and avoid the pitfalls of rote memorization.

Besides being useful, reciting can be fun. Experiment with any of the following options:

- **Just speak.** Talk informally about what you've read. Stop after reading a chapter or section and just speak off the cuff. Pretend that you've been called on to do an impromptu speech about the book or article. Talk about what you found significant or surprising in the material. Talk about what you intend to remember. Also talk about how you felt about the reading and whether you agree or disagree with the author.

- **Just write.** Stop at any point in your reading and write freely. Don't worry about following a particular format or creating a complete summary. Just note the points that emerge with the most clarity and force from your reading, along with your responses to them.

- **Structure your reciting.** Find a chapter title or heading in the text. Then close your book and summarize the text that follows that heading. When you're done, go back to the text and check your recitation for accuracy. Go on to the next heading and do the same. Or choose a passage that you've underlined and explain as much as you can about that particular point. For even more structure, put your recitation in writing following one of the note-taking formats explained in Chapters 12, 13, and 14.

- **Recite alone.** To make this technique more effective, do it in front of a mirror. It may seem silly, but the benefits can be enormous. Reap them at exam time.

- **Recite in the presence of people.** Friends are even better than mirrors. Form a group and practice teaching each other what you have read. One of the best ways to learn anything is to teach it to someone else, so talk about your reading whenever you can. Tell friends and family members what you're learning from your textbooks.

Think critically about your reading

Reading has been defined as borrowing the thoughts of others just long enough to stimulate your own thinking. To get lasting pleasure and benefit from reading, use it as fuel for critical thinking. Review the answers you uncovered by reading. Mull them over, ponder them, wonder about them, modify them, and make them your own.

Chapter 3 explains specific strategies for critical thinking. To get started with the process, remember that you can think critically about any body of ideas simply by asking the following questions:

- Are these ideas logical?
- Are these ideas supported by sufficient evidence?
- Do these ideas call on me to alter my thinking or behavior in significant ways? If so, how?

experiment WITH A STRATEGY FROM THIS CHAPTER

To get a feel for the reading system explained in this chapter, apply this tool to any read-ing assignment you have right now.

For purposes of this exercise, read a piece of nonfiction—something other than a novel, poem, or play. Choose a chapter or article that you can read in about 60 minutes. Also, gather some index cards to work with as you complete this exercise, or prepare to work at a computer.

When you've chosen your reading matter and gathered materials, go through each step described here. This is just for practice, so have fun.

Step 1: Ask questions about what you read (up to 10 minutes)

- *Preview by looking at each page of the text*. Notice any visual elements, along with any material that is highlighted graphically.
- *Create an outline from chapter headings and subheadings*. Focus on the major ele-ments. You don't have to include headings for exercises, journal entries, tables, charts, or similar elements in your outline. If you don't find any headings, then capture the major topics in single words or phrases.
- *Turn each item in your outline into a written question*. Don't worry about writing the perfect question. There are several possibilities for each heading, so just experiment. Record your questions on index cards or the computer.

Step 2: Read to answer your questions (up to 40 minutes)

- *Read through the chapter several times*. During your first pass through the material, scan and skim. Pick up more content than you did during your preview, but don't worry about getting all the details the first time. Read word for word only when you already feel familiar with the text.
- *As you read, look for answers to your questions*. Make a mental note of where these answers are located in the text.
- *After making at least one pass through the material, annotate the text*. Underline the sentences that most directly answer your questions, or make any other brief notes that you find helpful.

Step 3: Reflect on the answers

- *Write answers to the questions you listed in Step 1*. Record these answers on index cards or in a computer file.
- *Recite your reading*. Speak or write about what you've read. Explain the material in your own words. Explain the ideas to someone you know.
- *Think critically about your reading*. Go beyond listing the answers to your questions. Assess the quality of the material. Look for ideas that are presented logically and sup-ported by adequate evidence. Reflect on what you found significant in your reading, what you intend to remember, and what, if anything, was missing for you.

Follow up on these steps

Now turn your attention from the *content* of your reading to the *process* that you just used. In the space below, write answers to the following questions:

Are you already using any elements of the three steps listed?

What elements are of these steps are new to you?

Were any elements especially useful?

Which elements do you intend to keep using?

chapter 10

Becoming a Flexible Reader

Our culture abounds in high-tech tools: cellular phones, digital assistants, enhanced compact disks, high definition video, e-mail, wireless Internet connections, and more. Even so, we still depend on the written word. Consider that the World Wide Web borrowed its interface from the book (witness Web *pages*). And one of the first big merchants to emerge on the Internet—Amazon.com—got its start by peddling books.

Reading a printed page, Web page, or e-mail offers advantages not always found in audiovisual media, lectures, workshops, or other media:

- **Reading allows you to control the *content* of your learning.** You choose what books, articles, and other content to read and what to ignore. Even within a single publication, you can skip entire paragraphs, sections, or chapters and focus on what's most important to you.
- **Reading allows you to control the *sequence* of your learning.** You can read sections in any order and stop to reread a chapter whenever you want.
- **Reading allows you to learn at your own *pace*.** You can skim or scan text with all the techniques of speed reading at your command. You can also slow down to crawl through difficult paragraphs, or stop to savor your favorite passages and read them out loud.

Learning to enjoy all these benefits is the essence of becoming a flexible reader.

Make Choices About What to Read

Books about time management often mention the "80/20" principle. According to this principle, 80 percent of the value created by any group derives from only 20 percent of its members. If you have a to-do list of

10 items, for example, you'll get 80 percent of your desired results by doing only two items on the list.

You might find that the 80/20 principle applies to other aspects of your life. If you have 100 CDs, you might consistently listen to only about 20 of them. If you go to an hour-long meeting, you might find that the most valuable information is imparted in the first 12 minutes (20 percent of the meeting time).

The point is not to take these figures literally but to remember the underlying principle: *Focus on what creates the most value.* These things may be only a fraction of the total content or options available to you in any situation.

Apply the 80/20 principle when you read

Look at your reading in light of the 80/20 principle. For instance:

- In a 10-paragraph newspaper article, you might find 80 percent of the crucial facts in the headline and first paragraph. (In fact, journalists are *taught* to write this way.)
- If you have a 100-page assignment, you may find that the most important facts and ideas could be summarized in 20 pages.
- If you're asked to read five books for a course, you may find that most test questions come from just one of them—20 percent of the total reading load.

Keep a caution in mind

A caution is in order here. The 80/20 principle is not an invitation to attend only 20 percent of your classes. Nor is it a license to complete only 20 percent of your reading assignments. Making such choices will undermine your education.

Remember that in order to find the "top 20" items in any group, you must attend to 100 percent of the items. Likewise, to find the most important parts of anything you read, you first need to get familiar with the whole. Only then can you make sound choices about what you want to remember and apply.

Approach reading with an overall plan

After making some preliminary choices about what to read, create a reading plan. Planning dispels panic ("I've got 300 pages to read before tomorrow morning!") and helps you systematically finish off your entire reading load for a term.

Creating a reading plan is relatively simple:

1. **To begin, estimate the total number of pages that you'll read for each course.** To arrive at this figure, check each course syllabus and other relevant materials.

2. **Next, estimate how many pages you can read in each of your texts during one hour.** Remember that your reading speed will be different for various materials, depending on the layout of the pages and the difficulty of the text. To give your estimate some credibility, base it on actual experience: Spend an hour reading and see how many pages you complete.

3. **With these estimates in hand, project the total number of hours you'll need to complete reading assignments in all your current courses.** Remember to give yourself plenty of "wiggle room." Allow extra hours for rereading and unanticipated difficulties. Consider taking your initial number of projected hours and doubling it.

4. **Schedule reading time.** Block in hours on your calendar for reading. At the very least, take the total number of hours from Step 3 and divide it by the number of weeks in your current term. This is your weekly reading load. Remember that you can read for short "bursts" to fill holes in your schedule—for example, during an hour between classes, or even in 10 minutes before class begins.

5. **When you face a long reading assignment, break it into manageable chunks.** Textbooks are usually divided into chapters—a logical chunk. However, if the chapter is long or difficult, feel free to tackle it in smaller sections with study breaks between each section.

Planning your reading may take a few hours, but the benefits are beyond calculation. With a plan, you can be far more confident that you'll actually get your reading done. Even if your estimates are off, you'll still go beyond blind guessing or leaving the whole thing to chance. Your reading matters too much for that.

Keep asking: What's important?

In summary, flexible readers constantly make choices about what to read and what *not* to read. They realize that some texts are more valuable for their purposes than others and that some passages within a single text are more crucial than the rest. When reading, they constantly ask: What's most important here?

The answer to this question varies from assignment to assignment and even from page to page within a single assignment. Pose this question each time that you read, and look for clues to the answers. Pay special attention to:

- Parts of the text that directly answer the questions you generated while previewing.
- Any part of the text that's emphasized graphically—for example, headings, subheadings, lists, charts, graphs, and passages printed in boldface or italics.

- Summary paragraphs (usually found at the beginning or end of a chapter or section).
- Any passage that provokes a strong response from you or raises a question that you cannot answer.

Adjust Your Reading Pace

Another key aspect of flexible reading is choosing your pace. Most people can read faster simply by making a conscious effort to do so. In fact, you probably can read faster without any loss in comprehension. Your comprehension might even improve.

Experiment with this idea right now. Read the rest of this chapter as fast as you can. After you finish, come back and reread the material at your usual rate. Notice how much you remembered from your first sprint through. You might be surprised to find how well you comprehend material even at dramatically increased speeds.

Following are more strategies for adjusting your reading pace.

Set a time limit

When you read, use a clock or a digital watch with a built-in stopwatch to time yourself. The objective is not to set speed records, so be realistic.

For example, set a goal to read a chapter in an hour. If that works, set a goal of 50 minutes to read a similar chapter. Test your limits. The idea is to give yourself a gentle push, increasing your reading speed without sacrificing comprehension.

Notice and release tension

It's not only possible to read fast when you're relaxed, it's also easier. Relaxation promotes concentration. And remember, relaxation is not the same thing as sleep. You can be relaxed and alert at the same time.

Before you read, take a minute to close your eyes, notice your breathing, and clear your mind. Let go of all concerns other than the reading material that's in front of you. Then slowly open your eyes and ease into the text.

Notice and release regressions

Ineffective readers and beginning readers make many regressions. That is, they back up and reread words.

You can reduce regressions by paying attention to them. Use an index card to cover words and lines you have read. This can reveal how often you stop and move the card back.

Don't be discouraged if you stop often at first. Being aware of it helps you naturally begin to regress less frequently.

Notice and release vocalizing

Obviously, you're more likely to read faster if you don't read aloud or move your lips. You can also increase your speed if you don't subvocalize—that is, if you don't mentally "hear" the words as you read them. To stop doing it, just be aware of it.

Practice with simpler materials

When you first attempt to stop regression and vocalizing, read simpler material. That way, you can pay closer attention to your reading habits. Gradually work your way up to more complex material.

Remember that speed isn't everything

Skillful readers vary their reading rate according to their purpose and the nature of the material. An advanced text in analytic geometry usually calls for a different reading rate than the Sunday comics.

You also can use different reading rates on the same material. For example, you might sprint through an assignment for the key words and ideas, then return to the difficult parts for a slower and more thorough reading.

Read Across the Curriculum

Reflect for a moment on the quantity and variety of material that you're asked to read in higher education. A textbook in differential calculus demands to be read in a different way than does Shakespeare's *Hamlet*. Getting the most from either work means tailoring your approach to the subject matter.

Gaining this intellectual flexibility is one of the rewards of a liberal education. The question is: How do you read well across the entire curriculum?

Find the animating questions

That last question embodies a solution. To read well, remember that the essence of any subject consists of asking and answering questions. The humanities, the sciences, the arts, and other academic subjects did not arise out of a void. Rather, these subjects sprang from human curiosity. People asked questions about the nature of the world and about human nature. The subjects we study today began with those questions—and continue with the vast range of answers that have been created.

You can harness the power of questions every time you read. If you understand the specific questions that animate any subject matter, then you're already well on the way to finding answers.

To begin, group the courses that you take in higher education according to various purposes. Then translate each purpose to a series of fundamental questions. Some examples follow.

▶ sidebar

WAYS TO OVERCOME CONFUSION

Learning has been defined as the process of systematically overcoming confusion. One way to avoid becoming confused is to stop learning. By enrolling in higher education, you've already ruled out that option. Instead, you can embrace occasional confusion as a prelude to insight.

Experiment with the following options when you get confused while reading:

- **Collect data about your confusion.** When you feel stuck, stop reading for a moment and diagnose what's happening. At these stop points, mark your place in the margin of the page with a penciled S for "stuck." Seeing a pattern to your marks over several pages might indicate a question you want to answer before reading further. Or you might discover a reading habit you'd like to change.
- **Look for essential words.** If you are stuck on a paragraph, mentally cross out all the adjectives and adverbs and read the sentence without them. Find the important words. These will usually be verbs and nouns.
- **Read it again.** Difficult material—such as the technical writing of science—is often easier the second or third time around.
- **Read it aloud.** Make noise. Read a passage aloud several times, each time using a different inflection, emphasizing a different part of the sentence. Be creative. Imagine that you are the author talking.
- **Stand up.** Changing positions periodically can combat fatigue. Try standing as you read, especially if you get stuck on a tough passage and decide to read it aloud.
- **Skip around.** Jump immediately to the end of the article or chapter. You may have lost the big picture, and sometimes simply seeing the conclusion or summary is all you need to put the details in context. Retrace the steps in a chain of ideas and look for examples. Absorb facts and ideas in whatever order works for you—which may be different from the author's presentation.

Read for theories

Many of the subjects you'll study in higher education share a single purpose: to propose theories based on observations.

For example, the natural sciences—including physics, biology, and chemistry—offer theories to explain and predict events in the natural world. The social sciences, such as psychology and sociology, offer theories to predict and explain events in the human world—our patterns of thinking, feeling, and acting. Many of these disciplines are offshoots of philosophy, which at one time embraced all questions about the world and human behavior.

- **Summarize.** Pause briefly to summarize what you've read so far, verbally or in writing. Stop at the end of a paragraph and recite, in your own words, what you have read. Jot down some notes or create a short outline.
- **Find another published source of information.** Supplement your assigned reading with a good dictionary or encyclopedia. You may even want to look at other textbooks on the same subject. Look for a current publication filled with detailed explanations and examples. If it includes summaries, glossaries, and review questions (preferably with answers), that's all the better. Even children's encyclopedias can provide useful overviews of baffling subjects. Start with them and then look for more sources.
- **Ask for help.** Admit when you are stuck and make an appointment with your instructor. Most teachers welcome the opportunity to work individually with students. Be specific about your confusion. Point out the paragraph that you found toughest to understand. Find a tutor. Many schools provide free tutoring services. If tutoring services are not provided by your school, then other students who have completed the course can assist you.
- **Pretend you understand, then explain it.** We often understand more than we think we do. Pretend that the topic is clear as a bell and explain it to another person. Write your explanation down. You might be amazed by what you know. To go even further, volunteer to teach the topic to a study group.
- **Stop reading.** When none of these suggestions work, do not despair. Admit your confusion and then take a break. Catch a movie, go for a walk, study another subject, or sleep on it. The concepts you've already absorbed may come together at a subconscious level while you move on to other activities. Allow some time for that process. When you return to the reading material, regard it with fresh eyes.

In *How to Read a Book,* Mortimer Adler and Charles Van Doren list four questions that sum up the whole task of reading. They are especially useful when reading about theories:

1. **What is the book about as a whole?** To answer this question, state the main topic of the book in one sentence. Then list the major and minor topics covered throughout the book.
2. **What is being said in detail?** List the author's key terms and major assertions about each topic covered in the book. Determine which questions the author raises and which of those questions are answered.

3. **Is it true?** Use the techniques of critical thinking. Examine the logic and evidence for the author's assertions. Keep an eye out for missing evidence, faulty evidence, incomplete analysis of the evidence, and errors in reasoning.

4. **What of it?** After answering the first three questions, reflect on any changes in your thinking—and perhaps in your behavior—that are implied by the material you've just read.

Read to solve problems

Other subjects go beyond theory to tackle specific problems and propose solutions. Their subjects range from the abstract problems of pure mathematics to the practical problems of engineering or computer science.

As you read about subjects, keep in mind that your purpose is to clearly understand the nature of various problems and to acquire techniques for solving those problems. Ask questions such as these:

- What is the purpose of solving this problem, or what benefits will having a solution create?
- What are the key features of this problem—the elements that are already known and the elements that have to be discovered?
- If the problem is a technical one, can I restate it in plain English?
- Can I take a problem stated in plain English and restate it in mathematical or other technical terms?
- Have I encountered similar problems before, and if so, how did I solve them?
- Is there a standard formula or process that I can use to solve this problem?
- What are alternative methods that can I use to solve this problem?
- If I had to estimate or guess the answer right now, what would it be?
- Can I solve this problem using a single operation, or does it call for several steps?
- What will each step accomplish?
- Will solving this problem call on me to collect data or do any other research?
- Can I derive a formula from my solution or generalize the solution I reached to similar kinds of problems?

Read for interpretation and insight

Courses in literature, drama, and film do not propose carefully reasoned theories about the world or human nature. Nor do they focus on solving problems. Instead, they teach through *vicarious experience*.

When you read a novel, see a play, or watch a film, you see the world through another human being's eyes. You get a window into that person's thoughts and feelings as the events of his life unfold. Just as you gain insight from your own experiences, you can gain insights from the experiences of others.

Works of fiction call for a substantial shift in your reading approach. Some points to remember:

- **One of your purposes is pure enjoyment.** People love a good story. This is something that's easy to forget when you're dissecting a poem or analyzing a play in one of your literature classes.
- **Another purpose is interpretation.** When encountering literature, your concern is with both *what* is being said and *how* it is being said. You respond not only to *content* (the artist's essential message) but also to *technique* (the way that the artist gets her message across). For a literary artist, technique includes the challenges of creating characters, crafting plot lines, and writing dialogue. When you can notice these elements and explain how they affect you, you've done the job of interpretation.
- **Interpretation calls for more than one reading.** Read a poem, novel, or play once through simply for enjoyment. Then allow time for several more readings so that you can pick up the details of the plot and the nuances of the character's personalities.
- **Interpretation often means going beyond the page.** To get the full effect of a poem, for example, read it out loud. Also remember that a play is ultimately meant to be observed rather than simply read. Whenever possible, see a live or recorded performance of the work.

With these points in mind, you can ask useful questions to guide interpretation and promote insight:

- Who are the major characters in this work?
- What are each character's major traits?
- What does each character want, and what obstacles stand in his or her way?
- How does each character change throughout the course of the story?
- What is the key complication in the story—the early event that sets a major character in pursuit of what he or she wants?
- What are the major events in the story—the points at which the action takes a significant turn?
- Is the story told in chronological order? If not, why not?
- Where in time and place does the story take place, and are these details important?
- Who tells the story—a character or a narrator? How does this point of view shape the story?
- What is the theme of the story—the major topic it deals with or the fundamental point of view behind it?

Build Your Vocabulary

As a skilled reader, you will build your vocabulary. The benefits are many. A large vocabulary makes reading more enjoyable and increases the range of materials you can read. In addition, increasing your vocabulary gives you more options for self-expression when speaking or writing. When you can choose from a larger pool of words, you increase the precision and power of your thinking.

Keep a dictionary handy

One potent ally in building your vocabulary is a dictionary. Print dictionaries come in many shapes, sizes, and media: pocket dictionaries, desk dictionaries, and unabridged dictionaries (the heftiest and most complete). Ask a librarian to recommend specific titles.

Don't forget digital dictionaries. Computer software, such as Microsoft Word, comes with a built-in dictionary. Also look for dictionary sites on the World Wide Web (such as the *American Heritage Dictionary*, which you can access at http://education.yahoo.com). To find them, go to any search engine and use the key words *dictionary* or *reference*.

Put your dictionaries to active use. When you find an unfamiliar word, write it down on an index card. Copy the sentence in which it occurred below the word. You can look up each word immediately or accumulate a stack of these cards and look them up later. Write the definition on the back of the card and add the diacritical marks that tell you how to pronounce it. You can find a list of these marks in the front of many dictionaries.

☑ checklist

CREATE YOUR PERSONAL DIGITAL DICTIONARY

Consider the benefits of using a computer to create a specialized glossary for each of your courses. The process is simple:

❐ As you complete assigned readings and review your class notes, underline key terms.
❐ Use a computer to enter these terms into a word processing file.
❐ Armed with your dictionary, readings, and notes, write a definition of each term.
❐ Use the "sort" feature in your word processor to alphabetize the terms.
❐ Revise definitions and add new terms as the course proceeds.
❐ Create backup copies of your glossaries and print them out periodically.
❐ Use your glossaries to study for tests.
❐ Refer back to your glossaries when you take related courses.

Distinguish between word parts

Words consist of discrete elements that can be combined in limitless ways. These parts include roots, prefixes, and suffixes.

Roots are "home base," a word's core meaning. A single word can have more than one root. *Bibliophile*, for example, has two roots: *biblio* (book) and *phile* (love). A *bibliophile* is a book lover.

Prefixes come at the beginning of a word and often modify the meaning of the word root. In English, a common prefix is the single letter *a*, which often means *not*. Added to *typical*, for example, this prefix results in the word *atypical*, which means "not typical."

Suffixes come at the end of a word. Like prefixes, they can alter or expand the meaning of the root. For instance, the suffix *ant* means "one who." Thus, an *assistant* is "one who assists."

One strategy for expanding your vocabulary is to learn common roots, prefixes, and suffixes. Start with the following checklist and see an unabridged dictionary for more.

☑ checklist

DO YOU KNOW THESE PREFIXES, ROOTS, AND SUFFIXES?

Make an investment in your word power by learning the following word parts. Use each of the example words in a sentence and check off each prefix, root, or suffix as you do.

Prefixes

❐ a [not, without]
   Example: amoral (without a sense of moral responsibility)
❐ acro [high]
   Example: acrophobia (fear of height)
❐ anti [against]
   Example: anticommunist (someone who is against communism)
❐ bi [both, double, twice]
   Example: biweekly (occurring twice per week)
❐ cerebro [brain]
   Example: cerebral (relating to the workings of the brain)
❐ circum [around]
   Example: circumnavigate (to walk around an object)
❐ deca [ten]
   Example: decagon (a ten-sided figure)
❐ extra [beyond, outside]
   Example: extraneous (outside the topic)
❐ fore [before in time]
   Example: foreshadow (to predict an event before it happens)

❏ hyper [over, above]
Example: hypersensitive (to react over and above what is considered normal in a situation)

❏ infra [beneath]
Example: infrastructure (the underlying organization)

❏ macro [large]
Example: macrocosm (a large viewpoint or system)

❏ neo [new]
Example: neologism (a new word)

❏ oct [eight]
Example: octagon (an eight-sided figure)

❏ poly [many]
Example: polygamy (having many wives)

❏ quad [four]
Example: quadruple (to increase by a factor of four)

❏ retro [backward]
Example: retrospective (to look back over a body of work)

❏ sub [below]
Example: subhuman (beneath ordinary standards of human conduct)

❏ ultra [exceedingly]
Example: ultraconservative (extremely opposed to change)

Roots

❏ acu [sharp]
Example: acupuncture (treatment with needles)

❏ amor [love]
Example: amorous (feeling affectionate)

❏ brev [short]
Example: abbreviate (to make shorter)

❏ bio [life]
Example: biopsy (to take a sample of living tissue)

❏ cide [kill]
Example: fratricide (to kill a sibling)

❏ dorm [sleep]
Example: dormant (remaining in a state of sleep or otherwise inactive)

❏ dox [opinion]
Example: heterodox (embracing many opinions)

❏ erg [work]
Example: ergonomics (relating to working conditions)

❏ gastro [stomach]
Example: gastrointestinal (relating to the stomach and intestines)

❐ greg [herd, group, crowd]
Example: gregarious (enjoying the presence of crowds)
❐ hetero [different]
Example: heterogeneous (having many different elements)
❐ uni [one]
Example: unicorn (an imaginary horse with one horn)
❐ vor [eat greedily]
Example: voracious (eating many foods or absorbing many stimuli)

Suffixes
❐ algia [pain]
Example: neuralgic (a medication to relive pain)
❐ ate [cause, make]
Example: liquidate (to dissolve or make obsolete)
❐ escent [in the process of]
Example: obsolescent (in the process of passing or becoming extinct)
❐ ize [make]
Example: idolize (to make an object of worship)
❐ oid [resembling]
Example: spheroid (resembling a sphere)
❐ ology [study, science, theory]
Example: neurology (the study of the nervous system)
❐ tude [state of]
Example: multitude (a state of having many elements)
❐ ward [in the direction of]
Example: eastward (turning in the opposite direction of west)

Look for context clues

You can often deduce the meaning of an unfamiliar word simply by paying attention to context—the surrounding words or images. Later you can confirm your trial definition of the word by consulting a dictionary.

Practice looking for context clues such as:

- **Definitions.** A key word may be defined right in the text. Look for phrases such as *the definition is* or *in other words*.
- **Examples.** Authors often provide examples to clarify a word meaning. If the word is not explicitly defined, then study the examples. They're often preceded by the phrases *for example, for instance*, or *such as*.
- **Lists.** When a word is listed in a series, pay attention to the other items in the series. They may, in effect, define the unfamiliar word.

- **Comparisons.** You may find a new word surrounded by *synonyms*—words with a similar meaning. Look for synonyms after words such as *like* and *as*.
- **Contrasts.** A writer may juxtapose a word with its *antonym*—a word or phrase with the opposite meaning. Look for phrases such as *on the contrary* and *on the other hand*.

experiment WITH A STRATEGY FROM THIS CHAPTER

Close this book and, on a separate sheet of paper, write a summary of this chapter.

Next, compare your summary with the original text. Was your summary complete and accurate? Did you encounter any problems in reading this material, such as words you didn't understand or main points that you forgot? Sum up your reading experience by completing this statement:

I discovered that I . . .

Now list a specific suggestion from this chapter that you'll use to increase your comprehension and retention of reading material. Describe that suggestion here, and explain when and how you will use it during the coming week.

I intend to . . .

Finally, return to this page to evaluate your experience. Did using the suggestion make your reading more effective? If not, describe how you could modify the suggestion. Or choose another suggestion from this chapter and apply the same cycle of discovery and intention to it.

Using Seven Tools for Powerful Notes

You enter a lecture hall filled with dozens of students. A lone person stands at the front of the room behind a lectern. For the next hour, she will do most of the talking. Everyone else in the room is seated and silent, taking notes. One person—the lecturer—seems to be doing all the work.

Don't be deceived. Look more closely and you'll see some people taking notes in a way that radiates energy. They're awake and alert, poised on the edge of their seats. They're writing, a physical activity that expresses mental engagement—the ability to listen for levels of ideas and information, make choices about what to record, and create effective materials to review later.

While you are participating in higher education, you may spend hundreds of hours taking notes. Experimenting with ways to make those notes more effective is a direct investment in your success.

This chapter and the next four focus on notes. To get the maximum benefit, absorb the material in three stages:

- Use the seven suggestions in this chapter to immediately improve the power of your notes on lectures, discussions, and readings.
- Hone your skills even more by experimenting with the special formats for taking notes explained in Chapters 12, 13, and 14.
- See Chapter 15 for ways to refine and review your notes, increasing their effectiveness over the long term.

If you take these steps, you can turn even the most disorganized chicken scratches into tools for learning.

Set the Stage for Note-Taking

The process of note-taking begins well before you enter a classroom or crack a book. You can promote your success at the task by "psyching up"—setting the physical and mental stage to receive what your teachers have to offer. The following suggestions can help.

Complete required reading

Instructors usually assume that students complete reading assignments, and they construct their lectures accordingly. The more familiar you are with a subject, the easier it will be to understand in class. Nothing is more discouraging (or boring) than sitting through a lecture about the relationship of the Le Chatelier principle of kinetics if you have never heard of Le Chatelier or kinetics.

Arrive early to put your brain in gear

When students arrive at class late or with only seconds to spare, they create a level of stress that interferes with listening. You can avoid that interference by arriving at least five minutes before class begins. Use the spare time to warm up your brain:

- Review your notes from the previous class.
- If you brought your textbook, scan the latest reading assignment—especially sections you've underlined or otherwise annotated.
- Review assigned problems and exercises.
- Reflect on what you already know about the topic of the upcoming class and list questions you intend to ask.

Situate yourself to succeed

Sit in the front of the classroom. This signals your willingness to fully participate in class. The closer you sit to the front, the fewer distractions there will be. Also, material on the board is easier to read from up front, and the instructor can see you more easily when you have a question.

Take care of housekeeping details

Write your name and phone number in each notebook in case you lose it. Class notes become more and more valuable as a term proceeds.

Develop the habit of labeling and dating your notes at the beginning of each class. Number the page, too. Sometimes the sequence of material in a lecture is important.

Devote a specific section of your notebook to listing assignments for each course. Keep all details about test dates here, also, along with a course syllabus. You're less likely to forget assignments if you compile them in one place, where you can review them all at a glance.

If you store notes on a computer, create one file in which you list assignments for all your courses.

Choose Your Technology for Note-Taking

More technology is available for taking notes than ever before. You've got a lot to choose from, and each choice has consequences for the way you learn.

Consider the pros and cons of recorders

Some students are fond of recording lectures and class discussions on audiocassette, videocassette, or digital media. Before you do, consider the potential pitfalls:

- **Recorders can malfunction.** Even when everything works perfectly, you may find it hard to get a decent recording. The built-in microphones that come with many recorders vary greatly in quality.
- **Watching or listening to recorded lectures can take a lot of time.** In fact, it can take more time than reviewing written notes. When you take notes, you can condense a lecture to a handful of key ideas and facts. Often you can review your notes in a fraction of the time needed to review a recording. (Note that some recorders have a feature called compressed speech, which speeds up the voice on the recording. This feature can reduce listening time.)
- **When you record a lecture, you may be tempted to daydream.** After all, you can always listen to the lecture later. Unfortunately, if you let the recorder do all the work, you are skipping a valuable part of the learning process—your active participation in class.

With those warnings in mind, you might be able to use recordings effectively. Recordings can help you:

- **Catch up after an absence.** Recordings can help you stay on track if you have to miss a class. Ask a classmate to record the lecture for you. Some teachers may even be willing to do this.
- **Review your written notes.** To create a useful review tool, record yourself as you review the notes you took in class. Using your notes as a guide, see if you can recreate the essence of the lecture. Pretend you're teaching the class—a way to check what you understood and uncover any areas of confusion.
- **Create review materials.** In addition, you can use recordings to create tapes or burn CDs to listen to while you drive.

If you do choose to record lectures, do a trial run with the equipment beforehand to make sure it all works. During class, set the volume high enough to pick up the speaker. Sitting close to the front can help.

Also, back up your recording with written notes. Turn the recorder on and then take notes as if it weren't there. If the recording fails, you'll still have a record of what happened in class.

Note: Before recording, check with your instructors. Some prefer not to be recorded.

Consider the pros and cons of laptops

Laptop computers offer more technology for note-taking, along with several benefits. If you're a decent typist, you can probably take notes more efficiently at a keyboard than with paper and pen. Notes you take via computer also show up in attractive type rather than an illegible scrawl. Notes stored on a computer take up less space than stacks of notebooks, and the process of typing them up forces you to review the material. Also, you can easily edit your notes later and search for key words—two features that facilitate review.

As with recorders, however, there are downsides. Laptops can freeze, crash, or run out of battery power. Your notes, like other data, will also be vulnerable to power surges, magnetic fields, software glitches, or hardware failure.

You can get around these disadvantages in several ways:

- **Read your laptop manual and help screens.** Find out how to conserve battery power and prevent crashes.
- **Back up, save, and print.** Protect your work! Save your data often while taking notes. Regularly back up all your computer files. After class, connect to a printer and print out a hard copy of your notes.
- **Bring paper and pen—just in case.** If you have computer problems, you can keep taking notes without missing a beat. Also, you may find it easier to enter diagrams and formulas by hand rather than by keyboard.
- **Combine handwritten notes with computer-based notes.** This option gives you the best of both worlds. During class, take notes by hand. After class, type your notes into a word processing or database file. Enter all your handwritten notes or use the computer simply to outline or summarize your notes. Save your handwritten notes as a backup.
- **Keep track of emerging technology for note-taking.** Read computer magazines and visit local dealers to keep up on what's current. In particular, keep an eye on notebook computers, which store handwritten notes as digital data.

Consider the benefits of simplicity

When taking notes, you can always turn to the original word processors—pen or pencil and notebook. If you do, keep the following in mind:

- **Use a three-ring binder.** Three-ring binders have several advantages over other kinds of notebooks. First, pages can be removed and spread out when you review. This way, you can get the whole picture of a lecture. Second, the three-ring binder format will allow you to insert handouts right into your notes easily. Third, you can insert your own out-of-class notes in the correct order. You can easily make additions, corrections, and revisions.

- **Use only one side of a piece of paper.** When you use one side of a page, you can review and organize all your notes by spreading them out side by side. Most students find the benefit well worth the cost of the paper. Perhaps you're concerned about the environmental impact of consuming more paper. If so, you can use the blank side of old notes and use recycled paper.
- **Use 3x5 cards.** As an alternative to using notebook paper, use 3x5 cards to take lecture notes. Copy each new concept on a separate 3x5 card. Later, you can organize these cards in an outline form and use them as pocket flash cards.

Keep technology in perspective

A fancy pen and notebook or an expensive recorder or laptop computer are great note-taking devices. And they're all worthless, unless you participate as an energetic observer in class, make useful choices about what to capture in notes, and regularly review your notes after class. The format and structure of your notes are more important than how fast you write or how many gadgets you own.

Leave blank space

Notes tightly crammed into every corner of the page are hard to read and difficult to use for review. Give your eyes a break by leaving plenty of space, no matter what technology or note-taking format you use. Later, when you review, you can use the blank space in your notes to clarify points, write questions,

> ## sidebar

TAKE EFFECTIVE NOTES FOR ONLINE LEARNING

While you are in higher education, you can log lots of computer time related to course work. You might even sign up for classes in which you never set foot in a classroom—classes that take place entirely online.

Digital technology allows you to print out anything that appears on a computer screen: articles, e-mail messages, Web pages, chat room sessions, and more. The problem is that you might skip taking notes altogether, reasoning that you can just print out everything. Doing this deprives you of the chance to internalize a new idea by restating it in your own words.

To prevent this problem, find ways to actively engage with online course material:

- Talk about what you're learning (and consider running a recorder at the same time).
- Write summaries of online articles and chat room sessions.
- Save online materials in a word processing file on your computer and add your own notes.
- Keep a personal journal to capture key insights from the course and ways you plan to apply them outside of the class.
- Print out online materials and treat them like a textbook, applying the suggestions for reading explained in Chapters 9 and 10.

or add other material. Often instructors return to material covered earlier in the lecture. If you leave adequate space, you can add information.

Sharpen Your Listening Skills

Your ability to take notes in any course—from American history to zoology—can improve when you master a core set of listening skills. These skills apply across the curriculum and even beyond the classroom, in your personal relationships.

Limit distractions

Listening can be defined as the process of overcoming distraction. And distraction is a constant factor in human interaction.

In the classroom, you may have to deal with external distractions: noises from the next room, students who have side conversations, a lecturer who speaks softly, or audiovisual equipment that malfunctions. Internal distractions can be even more potent—for example, memories of last Saturday night's party, daydreams about what you'll do after class, or feelings of stress.

When the problem is an external distraction, you'll often know what to do about it. You may need to move closer to the front of the room, ask the lecturer to speak up, or politely ask classmates to keep quiet.

Internal distractions can be trickier. The following ideas can help:

- **Return to the present moment and the task at hand—taking notes.** Flood your mind with sensory data. Notice the shape and color of the pen in your hand. Run your hand along the surface of your desk. Bring yourself back to class by paying attention to the temperature in the room, the feel of your chair, or the quality of light in the room. Paying attention to the sensations associated with taking notes can bring you back to the here and now.
- **Don't fight daydreaming.** When you notice your mind wandering, look at it as an opportunity to refocus your attention. If you notice that your attention is wandering from thermodynamics to beach parties, let go of the beach. Don't grit your teeth and try to stay focused. Just notice when your attention has wandered and gently bring it back.
- **To clear your mind of distracting thoughts, write.** Pause for a few seconds and write distracting thoughts down. If you're distracted by thoughts of errands you want to run after class, list them on an index card and stick it in your pocket. Or simply put a symbol, such as an arrow or asterisk, in your notes to mark the places where your mind started to wander. Once your distractions are out of your mind and safely stored on paper, you can gently return your attention to taking notes.

Remember that you can listen and disagree
When you hear something you disagree with, note your disagreement and let it go. If your disagreement is persistent and strong, make note of this and then move on. Internal debate can prevent you from receiving new information. Just absorb it with a mental tag: *I don't agree with this and my instructor says. . . .*

▶ sidebar

COPE WITH FAST-TALKING LECTURERS

- **Ask the instructor to slow down.** This obvious suggestion is easily forgotten. If asking her to slow down doesn't work, ask her to repeat what you missed.
- **Take more time to prepare for class.** Familiarity with a subject increases your ability to pick out key points. If an instructor lectures quickly or is difficult to understand, conduct a thorough preview of material to be covered. Before class, take detailed notes on your reading and leave plenty of blank space. Take these notes with you to class and simply add your lecture notes to them.
- **Be willing to make choices.** Focus your attention on key points. Instead of trying to write everything down, choose what you think is important. Occasionally you will make a wrong choice and neglect an important point. Worse things could happen. Stay with the lecture, write down key words, and revise your notes immediately after class.
- **Exchange photocopies of notes with classmates.** Your fellow students might write down something you miss. At the same time, your notes might help them.
- **Leave empty spaces in your notes.** Allow plenty of room for filling in information you missed. Use a symbol that signals you've missed something, so you can remember to come back to it.
- **See the instructor after class.** Take your class notes with you and show the instructor what you missed.
- **Use a recorder.** Recording can be useful when a speaker presents technical material, especially on a topic that's new to you. Take as many notes as you can during class. Later, play back your recording and review the sections you didn't understand. Stop the recording periodically to expand your notes or list questions.
- **Go to the lecture again.** Many classes are taught in multiple sections. That gives you the chance to hear a lecture at least twice—once at your regular class time and again in another section of the class.
- **Learn shorthand.** Some note-taking systems, known as shorthand, are specifically designed for getting ideas down fast. Books and courses are available to help you learn these systems.
- **Ask questions even if you're totally lost.** Most instructors allow time for questions. This is a time to ask about the points you missed. There may be times when you feel so lost that you can't formulate a question. That's OK. One option is to just report this fact to the instructor. The instructor can often guide you to a clear question. Another option is to just ask any question. Often this will lead you to the question you really want to ask.

Later, as you review and edit your notes after class, think critically about the instructor's ideas. Take this time to list questions or write about your disagreements.

A related guideline is to avoid "listening with your answer running." This refers to the habit of forming your response to people's ideas *before* they've finished speaking. Give people the courtesy of letting them have their say, even when you are sure you'll disagree. Don't assume that you know in advance what they will say. This simple strategy can prevent countless misunderstandings—and improve the accuracy of your notes.

Focus on content over delivery

Human beings are judgment machines. We evaluate everything, especially other people. If another person's eyebrows are too close together (or too far apart), or if she walks a certain way or combs her hair a certain way, we instantly make up a story about her. We do this so quickly that the process is usually unconscious.

Don't let your attitude about an instructor's lecture style, habits, or appearance get in the way of your education. You can decrease the power of your judgments if you pay attention to them and let them go.

Give the speaker feedback

Speakers are human beings. They thrive on attention. They want to know that their audiences have a pulse. Giving lecturers some verbal and nonverbal feedback—everything from simple eye contact to insightful comments—can raise their energy level and improve the class.

Also ask questions. Questions contribute to the whole class and to the teacher. Chances are that the question you think is "dumb" is also on the minds of other people.

Use Abbreviations Carefully

Abbreviations can greatly speed up your note-taking if you use them consistently. Some abbreviations are standard. If you make up your own abbreviations, write a key explaining them in your notes.

Avoid vague abbreviations. When you use an abbreviation like *comm.* for *committee,* you run the risk of not being able to remember whether you meant *committee, commission, common, commit, community, communicate,* or *communist.*

If you key your notes into word processing files, you can use the "search and replace" command to replace abbreviations with full words.

Use Key Words

Your job is not to write down all a lecturer's words or even most of them. Taking effective notes calls for split-second decisions about which words are essential to record and which are extraneous.

An easy way to sort the extraneous from the essential is to take notes using key words. Key words or phrases contain the essence of communication. They include technical terms, names, numbers, equations, and words of degree: *most, least, faster,* and the like.

Key words are laden with associations. They evoke images and associations with other words and ideas. One key word can initiate the recall of a whole cluster of ideas. A few key words can form a chain from which you can reconstruct an entire lecture.

Focus on nouns and verbs

In many languages, there are two types of words that carry the essential meaning of most sentences: nouns and verbs. For example, the previous sentence could be reduced to: *nouns + verbs carry meaning. Carry* is a verb; the remaining words are all nouns.

There are additional ways to subtract words from your notes and still retain the lecturer's meaning:

▶ **sidebar**

USEFUL PRINCIPLES FOR ABBREVIATIONS

Principle: Leave out articles.
  Examples: omit *a, an, the.*
Principle: Leave out vowels.
  Examples: *talk* becomes *tlk, said* becomes *sd, American* becomes *Amrcn.*
Principle: Use mathematical symbols.
  Examples: plus becomes $+$, *minus* becomes $-$, *is more than* becomes $>$, *is less than* becomes $<$, *equals* or *is* becomes $=$.
Principle: Use arrows to indicate causation and changes in quantity.
  Examples: *increase* becomes $\uparrow$, *decrease* becomes $\downarrow$, *causes, leads to,* or *shows that* becomes $\uparrow$.
Principle: Use standard abbreviations and omit the periods.
  Examples: *pound* becomes *lb, Avenue* becomes *av.*
Principle: Create words from numbers and letters that you can sound out and combine.
  Examples: *before* becomes *b4, too* becomes *2.*
Principle: Use a comma in place of *and.*
  Example: *Freud and Jung were major figures in twentieth-century psychology* becomes *20th century psych: Freud, Jung = major figures.*

- **Eliminate adverbs and adjectives.** The phrase *extremely interesting* can become *interesting* in your notes or simply an exclamation mark (!).
- **Note the topic first; follow that with a colon and an assertion about the topic.** For instance, *There are seven key principles that can help you take effective notes* becomes *Effective notes: 7 principles.*
- **Use lists.** There are two basic types. A *numbered list* expresses steps that need to be completed in a certain order. A *simple list* includes ideas that are related but do not have to follow a sequential order. The list you're reading right now is a simple list.

To find more examples of key words, study newspaper headlines. Good headlines include a verb and only enough nouns to communicate the essence of an event.

example

To see how key words can be used in note-taking, take yourself to an imaginary classroom. You are enrolled in a course on world religions, and today's lecture is an introduction to Buddhism. The instructor begins with these words:

Okay, today we're going to talk about three core precepts of Buddhism. I know that this is a religion that may not be familiar to many of you, and I ask that you keep an open mind as I proceed. Now, with that caveat out of the way, let's move ahead.

First, let's look at the term *anicca*. By the way, this word is spelled *a-n-i-c-c-a*. Everybody got that? Great. All right, well, this is a word in an ancient language called Pali, which was widely spoken in India during the Buddha's time—about 600 years before the birth of Jesus. *Anicca* is a word layered with many meanings and is almost impossible to translate into English. If you read books about Buddhism, you may see it rendered as *impermanence*, and this is a passable translation.

Impermanence is something that you can observe directly in your everyday experience. Look at any object in your external environment and you'll find that it's constantly changing. Even the most solid and stable things—like a mountain, for example—are dynamic. You could use time-lapse photography to record images of a mountain every day for ten years, and if you did, you'd see incredible change—rocks shifting, mudslides, new vegetation, and the like.

Following is one way to reduce this section of the lecture to key words:

Buddhism: 3 concepts.

#1 = anicca = impermanence.

Anicca = Pali = ancient Indian language (600 yrs b4 Jesus).

Example of anicca: time lapse photos → changes in mountain.

Use complete sentences at crucial points

Sometimes key words aren't enough. When an instructor repeats a sentence slowly and emphasizes each word, she's sending you a signal. Technical definitions are often worded precisely because even a slightly different wording will render the definitions useless or incorrect. Write down these definitions word for word.

Listen for Levels of Ideas

When reading, you are constantly responding to clues about the levels of ideas in a text. Newspapers and magazines include headlines and photographs with captions to grab your attention and direct you to key points. Textbooks usually include tables of contents, headings, subheadings, illustrations, summaries, and other devices that alert you to what's important.

When you're listening, these visual clues are often absent. However, speakers usually provide verbal clues, and you can learn to spot them.

Listen for transitional words and phrases

These include such phrases as *the following three factors, in conclusion, the most important consideration, in addition to,* and *on the other hand.* These phrases and others signal relationships, definitions, new subjects, conclusions, cause and effect, and examples. They reveal the structure of the lecture. You can use these phrases to organize your notes.

Use visual devices to reveal the structure of ideas

As you listen, go beyond the lecturer's words to the core structure of that person's ideas. Lecturers in any subject tend to use a small number of structuring devices over and over again. You can indicate these structures in your notes with simple visual cues:

- **Use numbered lists to record the sequence of events.** When you want to indicate a series of events that take place in time, number each event in chronological order. This device applies naturally to subjects such as history. Also use numbers for procedures, especially those that call for performing tasks in a certain order.

- **Emphasize main points.** Most human speaking—and most published material—is based on the tension between generals and particulars. General statements are key points, the major ideas, the "bottom line" or "take-away" messages. To illustrate and support these statements, speakers offer examples, facts, statistics, quotations, anecdotes, stories, and other details. As you take notes, graphically emphasize the general statements: Underline them, write them in all upper-case letters, write them in a different color of ink, or go over them with a highlighter after the lecture. In your notes, record only the most vivid examples and details used to support each main point.

- **Create charts for contrasts and comparisons.** Lecturers signal comparison with phrases such as *in comparison . . . , compare this to . . . , contrast this with . . . , instead of . . . , in contrast . . . ,* and *on the other hand . . . .* See if you can create a chart to visually summarize comparisons and contrasts. If the lecturer is comparing two topics, create a two-column chart. List the main points about the first topic in the left-hand column; use the right-hand column to record the main points about the second topic. Structure your chart so that similarities and differences become clear. If this is too hard to do during class, go back to your notes and do it later.

Specialized formats for taking notes—such as maps, outlines, and the Cornell format—offer even more devices for revealing the structure of ideas. See Chapters 12 through 14 for more details.

example

FINDING LEVELS OF IDEAS

Imagine that you're sitting in a workshop about career planning. The speaker is a career counselor, and he begins his presentation with the following words:

Career planning is an adventure that involves exploration. There are many effective ways to plan your career. You can begin this adventure right now by remembering two ideas.

The first idea is this: You already know a lot about your career plan. You've already made many decisions about your career. Consider the student who can't decide if she wants to be a cost accountant or a tax accountant and then jumps to the conclusion that she is totally lost when it comes to career planning. Sure, she's debating tax accounting versus cost accounting, but she already knows she doesn't want to be a doctor, playwright, or taxicab driver. Contrast this with students who say, "I have no idea what to do with my life."

Second, career planning is a choice, not a discovery. Many people approach career planning as if they were panning for gold. They keep sifting through the dirt, clearing the dust, and throwing out the rocks. They are hoping to strike it rich and discover the perfect career. Other people believe they'll wake up one morning, see the heavens part, and suddenly know what they're supposed to do. Many of them are still waiting for that magical day to dawn.

We can approach career planning in a different way. Instead of seeing a career as something we discover, we can see it as something we choose. We don't find the right career. We create it. And we can create a career plan today.

To act on this second idea, you can take several steps. Perform a little experiment for me. Begin by looking up a Web site called *The Dictionary of Occupational Titles.* Just key those words into your favorite search engine and you'll get there. On this site you'll find dozens of common job titles listed. Next, print out a list of job titles from the fields that interest you most right now. Finally, sit down with your printout and cross out all the titles for jobs that you are definitely *not* interested in. You may be surprised to find out how many jobs you've already ruled out as career choices. The remaining jobs—those that are not crossed out—are possible career choices for you.

Following is one set of notes on this passage:

Career Planning (CP)

I've already made CP choices.

— what I don't want to do

CP = choice, not discovery

I don't find career—I create it

Steps to take:

1. Go to Web site—Dictionary of Occupational Titles
2. Print list of job titles
3. Cross out jobs I don't want
4. Remaining jobs = possible careers

CP AS A CHOICE	CP AS DISCOVERY
I know a lot about my CP	I know nothing about my CP
I can create CP now	I will create CP later

Bracket extra material

Bracketing refers to separating your own thoughts from the lecturer's as you take notes. This is useful in several circumstances:

- **Bracket your own opinions.** For the most part, avoid making editorial comments in your lecture notes. The danger is that when you return to your notes, you may mistake your own ideas for those of the instructor. If you want to make a comment—either a question to ask later or a strong disagreement —clearly label it as your own. Pick a symbol or code and use it in every class. Brackets—[and]—can work well.
- **Bracket material that confuses you.** No matter how attentive and alert you are, you might get lost and confused in a lecture. If it is inappropriate to ask a question, record in your notes that you were lost. Invent your own signal, for example, a circled question mark. When you write down your code for "I'm lost," leave space for the explanation or clarification that you will get later. The space will also be a signal that you missed something. Later, you can call your instructor with questions or ask to see a fellow student's notes. As long as you are honest with yourself when you don't understand, you can stay on top of the course.
- **Bracket digressions.** Let go of judgments about rambling, unorganized lectures. Turn them to your advantage. Take the initiative and organize the material yourself. While taking notes, separate the key points from the examples and supporting evidence. Note the places where you got confused and make a list of questions to ask.

Predict Test Questions

Predicting test questions can do more than get you a better grade on a test. It can keep you focused on the purpose of the course and help you design your learning strategies. Following are constructive ways to outsmart your teacher and reduce surprises at test time.

Get organized

Have a separate section in your notebook labeled "Test Questions." Add several questions to this section after every lecture and assignment.

Create a signal to flag possible test items in your notes

Use asterisks (***), exclamation points (!!), or a *T!* in a circle. Place these signals in the margin next to ideas that seem like possible test items.

Look for verbal cues from your teacher

Few teachers will try to disguise the main content of their courses. In fact, most offer repeated clues about what they want you to remember.

Many of those clues are verbal. In addition to focusing on *what* lecturers say, pay attention to *how* they say it:

- **Repetition.** Your teachers may state important points several times or return to those points in subsequent classes. They may also read certain passages word for word from their notes or from a book. Be sure to record all these points fully in your notes.
- **Common terms.** Also note your teachers' "pet phrases"—repeated terms that relate directly to course content. You could benefit from using these terms in essay exams, along with explanations in your own words to show that you truly understand the concepts.
- **Questions.** Pay attention to questions that the instructor poses to the class. These are potential test questions. Write them down, along with some answers.
- **Emphasis on certain types of content.** Some teachers have a penchant for detail—facts, names, dates, technical terms, and the like. Other teachers focus on broad themes and major events. Be alert to such differences; they are clues to the kinds of tests you'll have.
- **Placement of content.** Listen closely to material presented at the beginning and end of a lecture. Skilled speakers will often preview or review their key content at these points.
- **Comments on assigned readings.** When material from reading assignments is also covered extensively in class, it is likely to be on the test. The opposite can also be true: When your teacher emphasizes material that does *not* appear in any assigned reading, that material is likely to be important.

Look for nonverbal cues from your teacher

Sometimes a lecturer's body language will give potent clues to key content. She might use certain gestures when making critical points—pausing, looking down at notes, staring at the ceiling, or searching for words. If the lecturer has to think hard about how to make a point, that point is probably important. In addition:

- **Watch the board or overhead projector.** If an instructor takes time to write something down, consider this to be another signal that the material is important. Copy all diagrams and drawings, equations, names, places, dates, statistics, and definitions. Record all formulas, diagrams, and problems. Copy dates, numbers, names, places, and other facts. In short: If it's on the board, on a projector, or in a handout, put it in your notes. Use your own signal or code to flag this material.

- **Watch the instructor's eyes.** If an instructor glances at her notes and then makes a point, it is probably a signal that the information is especially important. Anything she reads from her notes is a potential test question.
- **Notice the instructor's interest level.** If the instructor is excited about something, it is more likely to appear on an exam. Pay attention if she seems more animated than usual.

Use the format of a test to predict questions

Ask your instructor to describe the tests she plans to give—how long they will be and what kinds of questions to expect (essay, multiple choice, true-false). Do this early in the term so you can be alert for possible test questions from the beginning.

Write practice test questions

Put yourself in your instructor's head. What kinds of questions would you ask?

Save all quizzes, papers, lab sheets, and graded material of any kind. Quiz questions have a way of appearing, in slightly altered form, on final exams. If copies of previous exams are available, use them to predict test questions. For science courses and other courses involving problem solving, practice working problems using different variables.

Also brainstorm test questions with other students. This is a great activity for study groups.

Remember the obvious

Instructors will often tell students point-blank that certain information is likely to appear on an exam. Instructors are not trying to hide what's important.

Listen for these words: *This material will be on the test.*

experiment **WITH A STRATEGY FROM THIS CHAPTER**

Recall a recent incident in which you had difficulty taking notes. Perhaps you were listening to an instructor who talked fast, or you got confused and stopped taking notes altogether. Describe the incident here:

Now review the seven suggestions in this chapter for taking notes. Choose one that you can use right away. Summarize that suggestion here and describe how and when you intend to use it:

After experimenting with this suggestion, evaluate how well it worked for you. If you thought of a way to modify the suggestion so that it worked more effectively, describe that modification:

Notes: Experimenting with the Cornell Format

Think of your notes as a textbook that *you* create—one that's more current and more in tune with your learning preferences than any book you could ever buy. An advantage of this "book" is that you can use it to actively experiment with the content of readings and lectures. And one key to this ongoing experimentation is playing with different options for note-taking.

An option that has worked for students around the world is the *Cornell format*. Originally developed by Walter Pauk at Cornell University during the 1950s, this approach is now taught across the United States and in other countries as well.

The simplicity of the Cornell format makes it a flexible tool. You can use this format for taking notes on anything—lectures, discussions, books, articles, Web sites, and more. You can even create a personal journal based on Cornell format principles.

Create Your Cornell Notes

The cornerstone of this system is simple: a wide margin on the left-hand side of the page. Pauk calls this the *cue column*, and using it is the key to the Cornell format's many benefits. To get started with this approach to note-taking, do two things.

1. Format your paper

On each page of your notes, draw a vertical line, top to bottom, about two inches from the left edge of the paper. This line creates the cue column—the space to the left of the line—that you will later use to condense and review your notes.

Some students avoid the Cornell format because they don't want to hand-draw this vertical line on every page of their note-taking paper.

There are several ways to get around this potential problem:

- Draw the vertical line on a blank page and make photocopies that you can use to take notes.
- Use word processing software to create a template page in Cornell format; print out pages as you need them.
- Check with your campus bookstore or an office supply store for paper that is preprinted in Cornell format.
- Take handwritten notes in any format; then use word processing software to create a two-column document and key in your notes.

In addition to creating a cue column, Pauk also suggests that you leave a two-inch space at the bottom of the page. He calls this the *summary area*. This space is also designed to be used at a later stage, as you review your notes.

Note: Some teachers of the Cornell format see the summary area as optional. Experiment with this feature to see if it makes a difference for you. You might choose to use the cue column only and skip the summary area.

2. Take notes, leaving the cue column and summary area blank

As you read or listen to a lecture, take notes on the right-hand side of the page. *Do not write in the cue column or summary area.* You'll use these spaces later.

As you take notes, don't worry about following any particular format. You can fill up the right-hand column with sentences, paragraphs, or outlines. Also, add visual notes such as mind maps or concept maps (see Chapter 13).

Study from Your Cornell Notes

A major benefit of the Cornell format is that it prompts you to go back to notes you took earlier, reflect on those notes, and actively review them. You can experience this benefit by taking the following steps.

Edit your notes

When you first review your notes, see if you can dress them up a bit:

- Fix words that are illegible.
- Write out abbreviated words that might be unclear to you later.
- If you can't read a passage or don't understand it, then mark it so that you can go to your instructor or another student for clarification.
- Check to see that your notes are labeled with the date and class and that the pages are numbered.

◆ example

CORNELL FORMAT NOTES TAKEN DURING A LECTURE

Following are notes from an early lecture in an introduction to philosophy course. Note that the cue column on the left and the summary area at the bottom of the page are both left blank.

	INTRO TO PHILOSOPHY, 1/10/05 **1**
	Philosophy—from the Greek <u>philosophia</u>—"lover of wisdom"
	Philosophers have different views of their main task:
	    —reflect on the nature of ultimate reality
	    —create a framework to unite all fields of knowledge
	    —critically evaluate all claims to knowledge
	Traditional topics in philosophy = 5 areas:
	1. Determine when a series of assertions is coherent and consistent (logic)
	2. Determine what is ultimately real (ontology)
	3. Determine what constitutes real knowledge (epistemology)
	4. Determine what is truly valuable (axiology and aesthetics)
	5. Determine what forms of behavior best sustain human society (ethics and politics)

If you want to distinguish between what you wrote in class and what you filled in later, make your edits with a different colored pen or pencil.

The main trick with this step is timing. Edit your notes right after class, preferably within 24 hours afterward. If you're using the Cornell format to take notes on a reading assignment, close the book and take a few minutes every hour to edit your notes.

Fill in the cue column

After making some initial "fixes" in your notes, begin the actual process of studying from them. The key to this step is summarizing and condensing your notes by making entries in the cue column. You can make several kinds of entries:

- **Reduce notes to key questions.** Normally you pose a question before answering it. In this case, you reverse the process. Think of the notes you took on the right-hand side of the page as a set of answers. In the cue column, write the corresponding questions. Write one question for each major term or point in your notes.
- **Reduce notes to key words.** Writing key words will speed the review process later. Also, reading your notes and focusing on extracting key words will further reinforce your understanding of the lecture or reading assignment. The trick is to use as few key words as possible. Search for words—usually specific nouns and action verbs—that are rich with associations, allowing you to recall whole sections of a lecture or reading assignment at once.
- **Reduce notes to headings.** Pretend that you are a copyeditor at a newspaper and that the notes you took are a series of articles. In the cue column, write a headline for each "article." You can use actual newspaper headlines and headings in your textbooks as models.

In any case, be brief. Leave space between your entries in the cue column. If you cram the cue column full of words, you defeat its purpose: to reduce your notes to the essentials.

Use the cue column to recite

When your cue column is full, you can use it as a series of prompts for one of the most powerful forms of review: recitation.

With a blank sheet of paper, cover the right-hand side of your notes; leave only the cue column showing. Then look at each item you wrote in the cue column and talk about it:

- If you wrote questions, answer each question.
- If you used the cue column for key words, then define each word and talk about why it's important.
- If you wrote headings in the cue column, then explain what the heading means and offer supporting details.

After reciting, uncover your notes and look for any important points you missed. Repeat this cycle of reciting and checking until you've mastered the material. Simply by taking these two steps, you are actively engaging with the material and applying many memory techniques at once.

Although speaking out loud is a common form of recitation, remember that you can also recite by writing. Writing engages different senses and areas of your brain than speaking does. In addition, writing promotes precision and clarity. You can sometimes bluff your way through a spoken recitation. However, seeing your own words on a page in front of you can quickly reveal any gaps in your understanding.

Whether you recite by speaking or writing, use your own words as much possible. Instead of simply repeating a lecturer's words, make the material your own.

Use the summary area to reflect

You'll probably find that your cue column fills up with a lot of content. If you choose to create a summary area on your page, use this space to continually remind yourself of the big picture:

- See if you can reduce all the notes on the page to a sentence or two.

 example:

FILLING IN THE CUE COLUMN AND SUMMARY AREA

Following are the notes from the previous example with the column and summary area added.

	INTRO TO PHILOSOPHY, 1/10/05 1
What is the derivation of the word <u>philosophy</u>?	<u>Philosophy</u>—from the Greek <u>philosophia</u>—"lover of wisdom" Philosophers have different views of their main task: —reflect on the nature of ultimate reality
What do philosophers do?	—create a framework to unite all fields of knowledge —critically evaluate all claims to knowledge
What are 5 traditional topics in philosophy?	Traditional topics in philosophy = 5 areas: 1. Determine when a series of assertions is coherent and consistent (logic) 2. Determine what is ultimately real (ontology) 3. Determine what constitutes real knowledge (epistemology) 4. Determine what is truly valuable (axiology and aesthetics) 5. Determine what forms of behavior best sustain human society (ethics and politics)

Even though philosophers have differing views of their main task, there are 5 traditional topics in philosophy.

- Add cross-references to topics elsewhere in your notes that are closely related.
- Explain briefly why the notes on this page matter; if you think the material is likely to appear on a test, note that fact here.

Also use the summary area to list any questions that you want to ask in class.

experiment WITH A STRATEGY FROM THIS CHAPTER

Find several pages of classroom notes that you took recently—ideally, during the past month. If you can find notes that seem confusing or incomplete, that's all the better for this exercise. Allow about one hour to complete the following five steps:

1. Spend a few minutes rereading your notes. Then re-create those notes in the Cornell format. You can use blank paper that's set up for Cornell-format notes. Or open up a blank document on your computer and format it in two columns. (The summary space at the bottom of the page is optional.)

2. Next, fill in the right-hand side of the page with the content of your old notes. As you do, make some quick edits for legibility and clarity.

3. Now turn your attention to the cue column. Use this space for questions, key words, or headings. If you chose to leave room for a summary area on each page, then use this space to condense your notes even more.

4. Cover the right-hand side of your notes and use the cue column to recite and review.

5. Finally, reflect on what you've just done. Do you think that the Cornell format would be a useful option for taking notes in the future? If so, describe when and where you will use this format. Also, could you modify this format in any way to make it more useful? If so, describe those modifications below:

Notes: Experimenting with Maps

To understand the benefits of maps as a format for taking notes, first reflect on the features of more traditional techniques for note-taking. Outlines, for example, contain main topics that are followed by minor topics, which, in turn, are subdivided further. They organize a subject in a sequential, hierarchical way.

In contrast, a map makes different areas of your brain come alive—the areas that focus on pattern making, visuals, and intuition. Like more traditional notes, maps can contain lists and sequences and show relationships. Yet maps also provide—literally—a picture of a subject. Maps are visual patterns that provide a framework for recall, working on both verbal and nonverbal levels.

Maps quickly, vividly, and accurately show the relationships between ideas. Also, maps help you think from general to specific. You focus first on the main topics, then zero in on minor topics. And by using only key words in your maps, you can condense a large subject into a small area of your notes. Many students find that they can review maps more quickly than long passages of notes that they have to read word for word.

As you build a map on paper or on a computer, you are also constructing a map in your mind. When you are finished, the picture of the map enters your memory. You could throw away your map and still retain many of the benefits gained by making it.

Two types of maps are especially useful for note-taking: mind maps and concept maps.

Create Mind Maps

Mind mapping, a note-taking system developed by author Tony Buzan, can be used in conjunction with other formats for note-taking. In some circumstances, you might want to use mind maps exclusively.

One key to successful mind mapping is to give yourself plenty of room. Use blank paper that measures at least 11x17 inches. If that's not available, turn regular notebook paper on its side so that you take notes in a horizontal (instead of vertical) format.

Another option is to use software with painting or drawing capabilities. Then you can generate mind maps on a computer.

With these basics out of the way, play with the following steps for creating your mind maps.

Write the main topic in the center of the page

Determine the main topic of a lecture—or, if you're taking notes on reading, the main topic of a chapter or article. Write that topic in the center of the page, expressing it in as few words as possible. (Buzan suggests using only one word per topic.) Circle this topic, underline it, or highlight it in some other way.

Add minor topics

Next, record minor topics related to the main concept. Connect topics with lines radiating outward from the center of the page. To give your map more depth, add topics that link to each minor topic.

Use key words only

As you add topics to your map, remind yourself to keep using key words only. Though this may seem awkward at first, it prompts you to summarize constantly and reduce ideas to their essence. There's also a practical benefit: Writing fewer words as you create your map means that you'll have fewer to slog through when it's time to review your notes later.

Key words are usually nouns and verbs that carry the bulk of a speaker's or writer's ideas. Choose words that spark a lot of associations in your mind, helping you recreate the essence of a lecture or chapter. As you practice making mind maps, you'll discover the kinds of key words that work especially well for you.

Add visuals and color

After taking the preceding steps to create your map, see if you want to jazz it up a bit. For instance, use color as an organizing device: If there are three main sets of topics covered in a lecture, record each set in a different color. Use red or another bright color to signal important topics. Or use one color for notes on your textbooks and another color for notes on lectures. Add symbols, pictures, and other images as well.

The general principle that's involved here is simple: Notes that are visually interesting are often easier to review.

Allow space

When creating mind maps, remember the virtue of visual simplicity. If you overload the page with key words and other elements, you could end up with a map that looks more like a piece of chaotic modern art than a tool for learning. Leave some blank space around each element in your map.

Link maps together

Remember that one mind map doesn't have to include all the ideas in a lecture or chapter. Instead, you can link mind maps. For example, draw a mind map that sums up the five key points in a chapter. Then make a separate, more detailed mind map for each of those key points. Within each mind map, include references to the other mind maps. This helps you see the relationships among many ideas.

 example

NOTES IN MIND MAP FORMAT

Following is an excerpt from notes taken during a psychology lecture about a mental illness called obsessive-compulsive disorder. Notice that the map covers three main "strings" of topics: symptoms, treatments, and other features.

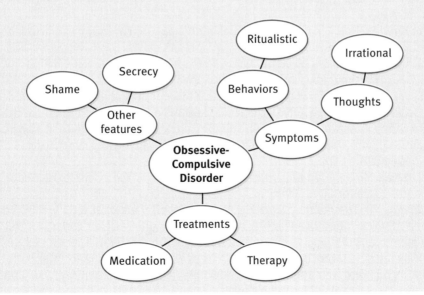

Some students pin several mind maps next to each other on a bulletin board or tape them to a wall. This gives a dramatic view of the big picture.

Combine mind maps with other types of notes

Mind maps can be used along with Cornell-format notes in a number of ways:

- Divide your note paper in half, reserving one half for mind maps and the other for information more suited to the traditional paragraph method: equations, long explanations, and word-for-word definitions.
- Incorporate a mind map into your paragraph-style notes wherever you feel one is appropriate.
- Use mind maps to summarize notes taken in other formats.

Another way to use mind maps is to modify the Cornell format: Draw a line down the center of the page. Then use the left-hand side for mind mapping and the right-hand side for more linear information—lists, graphs, and paragraphs.

▶ sidebar

STUDY FROM MIND MAPS

Using mind maps offers unique possibilities for reviewing your notes, reflecting on them, and preparing for tests:

- *Revise your mind maps.* Clean up your initial mind map or create a new and cleaner draft. Add key words, drawings, and color.
- *Recite from your mind maps.* Pretend that you are giving a lecture on the main topic of your mind map. Use your key words as cues for speaking.
- *Recreate your mind maps from memory.* Spend a few minutes reviewing your mind map. Close your eyes and see if you can visualize it in your mind. Then re-create the map strictly from memory, using a fresh sheet of paper or a new computer file. When you're done, compare your new mind map with the original one and check for any differences between the two.
- *Translate the content of your mind map into another format.* For example, re-create your notes in outline form or Cornell format.
- *Use mind maps for collaborative learning.* Mind maps offer an ideal activity for study groups and other collaborative learning projects. Get together with classmates and compare mind maps that you've created on the same topic. Or work together to create a single mind map on a large, complex topic. Assign each person a single "branch" of the map, working outward from the center. To allow plenty of room for writing, use poster board or tack large sheets of paper to a wall.

Create Concept Maps

Like mind maps, concept maps let you form visual connections between ideas. Yet concept maps are slightly more formal. People who find mind maps too unstructured or messy may find concept maps more appealing.

Concept mapping is a tool pioneered by Joseph Novak and D. Bob Gowin, psychologists who were deeply influenced by the work of David Ausubel. In *The Psychology of Meaningful Verbal Learning*, Ausubel wrote that the essence of learning a subject is integrating new concepts with concepts that we already know. We do this by creating propositions—statements that link familiar concepts to those that are unfamiliar.

Concept maps express this learning process in visual form. The key elements are:

- A main concept written at the top of a page.
- Related concepts arranged in a hierarchy, with more general concepts toward the top of a page and more specific concepts toward the bottom.
- Links—lines with words that briefly explain the relationship between concepts.

When you combine concepts with their linking words, you'll often get complete sentences (or sets of coherent phrases). These are the propositions described by Ausubel. With the nearly 460,000 words in the English language at your disposal, you have unlimited possibilities for creating new propositions about any topic.

Use the following steps to create concept maps.

Choose one concept as a focus

To begin, limit the scope of your concept map. Choose one general concept as a focus—the main topic of a chapter, article, or lecture. Express this concept in one to three words. Concept words are usually nouns and adjectives, including key terms and proper names. Circle your main concept.

List related concepts

Next, brainstorm a list of concepts that are related to the main concept. Don't worry about putting these concepts in any order yet. Just list them—again, expressing each concept in a single word or short phrase. For ease in rearranging and ranking the concepts later, you might wish to write each one on a single index card or on a single line in a word processing file.

Arrange concepts in a hierarchy

Rank concepts on a continuum from general to specific. Then create the body of your concept map by placing the main concept at the top and the most specific concepts at the bottom. Arrange the rest of the concepts in appropriate places throughout the middle. Again, circle each concept.

Allow some time for this step, and be willing to shuffle concepts around until you're satisfied with the arrangement.

Add links

Draw lines that connect the concepts, along with words that describe their relationships. Limit yourself to the fewest words needed to make accurate links. Linking words are often verbs, verb phrases, or prepositions.

Revise your map

Look for any concepts that are repeated in several places on the map. You can avoid these duplications by adding more links between concepts. Also add any missing concepts and see if you can clarify vague links.

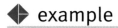 example

NOTES IN CONCEPT MAP FORMAT

The concept map below is an excerpt from notes on a reading assignment about nutrition.

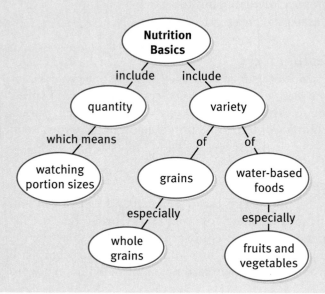

Avoid "string maps"—concepts that flow in basically a straight line from top to bottom. String maps are often a signal to expand your understanding by adding concepts, links, or both. In this way you create a richer set of relationships between concepts.

Use other graphic organizers

Mind maps and concept maps are just two examples of graphic organizers—ways to represent information and ideas in visual form. Consider the additional examples that follow, and feel free to invent more graphic organizers of your own.

The timeline. Events that take place in chronological order—such as historical events, the incidents in a novel, or the steps in a procedure—can be represented on a line. This line represents time as it flows from past to present to future. For example, you could use a timeline to represent major events in World War II:

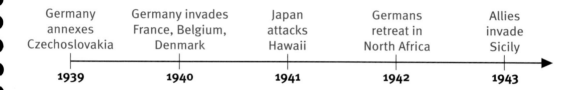

Germany annexes Czechoslovakia	Germany invades France, Belgium, Denmark	Japan attacks Hawaii	Germans retreat in North Africa	Allies invade Sicily
1939	1940	1941	1942	1943

The comparison and contrast chart. To show how two or more things resemble each other—and differ from each other—set up a comparison chart. The following chart compares the valence and atomic number for several items listed in the periodic table of the elements, a topic in chemistry and physics courses.

Element	Valence	Atomic Number
Actinium	3	89
Aluminum	3	13
Beryllium	2	4
Copper	3	96
Krypton	0	36
Magnesium	2	12

☑ checklist

STUDY FROM CONCEPT MAPS

You can study from concept maps in some of the same ways that you study from mind maps:

❑ *Revise your maps*. You may go through three or four drafts before you're satisfied that your concept map is pleasing to look at, complete, and accurate. Revision is generally easier when you create your maps on a computer.

❑ *Recite from your maps*. You may find it easier to recite from concept maps than from mind maps: Combining concepts with their links may often give you complete sentences.

❑ *Recreate your maps from memory*. Redraw your concept map without looking at the original. Then check it against the original for accuracy.

❑ *Translate the content of your concept map into another format*. Recreate your notes in outline form, Cornell format, mind-map format, or straight text.

❑ *Use your maps for collaborative learning*. Compare your concept maps with those created by others on the same material. Or work with a study group to create a large concept map on a complex topic.

experiment WITH A STRATEGY FROM THIS CHAPTER

Find several pages of classroom notes that you took recently—ideally, during the past month. If you can find notes that seem confusing or incomplete, that's all the better for this exercise. Set aside about one hour to complete the following steps:

1. Spend a few minutes rereading your notes. Then re-create those notes as a mind map. Work quickly, keeping your notes to key words. Feel free to add color or other visual elements to your map.

2. Next, translate the same pages of notes into the format of a concept map. Before drawing your map, you might find it helpful to brainstorm a list of topics on index cards—one topic per card—and then arrange the cards on a continuum from general to specific.

3. Now study from your maps. Use them as cues to recite, or see if you can recreate your maps from memory.

4. Finally, reflect on what you've just done. Do you think that concept maps or mind maps offer useful options for taking notes in the future? If so, describe when and where you will use either format. Also, could you modify or combine these note-taking formats in any way to make them more useful? If so, describe those modifications below:

Notes: Experimenting with Outlines

Perhaps you've had negative experiences with outlining in the past. Teachers may have required you to use complex, rigid outlining formats based exclusively on Roman numerals or an equally unfamiliar system.

If so, be willing to let go of those experiences and approach outlining in a more flexible way. The Roman-numeral style represents just one option for outlining. By playing with other options, you can discover the power of outlining to reveal relationships between ideas and to categorize large bodies of information.

One advantage of taking notes in outline form is that it can totally occupy your attention. You are not only recording ideas but also organizing them. This can be an advantage when you encounter material presented in a disorganized way.

Create Outlines

Outlines consist of *headings*—words, phrases, or sentences placed in a hierarchy that ranges from general to specific. To get the most from outlining, begin by choosing the styles you'll use for the various levels of headings. Then experiment with several types of outlines.

Distinguish between levels of headings

Headings in outlines are arranged in different levels:

- In the first or "top" level of an outline, record the major topics or points that are presented in a lecture or reading assignment.
- In the second level, record the key topics or points that are used to support and explain the first-level headings.
- In the third level, record more specific ideas, facts, and details that relate to each of your second-level headings.

To understand the concept of levels in an outline, consider the organization of this chapter. You can quickly outline this chapter just by listing the major headings at the first level and placing the minor headings at the second level. Consider the following example.

Theoretically, you can create outlines that extend to four, five, six, or even more levels of headings. An advantage of adding levels is that your outline gains more detail. However, your outline also becomes more bulky and complex. You may find it difficult to keep track of all the levels.

With some practice, you can learn to strike a balance: Consider how much detail is useful for your note-taking. When outlining, add just the number of levels you need to adequately summarize the material you're studying.

◆ example

OUTLINE OF THIS CHAPTER

Create Outlines
Distinguish between levels of headings
Choose your heading styles
Create topic outlines
Create sentence outlines

Create Outlines With a Computer
Create headings in various levels
Hide and reveal body text
Edit headings
Use outlining to think clearly and efficiently
Use outlines to collaborate

Study from Outlines

Experiment With a Strategy From This Chapter

Notes on this outline:
- *First-level headings are printed in all uppercase (capital) letters.*
- *Second-level headings appear in both uppercase and lowercase letters.*
- *Only two first-level headings are followed by second-level headings. You could add a third level of headings to this outline by listing the topic sentences for each paragraph in the chapter. These third-level headings would fall "underneath" the second-level headings.*

Choose your heading styles

When you first encountered outlines, you probably learned to use:

- Roman numerals for first-level headings.
- Uppercase letters for second-level headings.
- Numbers for third-level headings.

For additional levels, you may have used lowercase letters and numbers in parentheses. In addition, as you added levels of headings, you probably indented each level.

You may like this traditional format for an outline; many students do. At the same time, play with other possibilities. For instance, you can indicate different levels simply by indenting headlines. Other options are displayed in the box on the next page.

Caution: Trying to remember and use an elaborate set of styles for headings can distract you from the content of the material you want to learn. To make outlining an effective tool, stick to two or three levels and keep styles simple.

Create topic outlines

When you're brainstorming ideas for a paper or just want to record some quick reminders of the content of a lecture, consider creating a topic outline. This outlining format is ideal when you're pressed for time or just initially exploring a topic.

Topic outlines tend to be informal. Headings can be just a single word or a short phrase. Keep the styles simple, use minimal formatting, and limit yourself to two or three heading levels.

Be sure to save your topic outline, no matter how rough. It can help you prepare a more formal outline in the future on the same topic.

Create sentence outlines

Compared with topic outlines, sentence outlines are more formal and take more time to craft. The payoff is precision: By the time you finish a sentence outline, you'll have greater clarity about what you heard or read or about what you want to say.

Whereas topic outlines can indicate the *structure* of a lecture or reading assignment, sentence outlines give you a record of the point-by-point *content*. This level of understanding allows you to step deeper into the subject matter. Instead of merely being able to state what a lecture was about, you'll reconstruct the gist of what the lecturer actually said.

Another difference between topic outlines and sentence outlines relates directly to critical thinking. Topic outlines are fairly forgiving; often they are too brief to reveal gaps in logic or holes in

 example

HEADING STYLES FOR OUTLINES

Use traditional outline styles:
I. First-level heading
   A. Second-level heading
      1. Third-level heading
        (a) Fourth-level heading
          (1) Fifth-level heading

Distinguish styles with indentation only:
First-level heading
   Second-level heading
      Third-level heading
         Fourth-level heading

Distinguish styles with bullets and dashes:
First-level heading
  ■ Second-level heading
   —Third-level heading

Distinguish styles by size:
FIRST-LEVEL HEADING
  Second-level heading
   Third-level heading

 example

TOPIC OUTLINE

America's Health—Improvements
I. Key source: Government report, 2002
   A. Official announcement
   B. Key findings—quote
II. Life expectancy
   A. Infant mortality
   B. Length of life
III.Deaths from chronic illness, injury—lower
   A. AIDS deaths
   B. Smoking rates—1960s vs. 2000

example

HHS Issues Report Showing Dramatic Improvements in America's Health

I. Health and Human Services Secretary Tommy G. Thompson reports that Americans' health changed over the past 50 years.
   A. Thompson: "When you take the long view, you see clearly how far we've come in combating diseases, making workplaces safer, and avoiding risks such as smoking."
   B. Thompson referred to *Health, United States, 2002*, a report from the Centers for Disease Control and Prevention (CDC).
II. By 2000, infant mortality dropped to a record low, and life expectancy hit a record high.
   A. Death rates among children and adults up to age 24 were cut in half.
   B. Americans enjoyed the longest life expectancy in U.S. history—almost 77 years.
III. Among working-age adults, fewer are dying from unintentional injuries, heart disease, and stroke.
   A. After 1995, deaths from AIDS dropped due to powerful new drugs.
   B. More than 40 percent of adults were smokers in 1965, compared with 23 percent in 2000.

evidence. In contrast, sentence outlines are more complete, laying bare a speaker or writer's chain of assertions about a topic and the thread of that person's logic. Sentence outlines shine a light on contradictions and other fallacies in reasoning.

To create this type of outline, just make sure that each of your headings is a complete sentence. This means including a verb in each heading. A phrase such as *N. Scott Momaday—writer* is fine for a heading in a topic outline. But for a sentence outline, you'll need to say something about him, such as: *N. Scott Momaday won a Pulitzer Prize for his novel* House Made of Dawn.

Create Outlines With a Computer

With computer software, outlining becomes a flexible and intuitive tool for sharpening your thinking. The hallmark of outlining on the computer is the ability to insert headings at various points in your draft and to display those headings with or without the text that follows them.

To understand the benefits of this feature, consider how headings are used in the material you read. Most published material includes headings. These range from newspaper headlines to the chapter headings and subheadings found in textbooks. Headings offer capsule summaries and signposts that readers can use to navigate through long documents. Outlining software allows you to add such headings to everything you write.

Many software packages include an outlining feature. Microsoft Word allows you to toggle back and forth between "normal" document view (your complete draft) and outline view (a list of headings). PowerPoint, often used to create images for speeches and other presentations, allows you to view headlines and text apart from visuals.

Experiment with the following outlining features.

Create headings at various levels

Writing headings helps you plan your writing and divide a big writing project into small steps. Begin by writing major headings for the main sections; then write the text to follow each heading. To work your way through long sections, divide them up into subsections with minor headings. And to create more meaningful headings at every level, use brief but complete sentences rather than single words or short phrases.

Hide and reveal body text

With outlining software, a single click allows you to hide body text—the paragraphs that lie "beneath" each heading. In outline view, you can display headings only, giving you a functional table of contents for your document. This view allows you to reduce a document of many pages to a single screen full of headings, revealing the structure of your manuscript at a glance.

With another brief series of keystrokes you can reveal, read, and edit the body text under any heading, then switch back to headings only. In effect, you alternate between whole and parts, major points and minor details—from seeing the "forest" to inspecting the "trees."

Edit headings

Outlining makes it easy to rearrange headings, assign them to different levels, and insert sentences under each heading. You can also assign each level of heading a style, such as boldface for major headings and italics for minor headings.

What's more, the software allows you to "promote" headings (raise them from a minor to major level) or "demote" them (lower them from a major to a minor level). When you perform either operation, the heading style changes automatically.

Use outlining to think clearly and efficiently

Creating outlines can save you hours of writing time. By reflecting on the wording and sequence of headings, you can spot gaps in logic, missing topics, and topics that need to be deleted or rearranged. If you're writing narrative fiction, you can mark the key events in your story with headings, scan those headings to get the big picture of your plot, and reorder individual events. And you can do all these things before you draft hundreds or thousands of words.

Use outlines to collaborate

Computer outlining offers an ideal activity for study groups. Gather around a computer and assign one person to sit at the keyboard and type. Working as a group and checking the screen periodically, brainstorm headings to capture the main points of a lecture or reading assignment.

If you're working collaboratively to write a paper, create major headings as a group. Then print out copies of the outline and ask each person in the group, working alone, to fill in another level or two of headings below each major heading. Gather again as a group to assemble the completed outline and fine-tune it.

Study from Outlines

Outlines offer unique possibilities for reviewing your notes, reflecting on them, and preparing for tests:

- **Revise your outline.** You may go through three or four drafts before you're satisfied that your outline is complete and accurate. With each draft, your understanding of the subject increases. Also, the act of outlining in several "passes" reinforces your memory of the material. As with other forms of note-taking, revision is generally easier when you use a computer.
- **Recite from your outline.** Focus on one major heading in your outline. Then look away from your outline and talk about that heading. Pretend that you are giving a short, impromptu speech or writing a brief article about each heading. After a few minutes of reciting several headlines, look back at your written outline for any points you missed.
- **Recreate your outline from memory.** After drafting and revising an outline, put it away for a while. Then take out a blank sheet of paper or open up a new document file on your computer and see if you can reconstruct the entire outline without looking at the original. When you're done, compare the two outlines and check for accuracy.
- **Translate the content of your outline into another format.** Recreate your notes as a mind map or concept map or as a document in Cornell format. Doing so prompts you to view the subject from a new angle and experiment with different learning styles.

experiment WITH A STRATEGY FROM THIS CHAPTER

Find several pages of classroom notes that you took recently—ideally, during the past month. If you can find notes that seem confusing or incomplete, that's all the better for this exercise. Allow about one hour to complete the following five steps:

1. Spend a few minutes rereading your notes. Then, using blank paper or word processing software, re-create those notes as a topic outline. Keep this outline brief and informal—one page at most. Use a set of heading styles that is easy to remember and yet helps you distinguish between levels of ideas.

2. Next, expand your topic outline into a sentence outline. If you're writing by hand, start a new outline on a clean sheet of paper. If you're outlining on a computer, turn your topic outline headings into complete sentences and add another level or two of ideas.

3. Now study from your outlines. Use them as cues to recite, or see if you can recreate your outlines strictly from memory.

4. Finally, reflect on what you've just done. Do you think that topic or sentence outlines would be useful options for taking notes in the future? If so, describe when and where you will use either format. Also, could you modify or combine these note-taking formats in any way to make them more useful? If so, describe those modifications below:

Creating More Value from Your Notes

The purpose of taking notes is to consult them later. To some students, that means scanning them once or twice before a test. By that time, however, the notes may raise more questions than they answer. Notes that are not used continuously throughout a term can quickly become inaccurate, even useless.

You have another option: to add value to your notes. Do this by continuously updating, condensing, reorganizing, reviewing, and refining them. Also use your notes to predict test questions.

The key is to see your notes as living documents—words and images that gain clarity as your understanding of a subject deepens. Create notes that are clear enough for you to understand and useful enough to consult for weeks, months, or years to come.

Revise Your Notes

Approach your notes as works in progress—documents that can almost always be improved. You can revise those documents in two broad stages.

Stage 1: Clean up your notes

Take your first pass through your notes as soon after each class as possible. Use this time to:

- Fix passages that are illegible.
- Check to see that your notes are labeled with the date and the name of the class.
- Make sure that the pages are numbered.
- Expand on passages that are hard to understand.
- Write out abbreviated words or phrases that might be unclear to you later.
- List questions that you need answered in order to make sense of your notes.

You might find it useful to distinguish between what you wrote in class and what you filled in later. With handwritten notes, edit using a different colored pen or pencil. If you key your notes into a computer, you can use different colored fonts for your edits.

Stage 2: Recreate your notes in a new format

The goal of *taking* notes in the first place is to condense a lecture or discussion to its essence, leaving you with a compact set of ideas and information to study. A goal of *revising* your notes is to reflect on the subject matter and bring your insights into clear focus.

▷ sidebar

WAYS TO EVALUATE YOUR NOTES

The following table lists three broad goals of effective note-taking, along with strategies for meeting each goal. Review and revise your own notes with these criteria in mind. As you do, avoid vague and absolute judgments such as *I'm a lousy note taker*. Instead, be specific but nonjudgmental. Focus on ways to improve.

Goal	Strategies
Reduce course content to its essentials.	▪ Use meaningful abbreviations. ▪ Use key words. ▪ Focus on major topics, terms, and points; record only key details.
Clarify the organization of course content.	▪ Use concept maps, mind maps, and other visual devices to highlight key ideas and their relationships. ▪ Use outlines with headings that clearly distinguish between different levels of ideas. ▪ Create graphic cues to aid review: underline or capitalize key words and phrases; indent key passages or record them in a different color from the rest of your notes; use simple lists and numbered lists.
Reveal understanding of the material.	▪ Whenever possible, use your own words rather than the lecturer's. ▪ Take notes in several different formats. ▪ Use key words, but avoid condensing material so much that it becomes impossible to decode. ▪ Record essential points in complete sentences.

Sometimes it helps to get a different perspective on the material. You can do that by recreating your notes in a new format. If you took notes in Cornell format (see Chapter 12), try converting sections to outline format (see Chapter 14). If your original notes are outlined, try converting sections to mind maps or concept maps (see Chapter 13). Use all these formats at different points in your notes for a course, or invent new formats of your own.

The benefit of playing with all these formats is that they engage your mind in different ways. Taking notes in Cornell format can help you get a handle on details—key terms and facts. Outlines force you to pay attention to the way that material is structured. Maps are visual devices that help you see connections between many topics at once. Each format yields a different cross-section of the subject matter, and each format deepens your understanding.

Review Your Notes

In terms of reinforcing long-term memory, the process you use to *review* your notes can be just as crucial as the content or format of those notes. Think of unreviewed notes as leaky faucets, constantly dripping, losing precious information until you shut them off with a quick review.

Review notes within 24 hours

The sooner you review your notes, the better, especially if the class was difficult. In fact, you can start reviewing during class. When your instructor pauses to set up the overhead projector or erase the board, scan your notes. Dot the *i*'s, cross the *t*'s, and write out unclear abbreviations.

Another way to use this technique is to get to your next class as quickly as you can. Then use the four or five minutes before the lecture to review the notes you just took in the previous class.

If you do not get to your notes immediately after class, you can still benefit by reviewing later in the day. A review right before you go to sleep can also be valuable. And you can do it in just a few minutes—often 10 minutes or less.

Review notes weekly

Once a week, review all your notes again. The review sessions don't need to take a lot of time. Even a 20-minute weekly review period is valuable. Some students find that a weekend review, say on Sunday afternoon, helps them stay in continuous touch with the material. Scheduling regular review sessions on your calendar helps develop the habit.

▶ sidebar

REINFORCE MEMORY BY REHEARSAL

When you want to remember a fact or idea, you instinctively rehearse it. Rehearsal can be as simple as repeating the seven digits of a phone number a few times before you dial it, or as complex as an actor's practicing lines in order to learn a one-hour monologue.

The point is this: Information that you rehearse moves into your long-term memory. And information that you do not rehearse can fade completely from your memory in anywhere from a few seconds to a few hours. In more common parlance: If you don't use it, you lose it.

For more effective rehearsal:

- **Use a variety of strategies.** Recite the points in your notes that you want to remember. Explain these points to someone else. Lead a study group about the topic. Also, look for ways to summarize and condense the material. See if you can take the language from your notes and make it more precise. If you succeed, edit your notes accordingly.
- **Involve your senses.** Make rehearsal a rich, enjoyable experience. Read your notes out loud and use a variety of voices. Sing your notes, making up your own rhymes or songs. Record yourself as you recite your notes, and play music you like in the background.
- **Use elaborative rehearsal instead of rote memory.** Rehearsal is a sophisticated learning strategy that goes well beyond rote repetition. As you review your notes, use rehearsal to move facts and ideas off the page and into your mind. See if you can elaborate on your notes by using more of your own words and by supplying your own examples.
- **Build a feedback cycle into your rehearsal.** Create a list of key questions that cover the important sections of your notes. Then quiz yourself, or ask a friend to quiz you. To get maximum value from this exercise, evaluate the accuracy of your answers. If you're consistently missing key questions, then consider using a new strategy for reading or note-taking.
- **Allow adequate time.** Following the preceding suggestions means that rehearsal will take more time than mindlessly scanning your notes. It's worth it. Also remember that you can be selective. You don't have to rehearse everything in your notes. Save your most elaborate rehearsal for the most important material.

As you review, step back for the larger picture. In addition to reciting or repeating the material to yourself, ask questions about it:

- Does this relate to my goals?
- How does this relate to information I already know, in this field or another?
- Will I be tested on this material?
- What will I do with this material?
- How can I relate it to something that deeply interests me?
- Am I unclear on any points? If so, what exactly is the question I want to ask?

Conduct major reviews

A third and equally important level of review is the kind of studying you do during the week before a major test. This is an intensive phase of learning that can involve many types of activity: creating course summaries, writing mock tests, and taking part in study groups. For more details on this type of review, see Chapter 18.

Expand on Your Notes With a Personal Journal

There's a definition of note-taking: Words that go directly from the instructor's mouth to the student's notebook—without ever entering the student's mind.

You can avoid this fate by writing in a journal. Here is a chance for you to stretch out mentally: Reflect on the significance of your courses. Mine your own experiences for examples of the ideas you're learning about. Speculate about how you might apply what you're learning in class.

Writing this broadly can enhance almost all of the strategies explained in this book. Writing prompts you to think both creatively and critically. In addition, writing is a multisensory activity, one that involves touching, seeing, and even hearing (the sound of a pencil scratching across paper or fingers tapping a keyboard). Each sense mode opens up a channel to your brain of ways to make your learning more vivid and to transfer the content of your writing from short-term to long-term memory. Chances are that the things you write about with the most interest and passion are the things you will remember after you graduate.

Include many kinds of material

Remember that a journal can include any kind of writing. Examples are ideas for papers, responses to topics discussed in class, questions, ideas for articles or books you might like to publish some day, career plans, goals, and dreams. Also include poems, prayers, creative visualizations, drawings, paintings, and photographs. Also remember that you can create journal entries on paper or use a computer for this purpose.

Use a journal to go beyond assignments and tests. Explore connections between subjects and reflect on ways to apply what you're learning.

Use a journal to create dialogues

Imagine that you're sitting face to face with the author of your textbook or a historical figure that you're studying. Write what you would say to this person. Argue. Debate. Note questions you want to ask this person; later, pose these questions in class. In each case, you will build your skills at critical thinking.

You can make this process more formal with a two-column journal:

- Draw a vertical line down the middle of a blank sheet of paper, or open up a word processing file and create a two-column chart.
- In the left column, write summaries of readings or class discussions.
- In the right column, record your responses to these summaries—questions, disagreements, agreements, and additional comments.

Use a journal to increase writing skills

By keeping a journal, you can explore a variety of writing genres. For instance:

- Use a journal to sharpen your powers of observation. To begin, list as many details as you can about a person or an object in your environment. Make your description as complete, vivid, and detailed as you can.
- Review your journal for writing topics. Perhaps you've already written something in your journal that could become the basis for a research paper.
- Try your hand at fiction, too. Create characters for plays or novels. Write short stories that you could refine and perhaps submit for publication.

Use a journal to promote insight and change

To create a journal that has an impact on your daily life, experiment with writing two types of entries. (Both are explained in more detail in the book *Becoming a Master Student* by Dave Ellis.)

The first type is a Discovery Statement. These are statements about where you stand today and what you learn about yourself as a student—both strengths and weaknesses. Discovery Statements can also be descriptions of your attitudes, statements of your feelings, transcripts of your thoughts, and chronicles of your behavior.

Intention Statements are the second type. These can be used to alter your course. They are statements of your commitment to do a specific task, to take a certain action. An intention arises out of your choice to pursue a particular goal.

You may soon discover an intimate link between these two types of writing. A Discovery Statement (such as "I discovered that my notes don't create much value for me in studying for tests") can lead naturally to an Intention Statement ("I intend to review my notes within 24 hours after a class and to edit them once a month").

☑ checklist

JOURNALING WITH LISTS

A simple way to start a journal and gradually expand its content is to make lists. Experiment with many kinds of lists. For example:

❏ List new words and their definitions.
❏ List the top five ideas that you want to remember from your classes or assigned readings.
❏ List the five most influential people in your life and what they taught you.
❏ List the three most important things you want to teach your children.
❏ List your favorite quotations, including notable things that you and your friends say.

Use a journal to manage stress

Much stress has its source in negative self-talk—nagging voices in our heads that make dire predictions for the future and undermine our abilities: *Flunking this test is the worst thing that could ever happen to me* or *I never finish what I start.*

Getting these disempowering ideas outside your head and onto paper is one way to defuse them. Begin by listing any irrational, self-defeating beliefs you have. These statements tend to be judgmental and absolute, including words such as *never, can't, have to, must,* and *should.* Then write down more reasonable, empowering beliefs. These statements focus on the words *can, could, like to,* and *love to.* For example: *I can adopt new habits to create new results in my life.*

In this way a journal becomes a trusted confidant that always respects your safety and privacy. Here is a counselor that's available any place, any time—free.

Take Notes on Reading

There are two kinds of notes on reading: review notes and research notes.

Review notes will look like the notes you take in class. Sometimes you will want more extensive notes than you can write in a margin of your text. You can't underline or make notes in library books, so make separate notes when you use these sources.

Research notes—those you make in order to write papers and prepare for presentations—follow a different format. These notes are one element of a process that starts with planning what you want to say and creating several drafts of your material. For more details on this process, see Chapters 20 through 25.

To take more effective review notes:

- **Set priorities.** Single out a particularly difficult section of a text and make separate notes. Or make summaries of overlapping lecture and text material.
- **Use a variety of formats.** Translate text into Cornell notes, maps, or outlines. Combine these formats and create your own. Translate diagrams, charts, and other visual elements into words. Then reverse the process by translating straight text into visual elements.
- **On the other hand, don't let formats get in your way.** Even a simple list of key points and examples can become a powerful review tool. Another option is to just close your book and start writing. Write quickly about what you intend to remember from the text, and don't worry about following any format.
- **Condense a passage to key quotes.** Authors embed their essential ideas in key sentences. As you read, continually ask yourself: What's the point? Then see if you can point to a specific sentence on the page to answer your question. Look especially at headings, subheadings, and topic sentences of paragraphs. Write these key sentences word for word in your notes and put them within quotation marks. Copy as few sentences as you can and still retain the core meaning of the passage.
- **Condense by paraphrasing.** Pretend that you have to summarize a chapter, article, or book on a post card. Limit yourself to a single paragraph or a single sentence and use your own words. This is a great way to test your understanding of the material.
- **Take a cue from the table of contents.** Look at the table of contents in your book. Write each major heading on a piece of paper, or key those headings into a word processing file on your computer. Include page numbers. Next, see if you can improve on the table of contents. Substitute your own headings for those that appear in the book. Turn single words or phrases into complete sentences, and use words that are meaningful to you.
- **Enhance your memory.** Instead of taking notes sentence by sentence or paragraph by paragraph, turn away from the text and write notes from memory. Pretend that you're taking an essay exam on a topic presented in the text. Create an open-ended question on that topic and then write your answer.

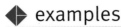 examples

TRANSLATING TEXT INTO REVIEW NOTES

Read the following passage from *Public Speaking* by Michael Osborn and Suzanne Osborn — an excerpt from a section about using clear language. Then consider the examples of notes on this passage.

One factor that impairs clarity is the use of **jargon**, the technical language that is specific to a profession. Such language is often referred to with an —*ese* at the end, as in "speaking in computerese." If you use jargon before an audience that doesn't share that technical vocabulary, you will not be understood. For example, "We expect a positive vorticity advective" may be perfectly understandable to a group of meteorologists, but to most audiences, simply saying, "It's going to rain" would be much clearer. Speakers who fall into the jargon trap are so used to using technical language that they forget that others may not grasp it. It does not occur to them that they must translate the jargon into lay language to be understood by general audiences. . . .

A problem similar to that of using jargon is using words that are needlessly overblown. A notorious example occurred when signmakers wanted to tell tourists how to leave the Barnum museum. Rather than drawing an arrow with the word *Exit* above it, they wrote "To the Egress." There's no telling how many visitors left the museum by mistake, thinking that they were going to see that rare creature—a living, breathing "Egress."

Although such misunderstandings may result from innocent incompetence, at other times jargon seems to be purposely befuddling. Some speakers like to satisfy their egos and intimidate others by displaying their technical vocabularies. The parent of a student in Houston received a message from the high school principal regarding a special meeting on a proposed educational program. The message read:

Our school's cross-graded, multiethnic, individualized learning program is designed to enhance the concept of an open-ended learning program with emphasis on a continuum of multiethnic, academically enriched learning, using the identified intellectually gifted child as the agent or director of his own learning. Major emphasis is on cross-graded, multiethnic learning with the main objective being to learn respect for the uniqueness of a person.

The parent responded:

Dear Principal: I have a college degree, speak two foreign languages and know four Indian dialects. I've attended a number of county fairs and three goat ropings, but I haven't the faintest idea as to what you are talking about. Do you?

Example #1—Condensing the passage to key quotes:

"One factor that impairs clarity is the use of **jargon**, the technical language that is specific to a profession."

"A problem similar to that of using jargon is using words that are needlessly overblown."

"Some speakers like to satisfy their egos and intimidate others by displaying their technical vocabularies."

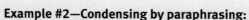

Example #2—Condensing by paraphrasing:
   Jargon—language that is understood only by experts—impairs clarity. So does overblown language, whether used accidentally or deliberately. An example is saying *egress* when you mean *exit*.

Example #3—Creating an outline:
I. Factors that impair clarity:
   A. Jargon—language specific to one profession
   B. Overblown language
      1. Example: Substituting "egress" for "exit"
      2. Can be accidental
      3. Can be deliberate—to impress or intimidate

Example #4—Creating a mind map:

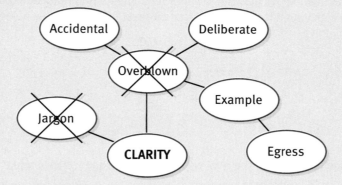

From Public Speaking, *Michael Osborn and Suzanne Osborn (Boston: Houghton Mifflin, 2003, pp. 268-269). Copyright © 2003 by Houghton Mifflin, Inc. Used with permission.*

experiment WITH A STRATEGY FROM THIS CHAPTER

Think of a time when you were disappointed with the notes you took during a lecture or on a reading assignment. Describe that incident here, along with some reflections on the source of your note-taking problem:

Based on that incident, review this chapter for a suggestion that could have prevented this frustration with your notes. Describe that suggestion in the space below:

List a time and place within the next week to use the suggestion you just described:

Finally, create an original technique for taking notes. Think about how you could modify or combine several of the methods mentioned in this book (Chapters 11 through 15). Summarize your original technique here:

BUILDING MEMORY AND TEST TAKING SKILLS

Quick Reference Guide to BUILDING MEMORY AND TEST TAKING SKILLS

16. MEMORY: STORING IDEAS AND INFORMATION

Memory is not a thing but a process—a series of strategies that we use to create mental representations of past events.

1. **Set the stage to remember (page 185)**
   The simple intention to remember something can be more powerful than any memory technique:
   - Keep in mind that stress in all its forms interferes with memory. Learn relaxation techniques. (See the checklist on page 186.)
   - To enhance your memory of events, do one thing at a time with full attention.
   - As an aid to remembering, avoid marathon study sessions and plan for shorter, spaced sessions.

2. **Elaborate on what you want to remember (page 188)**
   Move items from short-term into long-term memory by taking the time to *elaborate* on them through mental rehearsal:
   - Decide what's essential to remember from a reading assignment or lecture.
   - When you introduce new information, associate it with related information that you already know.
   - Create mnemonics—verbal associations that are designed to help you remember certain facts and ideas. (See the sidebar on page 191.)
   - Experiment with ways to organize the information you want to remember. (See the sidebar on page 192.)
   - Repeat a concept out loud until you know it; then say it five more times.

17. MEMORY: RECALLING IDEAS AND INFORMATION

"Storing" a memory means wearing neural traces in your brain—networks of nerve cells that connect by firing chemical messages to each other. Recalling a memory means reactivating cells that fired together in the past.

1. **Search your memory for specific information (page 196)**
   Accurately encode memories using the techniques explained in Chapter 16. Then, when you want to recall something but feel blocked:
   - Take some time to relax with a technique such as a body scan. (See the checklist on page 196.)
   - Recall information that is closely related to the item you want to remember.
   - Mentally recreate the original context in which you first learned the idea you want to remember.
   - Wait out memory lapses; clear a mental space for the answer to emerge in its own time.

2. **Recall key information regularly (page 200)**
   Use spaced reviews to move information and ideas securely into long-term memory:
   - Review new material within 24 hours.
   - Access the material often in a variety of ways; read about it, write about it, and speak about it.
   - Actively apply information that you want to remember.

18. PREPARING FOR TESTS

Preparing for a test means rehearsing—doing the kinds of tasks that you'll actually perform during a test, such as answering questions, solving problems, composing essays.

1. **Create effective materials to review (page 203)**
   Effective test preparation removes the guesswork and worry about what to study and when:
   - To begin your test preparation, make a list of what to study in each subject. (See the example of a study checklist on page 204.)
   - Create summary notes that condense and tie together content from readings, lectures, handouts, lab sessions, and any other course elements.

- Create flash cards: On one side of index cards, write key terms or questions; on the other side, write definitions or answers.
- Write up your own exam questions and take this "test" several times before the actual test.
- Review your answers to previous tests; reflect on any errors you made and ways to prevent them.
- Gear your review to the type of test. (See the sidebar on page 207.)

2. **Review regularly (page 206)**
   If you want to approach tests with greater confidence, then get into the habit of regular reviewing:
   - Each day, review any notes on lectures or readings that you made during the previous 24 hours.
   - Each week, do more extended reviews—about one hour per subject.
   - During the week before an exam, schedule several hours to review the topics that you will be tested on.

3. **Create study groups (page 208)**
   Harness the power of collaborative learning by forming study groups and planning activities for them. (See the checklist on page 209.)

4. **Cope with test anxiety (page 210)**
   To perform gracefully under the pressure of exams, put as much effort into working with test anxiety as you do into mastering the content of your courses:
   - Put grades in perspective by separating test scores from self-worth.
   - Instead of resisting feelings of test anxiety, simply notice them and let them pass away.
   - Cultivate a set of strategies to reduce test anxiety. (See the sidebar on page 212.)
   - Cultivate detachment by projecting days, weeks, or months into the future and asking how much the test will matter to you then.
   - During the 24 hours before the test, take specific steps to prevent test anxiety. (See the checklist on page 213.)
   - If you experience levels of anxiety that interfere with your daily life, then see a counselor.

19. USING TEST TIME EFFICIENTLY

Experiment with two kinds of test-taking strategies: those that work for any kind of exam and those that apply to specific kinds of tests (objective, short answer, essay, and more).

1. **Proceed with a plan (page 215)**
   At test time, instead of launching into the first question, take a few seconds to breathe deeply, clear your mind, and plan:
   - As tests are handed out, take a minute to record key ideas and facts that you've memorized.
   - Immediately after receiving your test, scan the whole thing.

- Read the test directions slowly and carefully; then reread them.
- Estimate how much time you can devote to each question or each section of the test.

2. **Avoid Common Errors in Test-Taking (page 217)**
   If you think of a test as a sprint, then remember that there are at least two ways that you can trip:
   - Errors due to carelessness, such as forgetting to answer a question.
   - Errors due to getting stuck. (See the checklist on page 218.)

3. **Tackle true-false tests (page 219)**
   Use the following strategies to answer true-false items:
   - Read each question entirely.
   - Look for qualifiers—words such as *all, most, sometimes,* and *rarely.*
   - Look for numbers that have been transposed or facts that have been slightly altered—signals of a false statement.
   - Watch for negatives, words such as *not* and *cannot.*

4. **Reduce the guesswork in multiple-choice tests (page 219)**
   After determining whether you are looking for *the* correct answer or the *most* correct answer:
   - Answer each question in your head *before* you look at the possible answers.
   - Read all possible answers before selecting one.
   - Combine the stem sentences with each possible answer.
   - Eliminate incorrect answers.
   - When all else fails, make an educated guess. (See the checklist on page 220.)

5. **Write essay tests with confidence (page 220)**
   To build momentum, start with easier questions, and allow extra time for the harder questions that can yield more points. In addition:
   - Write as legibly as possible.
   - Before you begin writing, briefly outline each answer.
   - Look for key direction words in essay questions. (See the sidebar on page 222.)
   - In your answers, avoid fluff; get directly to your point.
   - If you run short on time and are not able to finish a question, turn in an outline of your answer.

6. **Use strategies for other types of tests (page 223)**
   Consider ways to approach other kinds of tests as well:
   - Matching tests (page 223)
   - Open-book tests (page 224)
   - Computer-graded tests (page 224)
   - Math and science tests (page 224)

chapter 16

Memory: Storing Ideas and Information

Memory is not a *thing* but a *process*—a series of strategies that we use to create mental representations of past events. On a conscious level, a memory appears as a discrete mental event—an image, a series of words, the record of a sensation. On a biological level, each of those events involves millions of nerve cells firing chemical messages to each other. If you could observe these exchanges in real time, you'd see long chains of cells lighting up with electrical charges at speeds to put any computer to shame.

When a particular series of nerves connect several times in a similar pattern, the result is a stored memory. Psychologist Donald Hebb described this principle: "Neurons which fire together, wire together."

Talking about stored memories leads us to imagine a microscopic "closet" in the brain in which ideas and sensations are "shelved" for later retrieval. But there is no such closet. Memory is simply the *probability* that certain networks of nerve cells will "fire together" again in the future.

The whole art of improving memory lies in increasing that probability. You do this by activating neural networks in efficient ways—storing memories, the subject of this chapter. You also learn to reactivate those networks—recalling memories, which is explained in the next chapter.

Set the Stage to Remember

One step to a powerful memory often involves an attitude adjustment: reaching a state in which you are confident in your ability to remember and are open to new experiences. Allowing a few moments to make this shift will set the stage for wiring some new neural connections.

Relax

To begin, remember that stress in all its forms—including fear and anxiety—interferes with memory. When we're relaxed, we can absorb new information quickly and recall it with greater accuracy. That's why courses in accelerated learning and "whole mind" education often begin with relaxation techniques.

Being relaxed is not the same as being drowsy or zoned out. Relaxation is a state of alertness, free of excess tension. When you enter this state, you can play with new information, roll it around, and encode new memories. We can be active, relaxed, *and* alert.

Reduce distractions

The acceleration of technology provides us with ample means to divide our attention. We can watch television, play a CD, surf the Internet, talk on a cell phone—all at the same time, if we choose.

One memory-saving option is to do one thing at a time with full attention. Turn off the music when you study. Find a quiet place that is free from distraction. If there's a party at your house, go to the library. If you have a strong attraction to food, don't torture yourself by studying next to your refrigerator. Ten minutes of studying in a quiet place might be worth two hours of studying in front of the television.

☑ checklist

SIXTY SECONDS TO RELAXATION

You can learn relaxation techniques from books, audio and video recordings, and workshops. Some of these techniques are sophisticated and take time. The following are simple enough to use in 60 seconds or less.

❑ **Notice your breathing.** As long as you can breathe, you can relax. States of tension tend to manifest as irregular and shallow breathing. That means you can reduce tension simply by changing your breathing. Even the simple act of noticing your breathing will make it deeper and more regular.

❑ **Slow your breathing.** For a deeper relaxation, deliberately slow down your breathing. Take in more air with each inhalation and release more air with each exhalation.

❑ **Come to your senses.** Notice the sights, sounds, and smells in your immediate environment. If you're sitting, notice how the chair feels. If you're inside, become aware of the room temperature. By simply noticing your physical surroundings, you've taken control of your attention. You've also interrupted the flow of any negative thoughts that contribute to your tension. If negative thoughts persist, simply make a mental note of them. Then redirect your attention to input from any of your five senses.

Focus attention

Samuel Johnson, an eighteenth-century poet, wrote, "The art of true memory is the art of attention." The simple act of focusing your attention at key moments can do wonders for your memory. You can test this idea for yourself: The next time you're introduced to someone, direct 100 percent of your attention to hearing that person's name. Do this consistently and see what happens to your ability to remember names.

You can also train your attention by taking routines that you do unconsciously and making them conscious. An example is the sequence of actions you might take before you leave home for the day: grabbing your keys, turning off lights, and locking the front door. If you go through this series in a robotic trance of semiattention, you might get to school and wonder, *Did I remember to lock the door?*

You can eliminate such worries by saying to yourself before you leave home, *Now I am turning off the lights. . . . Now I am checking the stove. . . . Now I am turning the lock*. Instead of coasting through large portions of your life on automatic pilot, you'll wake up and remember.

Adopt attitudes that aid memory

"I never remember anything," some people say. "I've always had a poor memory. I'm such a scatterbrain." Such statements do little to help your memory, especially when repeated dozens of times.

Support your memory by consciously changing such attitudes. Go easier on yourself. Instead of saying, "I don't remember," say, "It will come to me." The latter statement implies that the information you want is stored in your mind and that you can retrieve it in due time.

Adopt an attitude that says, "I never forget anything that I make an effort to remember. I may have difficulty recalling something from my memory, but I will retrieve it."

The simple intention to remember something can be more powerful than any memory technique.

Distribute learning

As an aid to remembering, avoid marathon study sessions and plan for shorter, spaced sessions. You may find that you can recall far more from three two-hour sessions than from one six-hour session.

For example, when you are studying for your American history exam, study for an hour or two, and then wash the dishes. While you are washing the dishes, part of your mind reviews what you studied. Return to American history for a while, and then call a friend. Even while you are deep in conversation, part of your mind will be reviewing history.

You can get more done if you take regular breaks, and you can even use them as minirewards. After a productive study session, give yourself permission to make a short phone call, listen to a song, or play 10 minutes of hide-and-seek with your kids.

There is an exception to this idea. When you are engrossed in a textbook and cannot put it down, when you are consumed by an idea for a term paper and cannot think of anything else—keep going.

Elaborate on What You Want to Remember

Any idea that you want to remember has to successfully pass through three "gates":

1. *Sensory memory*, a buffer zone that that registers sights, sounds, smells, texture, and tastes for a second or so.
2. *Short-term memory*, a mental "chalkboard" on which sense impressions are registered and then "erased" if no conscious effort is made to remember them.
3. *Long-term memory*, a repository for information that's most useful to you—everything from your home phone number to the principles of sociology that you want to remember for Friday's test.

Ideas often make the transition from gate 1 to gate 2 at a level that is usually below your conscious awareness. You can make the most powerful intervention at the transition from gate 2 to gate 3. Move items from short-term into long-term memory by taking the time to elaborate on them.

Elaboration is a process of consciously encoding new information. One commonsense method of elaboration is simple repetition. For example, you look up a phone number and then say that number out loud several times as you close the phone book and dial.

"Any attempt to reduce transience should try to seize control of what happens in the early moments of a memory formation, when encoding processes powerfully influence the fate of a new memory," notes Harvard psychologist Daniel Schacter, author of *The Seven Sins of Memory: How the Mind Forgets and Remembers*. "All popularly available memory improvement packages recognize and build on this fundamental insight by trying to teach people to elaborate on incoming information."

Each of the following strategies offers a way to elaborate.

Choose what to remember

Decide what's essential to remember from a reading assignment or lecture. Extract the core concepts and key examples. Ask what you'll be tested on, as well as what you want to remember.

When meeting a group of people, for instance, concentrate on remembering just two or three names. Free yourself of any obligation to remember every one. Few of the people in mass introductions expect you to remember their names, anyway.

When you've chosen what you want to remember, then divide up the content into manageable chunks. Efficient elaboration calls for limiting the number of items in your short-term memory at one time. As a rough guide, remember the number seven. When reading a long list of terms, for instance, stop after the first seven or so and see if you can write definitions for them.

Elaborate with questions

One simple but powerful means of elaboration is to simply ask questions about incoming information and ideas. Asking questions forces you to slow down, focus your attention, and set priorities for what you intend to remember.

For starters, use the "five *W*" questions:

- *Why* (or *how*) would it create value for me to remember this new information?
- *Who* will ask me to remember this information?
- *What* are the main points and significant details to remember?
- *Where*—in what situations—could I use this information?
- *When* is such a situation likely to occur?

Create associations

The data already in your memory is arranged according to a scheme that makes sense to you. When you introduce new data, you can recall it more effectively if you associate it with similar or related data. In fact, the more you know about a subject, the easier it is for you to absorb new information about it.

Associations can be simple. You've used this technique since you were in grade school. When you learned to recognize Italy on a map of the world, for example, your teacher probably pointed out that the country is shaped like a boot. *Italy = boot* is an association.

You can use the same strategy in more sophisticated ways:

- **Create visual associations.** Invent a mental picture of the information you want to remember. You can remember how a personal computer stores files, for example, by visualizing the hard disk as a huge filing cabinet. That cabinet is divided into folders that contain documents.
- **Associate course material with something you want.** If you're bogged down in quadratic equations, stand back for a minute. Think about how that math course relates to your goal of becoming an electrical engineer. When information helps you get something you want, it's easier to remember.

Create mnemonics

Mnemonics are a form of verbal association. There are several varieties, including:

- **Acrostics.** The first letters of the words in the sentence *Every good boy does fine* (*E, G, B, D,* and *F*) are the music notes of the lines of the treble clef staff.
- **Acronyms.** *NASA* stands for the National Aeronautics and Space Administration.
- **Lists.** Theodore Cheney, author of *Getting the Words Right*, suggests that you remember the "three *R*'s" when editing a paper: *re*duce the paper to eliminate extraneous paragraphs, *re*arrange the paragraphs that remain into a logical order, and *re*word individual sentences so that they include specific nouns and active verbs.
- **Rhymes.** "In fourteen hundred and ninety-two, Columbus sailed the ocean blue." This simple technique is widely applied. Advertisers often use jingles—songs with rhyming lyrics—to promote products. You can invent original rhymes to burn course material into your long-term memory.

Mnemonics work with any subject. For example, the acronym *IPMAT* helps biology students remember the stages of cell division (*i*nterphase, *p*rophase, *m*etaphase, *a*naphase, and *t*elephase).

Mnemonics can be useful, but they also have two potential drawbacks. First, they rely on rote memorization rather than on understanding the material at a deeper level or thinking critically about it. Second, the mnemonic device itself is sometimes complicated to learn and time-consuming to develop. To get the most from mnemonic devices, keep them simple.

Organize the information you want to remember

When you're faced with a long list of items to remember, look for ways to organize them. Group them into larger categories or arrange them in chronological order.

If you have a long to-do list, for example, write each item on a separate index card. Then create a pile of cards for calls to make, for errands to run, and for household chores. Within each of these categories, you could also arrange the cards in the order in which you intend to do them.

The same concept applies to ideas and facts from your courses. When reading a novel, for example, organize your study in categories such as plot, characters, and setting:

- To remember the plot, create a timeline. List key events on index cards and arrange the cards to parallel the order of events in the book.

sidebar

USING MORE COMPLEX MNEMONICS

Two popular kinds of mnemonics can get fairly complex. Use them selectively.

The **loci system** involves associating items you want to remember with various parts of your body. To remember the five human sensory modes, for example, touch your eyes (visual), ears (auditory), nose (olfactory), tongue (gustatory, or taste), and fingers (tactile, or touch).

The **peg system** employs key words represented by numbers. For example:

```
 1 = bun
 2 = shoe
 3 = tree
 4 = door
 5 = hive
 6 = sticks
 7 = heaven
 8 = gate
 9 = vine
10 = hen
```

Each of these words becomes a mental "peg" on which you mentally "hang" items you want to remember. The key to using this system is to always use the same pegs in the same order. The only things subject to change are the items you hang on each peg.

Example: You can use the peg system to remember that the speed of light is 186,000 miles per second. Imagine a hamburger bun (1) entering a gate (8) made of sticks (6).

- Group the people in the story into major and minor characters. Again, use index cards to list each character's name, along with an identifying feature.
- If geographical setting is important, create a map of the major locations described in the story.

Note: When you're memorizing long lists of items, remember a principle from psychological research called the *primacy-recency effect*. This principle states that the first and last items in a list will be easier to remember than the items in the middle. If possible, place the more unfamiliar or complex items in the middle of the list and devote more of your study time to these.

Recite

Recitation is simply talking about ideas and facts that you want to remember. An informal version of this technique involves injecting summaries of your course work into ordinary conversation. When relatives

▶ sidebar

FIVE WAYS TO ORGANIZE ANY BODY OF INFORMATION

You'll probably find it easier to remember information that is logically organized. In his book *Information Anxiety*, Richard Saul Wurman proposes "five ultimate hat racks"—ways of organizing any large body of ideas, facts, or objects:

ORGANIZE BY *CATEGORY*
   Example: Items in a clothing store are organized into clothing for men, for women, and for children.

ORGANIZE BY *TIME*
   Example: Events in a novel flow in chronological order.

ORGANIZE BY *LOCATION*
   Example: Addresses for franchise stores across the country are grouped by region or state.

ORGANIZE BY *ALPHABET*
   Example: Entries in a phone book are listed in alphabetical order.

ORGANIZE BY *CONTINUUM*
   Example: Products rated in *Consumers Guide* are grouped from highest in price to lowest in price, or highest in quality to lowest in quality.

Source: From *Information Anxiety* by Richard Saul Wurman. Copyright © 1989 by Richard Saul Wurman. Used by permission of Doubleday, a division of Random House, Inc.

or friends ask what you're studying, seize the moment as an opportunity to recite. Explain what a course is about in one sentence and list the key topics covered. Describe the three most important ideas or startling facts that you've learned so far.

Informal recitation gains its power from the fact that you need to be brief, distinguishing between major concepts and supporting details. Another option is formal recitation, with which you can take more time and go into more depth. Pretend that you've been asked to speak about the topic you're studying. Prepare a brief presentation and deliver it, even if you're the only member of the audience.

Or agree to lead a study group on the topic. One of the best ways to learn something is to teach it.

Some points to remember about recitation:

■ **The "out loud" part is important.** Reciting silently, in your head, may be useful—in the library, for example—but it can be less effective than making noise. Your mind can trick itself into thinking it knows something when it doesn't. Your ears are harder to fool. When you repeat something out loud, you also anchor the concept in two different senses. First, you get the physical sensation in your throat, tongue, and lips when voicing the concept. Second, you hear it. In terms of memory, the combined result is synergistic.

■ **Recitation works best when you use your own words.** Say that you want to remember that the "acceleration of a falling body due to gravity at sea level equals 32 feet per second per second." You might say, "Gravity makes an object accelerate 32 feet per second faster for each second that it's in the air at sea level." Putting an idea in your own words forces you to think about it.

- **Recite in writing.** Like speaking, the act of writing is multisensory, combining sight and touch. The mere act of writing down a series of terms and their definitions can help you remember the terms, even if you lose the written list. In addition, writing down what you know quickly reveals gaps in your learning, which you can then go back and fill in. When you're done writing summaries of books or lectures, read what you've written out loud; this technique provides two forms of recitation.

- **Recite with visuals.** Create diagrams, charts, maps, timelines, bulleted lists, numbered lists, and other visuals. Even the traditional outline is a visual device that separates major and minor points. For more ideas, see Chapters 11 through 15 on note-taking.

Repeat

Repetition is the most common memory device because it works. Repetition blazes a trail through the pathways of your brain, making the information easier to recall. Repeat a concept out loud until you know it; then say it five more times.

Students often stop studying when they think they know material just well enough to pass a test. Another option is to pick a subject apart, examine it, add to it, and go over it until it becomes second nature. Learn the material so well that you could talk about it in your sleep.

This technique—overlearning the material—is especially effective for problem solving in math and science courses. Do the assigned prob-

☑ checklist

USE THE SEVEN *R*'s OF REMEMBERING

❐ **Relax.** Notice and release tension. Reduce distractions in the external environment and within yourself.

❐ **Reduce.** Distinguish between essential and nonessential information. Focus your attention on a limited number of items that you want to remember.

❐ **Restructure.** Organize the material you want to learn. Group items into logical categories and sequences.

❐ **Relate.** Create meaningful associations and connect new material to a topic that interests you or to personal experiences.

❐ **Recite.** Summarize facts and ideas by speaking, writing, and creating visuals.

❐ **Rephrase.** Go beyond rote learning by translating material into your own words.

❐ **Repeat.** Overlearn the material. Recite up to the point that the material feels like second nature.

lems, then do more problems. Find another text and work similar problems. Make up your own problems and work those. When you pretest yourself in this way, the potential rewards are speed, accuracy, and greater confidence at exam time.

experiment WITH A STRATEGY FROM THIS CHAPTER

Write a short paragraph describing the way you feel when you want to remember something but have trouble doing so. Think of a specific incident in which you experienced this problem. Examples might involve trying to remember someone's name or struggling to recall a fact you needed to answer a test question:

Now move into action. Pick a memory strategy from this chapter and set a goal to use it during the next week. Complete the following sentence, adding details about what you will do and when.

I intend to . . .

After the week is over, come back to this page and reflect on how well the technique worked for you. Describe the benefits you experienced. If the technique did not work, write about how you can modify it. Or choose another technique and write a goal to use it next.

While using this strategy, I discovered that . . .

To improve my memory, I now intend to...

Memory: Recalling Ideas and Information

eople sometimes describe memory in ways that resemble the process of photography:

- You witness an event—anything from a lecturer's gestures to a page of printed text—and make a mental "photograph" of it.
- You "store" that memory—a faithful replica of the original event—in an area of your brain, much like a photographer files prints in a folder.
- You "reach" into the appropriate mental folder and retrieve the photograph—that is, you *remember* it.

In some ways, this is an accurate description of memory. Memory researchers do talk about encoding, storing, and retrieving—three phases of memory that correspond roughly to the three steps just described.

However, the analogy breaks down at several points. Your brain does not store anything that resembles a photograph. Nor does your brain function like a filing cabinet full of drawers and folders that are idly waiting to be opened.

In reality, "storing" a memory means wearing neural traces in your brain—networks of nerve cells that connect by firing chemical messages to each other. Recalling a memory means reactivating cells that fired together in the past. In effect, you *re-create* the memory each time that you recall it.

One theory is that we recall memories in two phases. First we get the gist of an event—a dominant impression or general idea. Second, we fill in the details. If we did not accurately encode the original event, we might recall the gist of it but falter on the details. We might even fill in gaps by mixing details from several events. The result may be an interesting but inaccurate image, which may explain why eyewitnesses can give different accounts of the same event.

Search Your Memory for Specific Information

You don't have to rely on guesswork when you search your memory. First, learn to accurately encode memories using the techniques explained in Chapter 16. Later, when you want to recall information, draw on the suggestions explained next.

Focus your attention and relax

You've probably had this experience: You go into a test feeling some stress, worried about whether you'll remember the concepts you studied. During the exam, you feel blocked on a couple of questions. As the clock ticks away, your tension mounts. Finally you give up on answering the questions, leaving the answers blank or partially completed.

Feeling deflated, you turn in your exam paper, leave the exam room, and head back home. After a hearty meal, you lie down for a nap. Then, just as you're drifting into a blissful snooze, the missing answers pop into your head—fully formed, shimmering in precise detail, and too late to make a difference in your grade.

Although frustrating, such events make a vital point about memory: Stress interferes with recall, and relaxation promotes it. When you want to recall something but feel blocked, take some time to relax. At the very least, stop your mental search for the target item and go on to another task. Tell yourself that the answer will come on its own, when you need it.

☑ checklist

RELAX WITH A BODY SCAN

If you take the time to examine a state of tension, you'll find that it usually manifests in many areas of your body. You can detect and release tension in those areas, one by one. The result can be a deep relaxation that's as restful as sleep. To use this technique:

❏ Lie on the floor with a pillow supporting your head and another one placed under your knees.

❏ Close your eyes and carefully rest your attention on the soles of your feet. Notice and release any tension you sense in that area of your body.

❏ Use the same "notice and release" strategy as you slowly move your attention through your calves, knees, thighs, pelvis, stomach, chest, shoulders, neck, and arms.

Note: You can do a body scan even in situations in which you cannot lie down. Just sit in an upright (not rigid) position with your spine straight. Then scan each part of your body in turn. If possible, close your eyes as you do this.

Recall mnemonics

When you first learned something, you may have applied mnemonic devices such as:

- Acrostics
- Acronyms
- Lists
- Rhymes
- Reminders based on the loci or peg system

If you did, you can use these devices to prompt your memory. (For an explanation of mnemonics, see Chapter 16.)

Recall information in related categories

Even if you did not originally use an encoding technique, you can apply some on-the-spot memory prompts. One is to recall information that is closely related to the item you want to remember.

Say that your psychology class is reviewing the ideas of Sigmund Freud. In particular, you're studying his theory of defense mechanisms—the ways that people shield themselves from unpleasant events. In class, your teacher asks you to define a defense mechanism called *rationalization* and give an example. Your mind goes blank. You can't remember what Freud said about rationalization. But you can recall what he said about a defense mechanism called *denial.* While you are doing so, a definition of rationalization appears in your mind, along with a good example.

The principle here is to take advantage of the way you've organized ideas and information. We mentally group items in related categories. Accessing any one item in a category can help you recall others that are grouped with it.

Recreate the original context

You're out for a walk and somebody calls your name from across the street. The person runs over, shakes your hand, and greets you like a long-lost relative. He seems familiar. But when you want to say his name, your mind goes blank.

When something like this happens, back up to a bigger picture. See if you can mentally re-create the context in which you last saw this person. Perhaps this person is a former coworker. Try to recall a place where you were both employed. Or perhaps you once took a class together. Try to recall the name of the teacher and the room in which your class met. These prompts may be enough to help you recall the missing name.

The same principle applies to any fact or idea that you want to recall. If you're trying to remember a term defined in a textbook passage you read last night, for example, see if you can recall other terms defined in that passage. Visualizing the design of the page or the layout of the chapter headings may also help.

Reenter the original environment

Professional speakers know the value of rehearsing a presentation in the reserved room well *before* the audience shows up. The more time that speakers allow to get the feel of a room, the more confidence they gain. Bands do a sound check to an empty concert hall for the same reason.

You can use this principle as a memory aid: Practice in the same setting in which you will perform. When you learn something in a particular setting, you may be able to recall it faster in the same setting.

When studying for a test, for instance, create a practice test or ask your teacher for copies of a previous one. Then go to the classroom in which the scheduled test will actually take place and fill out the answers to your practice test. It may be late in the evening, and you might be the only person in the room. Even so, you are encoding memories in a new and useful way. When you can recall material in several contexts, you can truly say that you've learned the material.

Variation: A modification of this principle may help you during the actual test. If you cannot remember the answer to a question, see if you can mentally re-create the context in which you originally learned the material. Recall the physical setting—such as the desk in your bedroom—and mentally check off each topic that you studied. This may be enough to release your mental block and unleash the answer you seek.

Set "traps" to prompt your memory

Link items that you want to remember to events that are *certain* to occur. For example:

- You're walking to class and suddenly you realize that your accounting assignment is due tomorrow. Switch your watch from your left to your right wrist. Now you're "trapped." Every time you look at your watch, it becomes a reminder that you were supposed to remember something—in this case, the accounting assignment.
- To remember to write a check for the phone bill, picture your phone hanging on the front door of your house or apartment. In your mind, create the feeling of reaching for the doorknob and grabbing the phone instead. When you get home and reach to open the front door, the image is apt to return to you. Link two activities together in your imagination, and make the association unusual.

Rituals such as looking at your watch, reaching for car keys, and untying shoes are seldom forgotten. By associating items you want to remember with these rituals, or with unusual images, you can reduce absent-mindedness.

Wait out the memory lapse

Psychologists talk about the "tip-of-the-tongue" phenomenon—the feeling that you're just about to recall a name or fact but don't have it just yet. When this happens, don't force it. Just wait out the lapse and clear a mental space for the answer to emerge in its own time.

While you're waiting, avoid any interference with this process, such as repeating names or facts that are similar to the one you want to recall but obviously wrong.

Monitor your moods

One factor that affects your memory is your mood. Feeling elated, for example, can heighten your memory of pleasant events. And feeling sad can enhance your recall

> ### sidebar
>
> **SET EFFECTIVE MEMORY TRAPS**
>
> Effective memory traps are *timely* and *informative*. The sound of a whistling teapot is a perfect example. That sound is unique, it cues you to take immediate action, and you know exactly what to do.
>
> Traps such as changing the location of a watch or ring can fail to meet these criteria. Even though you notice the change, you might say to yourself: *I know I'm supposed to remember something, but what was it?*
>
> An alternative is the good old-fashioned reminder note written on an index card or a piece of brightly colored paper and placed in a prominent location. Even people with a prodigious memory use this technique.
>
> An example is Tatiana Cooley, who won the U.S. National Memory Championship in 1999. Participants in this contest were asked to memorize and recall lists that included hundreds of items. Even though she won, Cooley described herself as "horribly absent-minded" and said that she depends on Post-it™ notes to remember tasks.

of unpleasant events. This phenomenon may result from the way you place your attention: When you're in a certain mood, you're more likely to notice events that confirm your view of the world in that moment. Psychologists refer to this as *mood-congruent memory.*

Given this insight, you might find that stability in your moods supports your ability to recall what you learn. Of course, some variation in moods is normal, and trying to repress any strong emotion is seldom effective. While accepting your feelings, whatever they are, you can experiment with the following suggestions:

- **Notice your moods.** Observe your moods with a nonjudgmental attitude. Step back from your immediate situation and observe moods impartially. Moods may be pleasant or unpleasant, but they are not good or bad. Also, the simple act of observing your moods may even them out.
- **Collect data about your moods.** Imagine that you're a scientist in a laboratory. Your only job is to take measurements and record data about your moods. You could pause at key points in your day and rate your mood at each moment on a scale of 1 to 10: 1 for sad

and 10 for elated. You could even chart this data on a graph, look for patterns in the way your moods fluctuate, and discover correlations between external events and your moods.

- **Take action.** A negative, persistent mood may be a clue to solve a problem or change some external circumstance in your life. At other times, your moods may take a downturn even when your circumstances are pleasant or your life seems problem free. In these cases, practicing relaxation exercises (see page 196) and doing some form of aerobic exercise can help to even out your mood.
- **Monitor your overall health.** Besides taking a toll on your memory and overall ability to study, lack of sleep can negatively affect your moods and deplete your energy. So can a diet high in sugar and caffeine. Getting plenty of sleep, eating a variety of foods, and exercising regularly can improve your overall health and enhance your ability to study.
- **Note:** If moods of persistent sadness or anxiety interfere with your ability to carry out the tasks of daily life, see a doctor.

Recall Key Information Regularly

Review new material within 24 hours

Items in short-term memory tend to fade within a range of a few minutes to a few hours. A short review of new material can move it from

☑ checklist

EIGHT WAYS TO ENHANCE RECALL

❏ **Focus your attention and relax.** Clear away distractions and use relaxation techniques to release tension.

❏ **Use mnemonic devices.** These include acrostics, acronyms, lists, rhymes, and reminders based on the loci or peg system.

❏ **Recall related information.** Recalling any one item in a category can help you remember others that are grouped with it.

❏ **Recreate the original context.** Recall details about the setting in which you first learned information.

❏ **Reenter the original environment.** Practice a task in the same setting in which you will be asked to perform it.

❏ **Set "traps" to prompt your memory.** Link items you want to remember with events that are part of your daily routine.

❏ **Wait out the memory lapse.** When you want to recall something but feel blocked, allow a few moments to let your memory do its work.

❏ **Monitor your moods.** Respond to mood swings that affect your ability to remember.

this precarious holding zone into the more secure world of long-term memory.

Daily reviews include short pre- and postclass reviews of lecture notes. Also, conduct brief daily reviews when you read. Before reading a new assignment, scan your notes and the sections you underlined in the previous assignment.

You can review anytime, anywhere. Use the time you spend waiting for the bus or doing the laundry to conduct short reviews. Quick minireviews can save you hours of study time when finals week rolls around.

Review often

Even information stored in long-term memory becomes difficult to recall if we don't use it regularly. The neural pathways in our brains that were forged with learning become faint with disuse. For example, you know your current phone number, but what was your phone number five years ago?

To remember something, access it a lot. Read it, write it, speak it, listen to it, apply it. Find some way to make contact with the material regularly. Each time you do this, you widen the neural pathway to the material and make it easier to recall the next time.

Spaced review is a key principle of learning. Start with daily reviews and follow up with more detailed reviews of each course at regular intervals throughout the term, not just during finals week.

Review actively

According to an old saying, people remember 90 percent of what they do, 75 percent of what they see, and 20 percent of what they hear. These percentages might not be scientifically provable, but the idea behind them is sound: Action enhances memory.

Conduct reviews with the same energy you bring to the dance floor or the basketball court. To remember an idea, go beyond thinking about it. *Do* something with it.

As explained in Chapter 2, many courses in higher education lean heavily toward abstract conceptualization—lectures, papers, textbooks. Courses might not give you chances to *act* on the ideas, experiment with them, and test them in situations outside the classroom. So create those opportunities yourself. For example:

- Your introductory psychology text probably offers some theories about how people remember information. Choose one of those theories and test it for yourself. See if you can turn that theory into a new memory technique.
- Your English teacher might tell you that one quality of effective writing is clear organization. To test this idea, examine the docu-

ments you come in contact with daily—newspapers, popular magazines, Web sites, e-mail messages, and textbooks. Look for examples of clear organization and unclear organization. Then write goals for organizing your own writing more clearly.

- Your sociology class might include a section about how groups of people resolve conflict. See if you can apply any of these ideas to resolving conflict in your family.

experiment WITH A STRATEGY FROM THIS CHAPTER

To prevent memory glitches in the future, start developing a habit of regular reviews. As you plan each day, schedule 15-minute reviews to go over lecture and reading notes. Also use a monthly calendar and block out specific times to review key subjects. Schedule at least two major review periods for each course. The length of these review periods could range from two to five hours.

Next, think how you can conduct these reviews most effectively. Consider the major strategies presented in this chapter:

- Focus attention and relax
- Create mnemonics
- Recall information in related categories
- Re-create the original context
- Reenter the original environment
- Set memory "traps"
- Wait out memory lapses
- Monitor your moods and maintain overall health
- Review actively

From this list, choose one strategy. In the space below, describe how you will apply it to your review periods:

After one week of using the strategy, reflect on how well it worked for you. If you plan to modify the strategy, describe that modification in writing:

Preparing for Tests

One way to save hours of wasted study time is to see each test as a performance. From this point of view, preparing for a test means *rehearsing*. Study for a test in the way that a musician rehearses for a concert or an actor prepares for opening night—by simulating the physical and psychological conditions you'll encounter when you actually enter the exam room.

Rehearsing means doing the kinds of tasks that you'll actually perform during a test: answering questions, solving problems, composing essays. Start this process with regular reviews of course content. Also, create special review materials, explore the power of study groups, and discover ways to reduce test anxiety.

Create Effective Materials to Review

Study checklists and review materials can remove much of the guesswork and worry about what to study and when.

Create study checklists

To begin your test preparation, make a list of what to study in each subject. Include items such as:

- Reading assignments by chapters or page numbers.
- Dates of lectures and major topics covered in each lecture.
- Skills you must master.
- Key course content—definitions, theories, formulas, sample problems, and laboratory findings.

A study checklist is not a review sheet; it is a to-do list. Study checklists contain the briefest possible description of each type of material that you intend to study.

Keep a study checklist for each course, starting the first day of class. Create a master copy of each checklist and add to it as the term progresses. Also, compare your checklist against the syllabus. When you conduct your final review sessions, cross items off each checklist as you study them.

◆ example

American History Test
Date: 11/1
Materials:
- ❏ Lecture notes: 9/14–10/29
- ❏ Textbook, pages 190–323
- ❏ The Federalist, chapters 1, 2, 4, 6

Topics:
- ❏ Hamilton and bank policies
- ❏ Frontier crisis
- ❏ Jay's treaty and foreign policy
- ❏ Election of 1796
- ❏ Alien and Sedition Acts

Create summary notes

Summary notes are materials that you create specifically to review for tests. They are separate from notes that you take throughout the term on lectures and readings. Summary notes tie together content from all sources—readings, lectures, handouts, lab sessions, and any other course elements.

Because they condense large bodies of information and ideas and display them in reduced form, mind maps and concept maps make ideal summary sheets. (For more information on maps, see Chapter 13.) There are several ways to make maps as you study for tests:

- Go through your notes and pick out key words.
- Put your notes away and create a map of everything you can recall about each key word.
- Go back to your notes and fill in material you left out.

When you create a summary map totally from memory, you might be surprised by how much you remember. Celebrate the fact. Then consult your notes to fill in any gaps in your map.

You can also create summary notes with a computer. Key in all your handwritten notes and edit them into outline form. (See Chapter 14 for suggestions on outlining.) Or simply create an annotated table of contents for your handwritten notes: Note the date of each lecture, the major topics covered in the lecture, and the main points about each topic.

Caution: Even if you study largely from summary notes, keep the rest of your notes on file. They'll come in handy as backup sources of information.

Create flash cards

Flash cards are like portable test questions. Write them on index cards, take them with you anywhere, and use them anytime. On one side of the cards, write key terms or questions. On the other side, write definitions or answers. It's that simple.

Use flash cards for formulas, definitions, theories, key words from your notes, axioms, dates, foreign language phrases, hypotheses, and sample problems. Create flash cards regularly as the term progresses. Buy an inexpensive card file to keep your flash cards arranged by subject.

Carry a pack of flash cards with you whenever you think you might have a spare minute to review them. Also keep a few blank cards with you. That way, you can make new flash cards whenever you recall new information to study.

Create a mock test

Write up your own exam questions and take this "test" several times before the actual test. Before writing questions, make some predictions about the exam:

- What course material will the test cover—readings, lectures, lab sessions, or a combination?
- Will the test be cumulative, or will it cover just the most recent material you've studied?
- Will the test focus on facts and details or on major themes and relationships?
- Will the test call on you to solve problems or apply concepts?
- What types of questions will be on the test—true-false, multiple choice, short answer, essays?
- Will you have a choice about which questions to answer?
- Will your teacher write and score the test, or will a teaching assistant perform those tasks?
- Does your teacher have any strong points of view on certain issues—opinions that you disagree with and will need to carefully support with evidence?

Note: Your teacher may be willing to answer many of these questions directly. Just ask.

Type up your mock test so that it looks like the real thing. And, if possible, write out your answers in the room in which the test will actually take place. When you walk in for the real test, you'll be in familiar territory.

Get copies of previous tests

Copies of previous exams for a class may be available from the instructor, other students, the instructor's department, the library, or the counseling office. Old tests can help you plan a review strategy. In addition, keep a file of tests that have been returned to you.

Caution: If you rely on old tests exclusively, you may gloss over material the instructor has added since the last test. Also check your school's policy about making past tests available to students. Some may not allow it or allow it on only a limited basis.

Learn from tests you've already taken

A test is a learning experience—*if* you make it one. Use past tests to create feedback that can help you ace the next one.

As you review test items and the way you answered them, look for patterns:

- Answers on which you gained or lost points and why.
- Concept errors—ideas or techniques you simply did not understand.
- Application errors—mistakes you made even though you understood the concepts.
- Careless errors, such as forgetting to answer questions or misreading instructions.
- Repeated themes in your teacher's comments on your answers.

Summarize your discoveries about ways you could have done better on past tests. Then create clear and specific intentions about what you intend to do differently in the future. If you understood key concepts but made application errors, for example, then plan to spend extra time working sample problems or reviewing case studies.

Remember that you can learn even from failures. From now on, imagine that the letter *F*, when used as a grade, represents the word *feedback*. An *F* is simply a message to do something differently before the next test. If you interpret *F* as failure, you don't get to change anything. But if you interpret *F* as feedback, you get to change your thinking and behavior in ways that promote your success.

Review Regularly

If you want to approach tests with greater confidence, then get into the habit of regular reviewing. The biggest benefit of early review is that facts and ideas from your courses have time to roam around in your head. A lot of learning takes place when you are not "studying." Your brain has time to create relationships that can show up when you need them, such as during a test.

Daily reviews

Daily reviews include your short pre- and postclass reviews of reading and lecture notes. This is a powerful tool for moving ideas from short-term to long-term memory. Concentrate daily reviews on two kinds of material: material you have just learned in class or in your reading and material that involves simple memorization (equations, formulas, dates, definitions).

Conduct short daily reviews several times throughout the day. Reviews are ideal tasks for small pockets of time, such as waiting for a bus or doing laundry. To make sure you complete these reviews, include

sidebar

GEAR YOUR REVIEW TO THE TYPE OF TEST

If you predict . . .	Study this kind of information . . .	Rehearse by . . .
Objective questions (true-false, multiple choice, matching)	■ Definitions of key terms ■ Details, such as names and dates ■ Information presented in diagrams or lists in your notes or readings	■ Writing true-false, multiple choice, and matching questions ■ Working with a study partner to exchange practice questions ■ Timing yourself as you answer questions
Short-answer items	■ Information presented in diagrams or lists in your notes or readings ■ Definitions of key terms ■ Details, such as names and dates ■ Material from the recall column of Cornell-format notes (see Chapter 12) ■ Chapter previews, reviews, and study questions in your readings	■ Reciting information in full sentences and in your own words ■ Writing a short summary to practice expressing ideas on paper ■ Writing answers to the questions you created while previewing your assigned readings ■ Writing your own questions for fill-in-the-blank items, listings, words to define, and short answers ■ Working with a study partner to exchange practice questions
Essay questions	■ Themes ■ Major concepts ■ Relationships between concepts	■ Looking for concepts that appear in lectures *and* readings ■ Creating sample questions ■ Writing answers in complete sentences and several paragraphs ■ Timing yourself as you write answers

Adapted from Linda Wong, *Essential Study Skills,* 4th ed. (Boston: Houghton Mifflin, 2003), p. 157. Copyright © 2003 by Houghton Mifflin, Inc. Used with permission.

them on your daily to-do list. Write down *5 min. review of biology* or *10 min. review of economics.* When you're done, give yourself the satisfaction of crossing each item off your list.

Begin to review on the first day of class. The first day, in fact, is important. Most instructors outline the whole course at that time.

Weekly reviews

Weekly reviews are longer than short daily reviews—about an hour per subject. They are also more structured. When a subject is complex, the brain requires time to dig into the material.

Review each subject at least once a week. Review assigned readings and lecture notes and do something that forces you to rehearse the material. For example:

- Look over any course summaries you've created; then see if you can recreate them from memory.
- Answer study questions and sample problems from your textbooks.
- Recite the points in your notes that you want to remember.
- Rewrite your notes for greater precision and clarity.

Major reviews

Major reviews are usually conducted the week before finals or other major exams. They integrate concepts and deepen your understanding of material presented throughout the term. *To uncover gaps in knowledge, start major reviews at least three days before the test.*

These are longer review periods—several hours at a stretch, punctuated by sufficient breaks. During long sessions, study the most difficult subjects when you are the most alert: at the beginning.

Remember that the effectiveness of your review begins to drop after an hour or so unless you give yourself a short rest. And, after a certain point, short breaks every hour might not be enough to refresh you. That's when it's time to quit.

Learn your limits by being conscious of the quality of your concentration. When you find it difficult to focus your attention, quit for the day and go back to it the next day. Being able to allow yourself this leeway is a powerful reason for conducting major reviews over several days.

Create Study Groups

Study groups feed you energy. Aside from offering camaraderie, fellowship, and fun, study groups can elevate your spirit on days when you just don't want to work at your education. You may find that you'll keep an appointment to study with a group in situations in which you might skip studying by yourself.

As you enlist people in your study group, look for students who participate actively and successfully in class. To conduct an effective group:

- **Go for diversity.** Choose people with different backgrounds and learning styles. You can gain from seeing the material from a new perspective.

- **Limit numbers.** Aim for groups of five or six people. Larger groups are unwieldy.
- **Do a trial run.** Test the group first by planning a one-time session. If that session works, plan another. After several successful sessions, you can schedule regular meetings.

Set an agenda for each meeting, along with approximate time limits for each agenda item and a quitting time. Finally, end each meeting with assignments for each member before the next meeting.

☑ checklist

ACTIVITIES FOR STUDY GROUPS

❏ *Compare notes.* Make sure you all heard the same thing in class and that you all recorded the important information. Ask other students about material in your notes that is confusing to you.

❏ *Work in groups of three at a computer to review a course.* Choose one person to operate the keyboard. Another person can dictate summaries of lectures and assigned readings. A third person can act as fact checker, consulting textbooks, lecture notes, and class handouts.

❏ *Brainstorm test questions.* Set aside 5 or 10 minutes each study session to use brainstorming techniques (described in this book as a technique for creative thinking). You can add these to the "Test Questions" section of your notebook.

❏ *Take a mock test and share results.* Ask each group member to bring four or five sample test questions to a meeting. Create a mock test from these questions, take the test under timed conditions, and share answers.

❏ *Practice teaching each other.* Teaching is a great way to learn something. Turn the material you're studying into a list of topics. Then assign specific topics for each person to teach the group. When you teach something, you naturally assume a teacher's attitude—"I know this"—as opposed to a student's attitude—"I still have to learn this." Also, the vocalization involved in teaching further reinforces your memory.

❏ *Create wall-sized mind maps or concept maps to summarize a textbook or series of lectures.* Work on large sheets of butcher paper, or tape together pieces of construction paper. When doing a mind map, assign one "branch" of the mind map to each member of the study group. Use a different colored pen or marker for each branch. (For more information on concept maps and mind maps, see Chapter 13.)

❏ *Pair off to do "book reports."* One person can summarize an assigned reading. The other person can act like an interviewer on a talk show, posing questions and asking for further clarification.

❏ *Ask for group support in personal areas.* Other people might have insight into problems involving transportation, child care, finances, time scheduling, and a host of other subjects. Use groups as personal support for getting what you want from school.

Cope with Test Anxiety

To perform gracefully under the pressure of exams, put as much effort into preventing test anxiety as you do into mastering the content of your courses. Think of test-taking as the "silent subject" on your schedule, equal in importance to the rest of your courses. If nervousness about tests is a consistent problem for you, then you are an ideal candidate to begin "test-taking 101."

Put tests and grades in perspective

As a way to begin defusing test anxiety, reflect on a basic fact: A test score is a measure of what you score on a test. This seems obvious. Yet some people think that a test score measures what you accomplished in a course. That is false. If you are anxious about a test and blank out, then the grade cannot measure what you learned.

The reverse is also true: If you are good at taking tests and a lucky guesser, the score won't reflect what you actually learned.

Related to this is another fact: Grades are not a measure of self-worth. The truth is that if you do badly on a test, you are a worthy person who did badly on a test—nothing more.

It is easier to do well on exams if you don't exaggerate the pressure on yourself. Don't give the test some magical power over your worth as a human being. Academic tests are not a matter of life or death.

▶ sidebar

GET PAST THE MYTHS ABOUT TEST ANXIETY

Myth	Reality
All nervousness relating to testing is undesirable.	Up to a certain point, nervousness can promote alertness and help you prevent careless errors.
Test anxiety is inevitable.	Test anxiety is a learned response—one that you can also learn to replace.
Only students who are underprepared feel test anxiety.	Anxiety and preparation are not always directly related. Students who are well prepared may experience test anxiety. And students who underprepare for tests can be free of anxiety.
Successful students never feel nervous about tests.	Anxiety, intelligence, and skill are not always directly related. Gifted students may consistently feel stressed by tests.
Resisting feelings of test anxiety is the best way to deal with them.	Freedom from test anxiety begins with accepting your feelings as they exist in the present moment—whatever those feelings are.

Overprepare for tests

Performing artists know that stage fright can temporarily reduce their level of skill. That's why they often overprepare for a performance. Musicians will rehearse a piece so many times that they can play it without thinking. Actors will go over their parts until they can recite lines in their sleep.

As you prepare for tests, you can apply the same principle. Read, recite, and review the content of each course until you know it cold. Then review again. For math courses, work most or all of the problems in your textbook, even problems that are not assigned. The idea is to create a margin of mastery that can survive even the most extreme feelings of anxiety.

Accept your feelings

Telling someone who's anxious about a test to "just calm down" is like turning up the heat on a pan that's already boiling over: The "solution" simply worsens the problem. If you take such advice to heart, you can end up with two problems. First, there's your worry about the test. Second, there's your worry about the fact that you're worried!

There's a way to deal with both problems at the same time: Simply accept your feelings, whatever they are. Fear and anxiety tend to increase with resistance. The more you try to suppress them, the more intensity the feelings gain.

As an alternative, stop resisting. See anxiety as a cluster of thoughts and body sensations. Watch the thoughts as they pass through your mind. Observe the sensations as they wash over you. Let them arise, peak, and pass away. No feeling lasts forever. The moment you accept fear, you pave the way for its release.

Exaggerate your fear until it disappears

Imagine the catastrophic problems that might occur if you fail the test. You might say to yourself, *Well, if I fail this test, I might fail the course, lose my financial aid, and get kicked out of school. Then I won't be able to get a job, so the bank would repossess my car, and I'd start drinking. Pretty soon I'd be a bum on skid row, and then. . . .*

Keep going until you see the absurdity of your predictions. After you stop chuckling, you can backtrack to discover a reasonable level of concern.

Your worry about failing the entire course if you fail the test might be justified. At that point ask yourself, "Can I live with that?" Unless you are taking a test in parachute packing and the final question involves demonstrating jumping out of a plane, the answer will almost always be yes.

sidebar

SEVEN WAYS TO REDUCE ANXIETY

As you prepare for tests, set aside a few minutes each day to practice one of the following techniques. Achieve a baseline of relaxation that you can draw on during a test.

- *Breathe.* If you notice that you are taking short, shallow breaths, begin to take longer and deeper breaths. Fill your lungs so that your abdomen rises, then release all the air. Imagine yourself standing on the tip of your nose. Watch the breath pass in and out as if your nose were a huge ventilation shaft for an underground mine.

- *Describe it.* Focus your attention on your anxiety. Tell yourself how large it is, where it is located in your body, what color it is, what shape it is, what texture it is, how much water it might hold if it had volume, and how heavy it is. As you describe anxiety in detail, don't resist it. If you can completely experience a physical sensation, it will often disappear.

- *Tense and relax.* Find a muscle that is tense and make it even tenser. If your shoulders are tense, pull them back, arch your back, and tense your shoulder muscles even more tightly; then relax. The net result is that you can be aware of the relaxation and allow yourself to relax more. You can use the same process with your legs, arms, abdomen, chest, face, and neck.

- *Use guided imagery.* Relax completely and take a quick fantasy trip. Close your eyes, relax your body, and imagine yourself in a beautiful, peaceful, natural setting. Create as much of the scene as you can. Be specific. Use all your senses.

- *Focus.* Focus your attention on a specific object. Examine details of a painting, study the branches on a tree, or observe the face of your watch (right down to the tiny scratches in the glass). During an exam, take a few seconds to listen to the hum of the lights in the room. Touch the surface of your desk and notice the texture. Concentrate all your attention on one point. Don't leave room in your mind for anxiety-related thoughts.

- *Yell "Stop!"* When you notice that your thoughts are racing, that your mind is cluttered with worries and fears, that your thoughts are spinning out of control, mentally yell, "Stop!" If you're in a situation that allows it, yell it out loud. Stay in the present moment. Release all thoughts beyond the test.

- *Exercise aerobically.* This is one technique that won't work in the classroom or while you're taking a test. Yet it is an excellent way to reduce body tension. Do some kind of exercise that will get your heart beating at twice your normal rate and keep it beating at that rate for 15 or 20 minutes. Aerobic exercises include rapid walking, jogging, swimming, bicycling, basketball, or anything else that elevates your heart rate and keeps it elevated.

- *Adopt a posture of confidence.* Even if you can't control your feelings, you can control your posture. Avoid slouching. Sit straight, as if you're ready to sprint out of your seat. Look like someone who knows the answers. Notice any changes in your emotional state.

- *Show up ready to perform.* Show up just a few minutes before the test starts. Avoid talking to other students about how worried you are, which may only fan the fire of your fear. If other people are complaining or cramming at the last minute, tune them out. Look out a window and focus on neutral sights and sounds. You don't have to take on other people's nervous energy.

Zoom out

When you're in the middle of a test or another situation in which you feel distressed, zoom out. Think the way film directors do when they dolly a camera out and away from an action scene. In your mind, imagine that you're floating away and viewing the situation as a detached outside observer.

From this larger viewpoint, ask yourself whether this situation is worth worrying about. This is not a license to belittle or avoid problems; it is permission to gain some perspective.

Another option is to zoom out in time. Imagine yourself one week, one month, one year, one decade, or one century from today. Assess how much the current situation will matter when that time comes. Then come back to the test with a more detached perspective.

Resign yourself to failure—and continue

During a test, you may feel a panic so intense that you see no way out. You might apply all the suggestions listed here and find that none of them work for you in the moment.

If this happens, one option is to simply resign yourself to getting an *F* on the test. Most of the time, you'll be able to live with the consequences. They may not be ideal, but they won't be catastrophic, either. Even on important tests—entrance tests for college or medical school, law boards, CPA exams—a low score usually means only a delay.

Once you've taken the pressure off yourself, find just one question you think you can answer, anywhere on the test. When you finish that one, find another. Place 100 percent of your attention on answering the easier questions, one by one. This might be enough to gradually rebuild your confidence and help you complete the test.

☑ checklist

WHAT TO DO RIGHT BEFORE THE TEST

The actions you take in the 24 hours before a test can increase your worries—or reduce them. To manage stress:

❒ During the day before a test, review only the content that you already know; avoid learning facts and ideas that are entirely unfamiliar.

❒ On the night before a test, do a late review and then go directly to bed.

❒ Set up conditions so that you sleep well during the night before a test.

❒ On the morning of the test, wake up at your usual time and immediately do a quick review.

❒ Before a test, eat a nutritious breakfast. Go easy on caffeine, which can increase nervousness—and send you to the bathroom during the exam.

Get help for prolonged anxiety

If stress management techniques don't work, and if anxiety persists well beyond test times, get help. If you become withdrawn, have frequent thoughts about death or suicide, or feel hopeless or sad for more than a few days, talk to someone. Seek out a trusted friend. Also see your academic advisor or a counselor at your student health center.

experiment WITH A STRATEGY FROM THIS CHAPTER

Mentally re-create a time when you had difficulty taking a test. Do anything that helps you reexperience this event. List the types of questions you had difficulty answering, recall the feelings you experienced during the test, or describe the reactions you had after finding out your score. Describe that experience here:

Now review this chapter, looking for the most important suggestion you can find—one that could prevent the incident you just described from happening again. Summarize that suggestion in the space below:

Next, list specific ways that you can apply this suggestion in preparing for an upcoming test. Explain what exactly you intend to do and when:

After the test, reflect on your experience with this new behavior. Describe how well it worked for you, whether you would use it again, or how you could modify the behavior to make it more effective:

chapter 19

Using Test Time Efficiently

Many jobs can lead to an occasion on which you're asked to perform under pressure. For students, that occasion is often a test.

And it's no wonder. *Taking* a test is much different from *studying* for a test. While studying, the only time constraints are those that you place on yourself. You can take breaks for a nap or a walk. If you forget a crucial fact or idea, you can go back to your textbooks or your notes and look it up.

During a test, you usually can't do those things. There's far less leeway. And the stakes are higher.

Even so, test conditions are predictable, and you can prepare for them. There are strategies you can use to succeed on any type of test. Once you've mastered those, you can adopt specific strategies for certain kinds of tests—objective, short answer, essay, and more.

Proceed with a Plan

At test time, instead of launching into the first question, take a few seconds to breathe deeply and clear your mind. Then take one minute to plan your test-taking strategy. Doing this can actually save you time during the test, allowing you to answer more items and recall more facts and ideas.

Mentally "download" key material

As tests are handed out, you may find that material you studied pops into your head. Take a minute to record key items that you've memorized, especially if you're sure they will appear on the test. Make these notes before the sight of any test questions shakes your confidence.

Items you can jot down include:

- Formulas.
- Equations.
- Facts.
- Key words and definitions.
- Major points you want to make in essay questions.

Make these notes in the margins of your test papers. If you use a separate sheet of paper, you may appear to be cheating.

Do a test reconnaissance

Immediately after receiving your test, scan the whole thing. Make sure you got all the test materials: instructions, questions, blank paper or blue books, and anything else that was passed out.

Check the back sides of all sheets of paper you receive. Don't get to the "end" of a test and then discover questions you overlooked.

Next, read over *all* the questions. Get a sense of which ones will be easier for you to answer and which will take more time.

Decode the directions

Read the test directions slowly. Then reread them. It can be agonizing to discover that you lost points on a test only because you failed to follow the directions. If the directions call for short answers, for instance, give only short answers—not full-blown essays.

Sometimes you will be asked to answer two out of three questions. It's frustrating to find that out as you finish your third answer. When the directions are confusing, ask about them.

Pay particular attention to verbal directions given as a test is distributed. Find out:

- Exactly how much time you have to complete the test.
- Whether all the questions count equally or, if not, which count the most.
- Whether you can use resources, such as a dictionary, calculator, class handout, or textbook.
- Whether there are any corrections or other changes to test questions.

Budget your time

Check the clock and count up the number of questions you need to answer. With these two figures in mind, estimate how much time you can devote to each question or each section of the test. Adjust your estimate as needed if certain questions or sections are worth appreciably more than others. Plan to give point-laden items more time.

After quickly budgeting your time, tackle test items in terms of priority:

- Answer the easiest, shortest questions first. This gives you the experience of success. It also stimulates associations and prepares you for more difficult questions.
- Next, answer multiple-choice, true-false, and fill-in-the-blank questions.
- Then proceed to short-answer and essay questions.

Pace yourself. Watch the time; if you are stuck, move on. Follow your time plan.

Avoid Common Errors in Test-Taking

If you think of a test as a sprint, then remember that there are at least two ways that you can trip. Watch for errors due to carelessness and errors that result from getting stuck on a question.

Errors due to carelessness

These kinds of errors are easy to spot. Usually you'll catch them immediately after your test has been returned to you—even before you see your score or read any comments from your teacher.

You can avoid many common test-taking errors simply through the power of awareness. Learn about them up front and then look out for them. Examples are:

- Mistakes due to skipping or misreading test directions.
- Missing several questions in a certain section of the test—a sign that you misunderstood the directions for that section or neglected certain topics while studying for the test.
- Failing to finish problems that you knew how to answer, such as skipping the second part of a two-part question or the final step of a problem.
- Consistently changing answers that were correct to answers that were incorrect.
- Spending so much time on certain questions that you failed to answer others.
- Making mistakes in copying an answer from scratch paper onto your answer sheet.
- Turning in your test and leaving early, rather than taking the extra time to proofread your answers.

Errors due to getting stuck

You may encounter a test question and discover that you have no idea how to answer it. This situation can lead to discomfort, then fear, then panic—a downward spiral of emotion that can undermine your ability to answer even the questions you *do* know.

To break the spiral, remember that this situation is common. If you undertake 16 or more years of schooling, then the experience of getting utterly stuck on a test is bound to happen to you at some point.

When it occurs, accept your feelings of discomfort. Take a moment to apply one of the stress management techniques for test anxiety explained in Chapter 18. This alone may get you "unstuck." If not, continue with the ideas explained in the following checklist.

☑ checklist

WHAT TO DO WHEN YOU GET STUCK ON A TEST QUESTION

❏ **Read it again, Sam.** Eliminate the simplest sources of confusion, such as misreading the question.

❏ **Skip the question for now.** Simple, but it works. Let your subconscious mind work on the answer while you respond to other questions. The trick is to truly let go of answering the puzzling question—for the moment. If you let this question nag at you in the back of your mind as you move on to other test items, you can undermine your concentration and interfere with the workings of your memory.

❏ **Look for answers in other test questions.** A term, name, date, or other fact that escapes you might appear in another question on the test itself. Use other questions to stimulate your memory.

❏ **Treat intuitions with care.** In quick-answer questions (multiple choice, true-false), go with your first instinct as to which answer is correct. If you think your first answer is wrong because you misread the question, then do change your answer.

❏ **Visualize the answer's "location."** Think of the answer to any test question as being recorded someplace in your notes or assigned reading. Close your eyes, take a deep breath, and see if you can visualize that place—the answer's location on a page in the materials you studied for the test.

❏ **Rewrite the question.** See if you can put the question that confuses you into your own words. Doing so may release the answer.

❏ **Free write.** Just start writing anything at all. On scratch paper, record any response to the question, noting whatever pops into your head. Instead of just sitting there, stumped, you're doing something, a fact that can reduce anxiety. You may also trigger a mental association that answers the test question.

❏ **Write a close answer.** If you simply cannot think of a direct, accurate answer to the question, then give it a shot anyway. Answer the question as best as you can, even if you don't think your answer is fully correct. This technique may help you get partial credit for short-answer questions, essay questions, and problems on math or science tests.

Tackle True-False Tests

Often, true-false questions are not worth many points individually. Yet they can be tricky and turn into a source of lost credit. Use the following strategies to complete these test items efficiently:

- **Read the entire question.** Remember that for a statement to be true, all *parts* of the statement must be true. Separate the statement into its grammatical parts—individual clauses and phrases—and then test each one. If any part is false, the entire statement is false.
- **Look for qualifiers.** These include words such as *all, most, sometimes,* or *rarely.* These are the key words upon which the question depends. Absolute qualifiers such as *always* or *never* generally indicate a false statement.
- **Find the devil in the details.** Read true-false items to double-check each number, fact, and date in a statement. Look for numbers that have been transposed or facts that have been slightly altered. These are signals of a false statement.
- **Watch for negatives.** Look for words such as *not* and *cannot.* Read the sentence without these words and see if you come up with a true or false statement. Then reinsert the negative words and see if the statement makes more sense. Watch especially for sentences with two negative words. As in math operations, two negatives make a positive statement. *We cannot say that Chekhov never succeeded at short-story writing* means the same as *Chekhov succeeded at short-story writing.*
- **Write clearly.** Don't let your handwriting cost you points. Make a clear difference in the way you write the letters *T* and *F.* When written hastily, they can look alike.

Reduce the Guesswork in Multiple-Choice Tests

The suggestion to read directions carefully is one that applies with special force to multiple-choice tests. Start by determining whether you are looking for *the* correct answer or the *most* correct answer. This distinction can make a huge difference. Also check to see whether some questions can have two or more correct answers.

When you're clear about the type of answers you're looking for, keep the following in mind:

- **Answer each question in your head first.** Do this before you look at the possible answers. If you come up with an answer that you're confident is right, look for that answer in the list of choices.
- **Read all possible answers before selecting one.** This is essential for multiple-choice questions for which you must select the best

answer or more than one answer. Sometimes two answers will be similar, but only one will be correct.

- **Combine the stem with each possible answer.** Multiple-choice questions consist of two parts: the stem (an incomplete statement at the beginning) and a list of possible answers. Each answer, when combined with the stem, makes a complete statement that is true or false. Turn each multiple-choice question into a small series of true-false questions. Choose the answer that makes a true statement.

- **Eliminate incorrect answers.** Sometimes you can "back in" to the correct answer by using the process of elimination. Cross off the answers that are clearly incorrect. The answer you cannot eliminate is probably the best choice.

Write Essay Tests With Confidence

Begin essay tests by evaluating your options. Weigh the point value of different questions. Read the directions to see if you're required to answer all questions or whether you can choose from a list. Note any questions that seem particularly easy or difficult. To build confidence and momentum, start with easier questions, and allow extra time for the harder questions that can yield more points.

☑ checklist

WHEN ALL ELSE FAILS, MAKE AN EDUCATED GUESS

When none of the previous suggestions help you answer multiple-choice items, you can use the following guidelines to make a guess. Do this only if incorrect answers are not deducted from your score—and only as a last resort.

❏ If two answers differ by only one or two words, choose one of these answers.

❏ If two answers have similar-sounding or similar-looking words *(intermediate, intermittent)*, choose one of these answers.

❏ If the answer calls for a sentence completion, eliminate the answers that would not form grammatically correct sentences.

❏ If two quantities are almost the same, choose one.

❏ If answers cover a wide range (4.5, 66.7, 88.7, 90.1, 5000.11), choose one in the middle of the range.

❏ Choose the answer that is longest, most detailed, or most inclusive.

❏ If you're completely stumped and time is short, guess.

Note: None of these suggestions for guessing is meant to take the place of studying for a test.

Make your test easy to read

Grading essay questions is in large part a subjective process. Sloppy, difficult-to-read handwriting might actually lower your grade. Take care with the details that promote legible writing. For example:

- Write with an erasable pen so that you can make corrections without crossing anything out.
- Write on one side of a page in essay-test booklets; use the blank side of a page to add any points you missed.
- Give yourself room to revise; write only on every other line.
- Use abbreviations only when you're sure that the person who grades your test will understand them.
- Leave a generous left-hand margin and plenty of space between your answers in case you want to add to them later.
- If you have time, review your answers for grammar and spelling errors, clarity, and legibility.

Briefly outline each answer

Before you write an essay answer, make a quick outline. There are three reasons for doing this. First, you might be able to write faster. Second, you're less likely to leave out important facts. Third, if you don't have time to finish your answer, your outline could win you some points.

One way to get to the point is to include part of the question in your answer. Suppose the question is: *Explain whether increasing a city's police budget will lead to a decrease in street crime.* Your first sentence might be: *An increase in police expenditures will not have a significant effect on street crime for the following reasons.* Your position is clear. And you've alerted the reader to expect a list of reasons that support your position. You are on your way to an answer.

To finish your answer, pick your two or three strongest reasons and state them in one sentence each. Then make these the topic sentences of your next two or three paragraphs.

Get to the point

Answer essay questions directly, without "padding." This approach can save you time and endear you to instructors. Forget vague, rambling introductions. Sentences such as "There are many interesting facets to this difficult question" can cause acute irritation for teachers grading tests.

When you expand your answer with supporting ideas and facts, start out with the most solid points. Don't try for drama by saving the best for last. Avoid filler sentences that say nothing, such as: "The question certainly bears careful deliberation in order to take into account all the many interesting facts pertaining to this important period in the history of our great nation."

▶ sidebar

KEY DIRECTION WORDS IN ESSAY QUESTIONS

The first step to success on essay tests is to discover precisely what each question is asking. To do that, reread each question until you find the *key direction word*. Often this is a single word—usually a verb—that describes what your answer is supposed to do.

Say that an essay question on a psychology test asks that you *compare* psychoanalysis and cognitive-behavioral therapies. This is far different from a question that asks you to *explain* either form of therapy. Missing the difference between *compare* and *explain*—key direction words—can quickly lead you astray and cost you points.

The words printed in boldface in the following list are key direction words commonly found in essay test questions. If you want to do well on essay tests, then know these words backward and forward. To heighten your awareness of them, underline the words when you see them in a test question.

Analyze: Break into separate parts and discuss, examine, or interpret each part. Then give your opinion.

Classify: Take a general concept and divide it into parts, or take a specific concept and place it in a larger category.

Compare: Examine two or more things. Identify similarities and differences.

Contrast: Show differences. Set in opposition.

Criticize: Make judgments. Evaluate comparative worth. Criticism often involves analysis.

Define: Give the meaning, usually a meaning specific to the course or subject. Explain the exact meaning. Definitions are usually short.

Describe: Give a detailed account. Make a picture with words. List characteristics, qualities, and parts.

Write as if you expect the person grading your test to be tired, bored, and overworked. Even a well-rested instructor doesn't like to wade through a swamp of murky writing in order to spot an occasional lonely insight.

Answer all questions

As in objective tests, managing your time is important. Note how many questions you have to answer and monitor your progress during the test period. Writing shorter answers and completing all of the questions on an essay test can yield a better score than leaving some questions blank.

If you run short on time and are not able to finish an answer, shift into outline mode. List the points you *intended* to make, capturing each point in at least one full sentence or a meaningful phrase.

Diagram: Create a chart that displays the main features of an object, the steps in a process, or the relationship between several concepts.

Discuss: Consider and debate or argue the pros and cons of an issue. Write about any conflict. Compare and contrast.

Evaluate: Judge the worthiness or value of a viewpoint or theory.

Explain: Make an idea clear. Show logically how a concept is developed. Give the reasons for an event.

Illustrate: Answer by including specific examples or a visual device, such as a chart or diagram.

Justify: Give acceptable reasons for a point of view or course of action.

Outline: Divide a theory or viewpoint into topics and subtopics and explain each of these in turn.

Prove: Support with facts (especially facts presented in class or in the text).

Relate: Show the connections between ideas or events. Provide a larger context.

Review: Narrate events in the order they happened and explain the significance of each event.

State: Explain precisely.

Summarize: Give a brief, condensed account. Include conclusions. Avoid unnecessary details.

Trace: Show the order of events or progress of a subject or event.

Note: The meanings of any key direction word can vary across different contexts. If you're unsure what any word requires you to do, ask for help.

Use Strategies for Other Types of Tests

True-false, multiple-choice, and essay questions may compose the bulk of test items that you encounter in higher education. To increase your confidence level, consider ways to approach other kinds of tests as well, including those described next.

Matching tests

Matching tests ask you to link a key term to its definition or to connect a concept with one of its examples. These tests are usually formatted as two lists of items, with each list appearing in a separate column.

- Begin by reading through each column, starting with the one with fewer items.
- Check the number of items in each column to see if they're equal; if they're not, look for an item in one column that you can match with two or more items in the other column.

- Look for any items with similar wording and make special note of the differences between these items.
- Match words that are similar grammatically; for example, match verbs with verbs and nouns with nouns.
- When matching individual words with phrases, read the phrase, then look for the word that logically completes the phrase.
- Cross out items in each column as you finish with them.

Open-book tests

Review thoroughly for open-book exams. They can be difficult. As you study, carefully organize your notes, readings, and any other materials you plan to consult when writing answers:

- Bookmark the table of contents and index in each of your textbooks.
- Place Post-it® notes or paper clips on other important pages of books (pages with tables, for instance); don't waste time flipping through the pages.
- Create an informal table of contents or index for the notes you took in class.
- Predict which material will be covered on the test and highlight relevant sections in your readings and notes.
- On a separate sheet, compile lists of formulas or other key facts you will need.

Computer-graded tests

To prevent missed points on answer sheets that are scored by a computer:

- Make sure the answer you mark corresponds to the question you are answering.
- Check the test booklet against the answer sheet whenever you switch sections and whenever you come to the top of a column.
- Watch for stray marks; they can look like answers.

Math and science tests

Aim for a high grade on the first test—often the easiest and one that counts as much as later, harder tests. In addition:

- Right before the test, review any formulas you'll need to use; write them on the margin of the test or on the back of the test paper.
- Check your work systematically by asking questions: Did I read the problem correctly? Did I use the correct formula or equation? Is my arithmetic correct? Is my answer in the proper form?
- Practice using the necessary functions on your calculator *before* you take it to a test.

▶ experiment WITH A STRATEGY FROM THIS CHAPTER

Write a short paragraph that explains ways you are already using any of the techniques described in this chapter.

Now, list any new techniques for taking tests that you gained from reading this chapter.

Of the new techniques you just listed, choose one that you will actually use. Describe when and where you will apply it.

Evaluate how well this new technique worked for you. Also, describe possible ways to use this technique outside test situations. For example, consider ways that the suggestions for taking essay tests could help you write better papers.

 **DEVELOPING AND PRESENTING IDEAS**

Quick Reference Guide to DEVELOPING AND PRESENTING IDEAS

20. RESEARCH: DEFINING WHAT YOU WANT TO DISCOVER

When researching, gather more information than you can include in your final paper or presentation. This allows you to sift through any relevant statistics, quotations, and examples and select the gems.

1. **Brainstorm topics (page 231)**
   Unless your teacher has already defined a topic for your paper or presentation, you can exercise your creativity to choose one:
   - Get together with a study group or online community to brainstorm topics.
   - Use free writing—that is, list topics randomly, free associate, and let one thought lead to another.
   - Use mind mapping: List a broad topic as a key word in the center of a blank piece of paper; then, on lines radiating outward from the center, write down words that pop into your head when you think about that key word.
   - Admit your confusion about a topic for your paper or presentation. Then just think out loud, speaking your first thoughts about possible topics.

2. **Refine your topic (page 232)**
   If you can accurately summarize your topic in one sentence, then you've refined it. If not, take the time to define it further:
   - Choose one topic.
   - Avoid topics that are too broad or too narrow. (See the examples on page 233.)
   - Ask leading questions, such as: *Why does this topic matter?* and *Who are the main people associated with this topic?*
   - Imagine what your final paper will look like; visualize different titles at the top of the first page.
   - Do initial research to discover the overall structure of your topic—its major divisions or subtopics.

   - Use an Internet search engine to define your topic. (See the sidebar on page 234).

3. **State your thesis (page 235)**
   Clarify what you want to say in your paper or presentation by summarizing it in one concise sentence—your thesis:
   - For maximum clarity, state your thesis in a complete sentence. (See the examples on page 236.)
   - As you do more research, be willing to revise your thesis.
   - To stay focused on your topic, keep your thesis in front of you as you write.

4. **Clarify your purpose (page 236)**
   To focus your thinking and make a stronger impression on your audience, get clear about your purpose:
   - Consider three types of purpose that refer to the kinds of change you want to produce in your audience: cognitive (intellectual change), affective (emotional change), and behavioral (a change in action).
   - To clarify your purpose, state it in one sentence that includes your topic and thesis. (See the sidebar on page 237.)
   - After defining your purpose, ask what kinds of information you'll need to achieve it.
   - Analyze your audience, considering what they already know about your topic, how they feel about it, and any actions you want them to take.

4. **List the questions you want to answer (page 239)**
   Create a list of questions to guide your research:
   - To discover your main research question, take your purpose statement and convert it into a question.

- List supporting questions—questions you'll need to answer in order to answer your main research question. (See the examples on page 239.)

21. RESEARCH: USING SOURCES OF INFORMATION

Think of research as an intellectual adventure and path of continuous discovery.

1. **Use general research strategies (page 241)**
   Before diving into the library or mining Web sites for information, choose what type of sources to consult and evaluate their quality:
   - Whenever possible, find primary sources, such as letters, speeches, government documents, scientific experiments, and interviews with recognized experts.
   - Think critically about your sources, evaluating the currency, credibility, and relevance to your topic. Evaluate Internet sources carefully. (See the checklist on page 244.)

2. **Find published sources (page 243)**
   Explore a wide range of sources published in print and online:
   - Use the library, remembering that its basic elements are catalogs, collections of materials, and computer-based resources.
   - Ask a librarian for help—if possible, someone with a specialty related to your topic.
   - Look for reference works, both print and online, that are relevant to your topic. (See the sidebar on page 246.)
   - Before using computer-based catalogs and search engines, assemble a list of key words that are related to your topic.

3. **Turn to people as sources (page 248)**
   Making direct contact with people as you complete your research can offer a welcome relief from hours of solitary library time. Find and interview experts on your topic. In addition to gathering ideas and information from other people, make note of your own insights.

4. **Take notes on your sources (page 249)**
   Keep a careful record of all the ideas and information that you gather in your research:
   - Know what information to record about each source that you consult. (See the checklist on page 250.)
   - When appropriate, summarize a source in a few sentences or paragraphs.
   - When appropriate, take more detailed notes by paraphrasing—capturing an author's ideas in your own words. (See the examples on page 252.)

- When an author makes a point in a forceful or memorable way, consider capturing that person's exact words in your notes.
- As you take notes, take care to credit your sources and avoid plagiarism. (See the sidebar on page 253.)
- Before writing a first draft of your paper or presentation, take time to reflect on your notes.

22. PREPARING TO WRITE

Writing is a process of discovering what you want to say, starting with research and continuing through multiple drafts of a paper or presentation.

1. **Plan the project (page 255)**
   Set due dates for major writing tasks. (See the checklist on page 256.)

2. **Create an outline (page 257)**
   Before writing, create an outline to clarify the core structure of your ideas:
   - Start with a basic organizing pattern—anything from a numbered list to a detailed chronology of events.
   - As you outline, create an introduction that will grab your audience's attention. (See the sidebar on page 258.)
   - To clarify your thinking even more, create a formal outline in complete sentences. (See the example on page 260.)
   - Choose whether to directly state your thesis in your paper or presentation.
   - If you plan to collaborate with others on a writing project, find an appropriate task for each team member.

23. WRITING A DRAFT

Based on your research and outline, do a complete first draft of your paper or presentation.

1. **Reduce resistance to writing (page 263)**
   To ease any difficulty associated with producing a first draft, make a habit of writing, even when you're not assigned to do so:
   - Practice free writing—writing continuously, without editing, for a predetermined time period.
   - Use features of a computer that promote free writing. (See the checklist on page 264.)
   - Instead of waiting to feel inspired before you write, make a practice of writing regularly.
   - Use techniques to overcome writer's block. (See the sidebar on page 265.)

2. **Finish the first draft quickly (page 265)**
   To create your first draft, expand the ideas in your outline:
   - Experiment with writing a first draft before you reread your notes.

- Draft the sections of your paper or presentation in any order that appeals to you.
- Write in your own voice, letting go of the urge to sound "official" or "scholarly."
- Write through to the end of your draft, remembering that you can revise later.
- Save your drafts—including the material you eventually cut—for possible use in the future.

3. **Get some distance from your draft (page 267)**
   To get perspective on your draft, put it on the shelf for a while before you revise it.

24. REVISING YOUR DRAFT

The act of rewriting may teach you more about your topic than any other step in the creative process.

1. **Get feedback about your writing (page 269)**
   Before you start revising, consider sharing your first draft with a few people and asking them for feedback:
   - Request feedback on the overall organization and clarity of your writing, as well as the organization and clarity of individual sentences.
   - Let people offer their feedback in a variety of ways. (See the sidebar on page 270.)
   - Consider sharing your word processing files with other people and using software features that allow them to insert their comments.
   - Learn to welcome feedback by separating your self-esteem from your first draft.
   - When you're asked to give feedback on someone else's writing, make it constructive.

2. **Consider the scope of your writing (page 271)**
   Start revising from the "big picture"—an overall view of your paper's length and content:
   - Use word processing software to count the total number of words in your paper.
   - Read your paper out loud, listening for any gaps in content.
   - Cut material from your paper that does not support your purpose.
   - Add material to your paper when it will help you achieve your purpose for writing.

3. **Consider the structure of your writing (page 272)**
   Put the sections of your paper in a logical order:
   - Check your first draft against your outline.
   - Make changes as needed to your outline.

4. **Consider the style of your writing (page 273)**
   After refining the scope and structure of your paper or presentation, take a microscope to individual sentences and words:
   - Write mainly with specific nouns and action verbs; reduce the number of adjectives and adverbs. (See the examples on page 274.)
   - Revise your sentences to create a variety of lengths and structures.

- Proofread to catch errors in grammar, spelling, and punctuation. (See the examples on page 275.)
- Prepare a final draft of your paper to submit. (See the checklist on page 276.)

25. MAKING EFFECTIVE PRESENTATIONS

Remember that speeches and other presentations can move people to change their opinions, change their votes, or change their lives.

1. **Plan your presentation (page 278)**
   When the choice is yours, talk about topics that hold your interest and develop them in ways that follow your interests:
   - Determine your purpose—whether you want to inform, persuade, motivate, or simply entertain your audience.
   - Tailor the length and formality of your presentation to the setting in which you will speak.
   - Choose a format for your speaking notes, ranging from a simple list of key words to a complete manuscript that you will read word for word. (See checklist on page 280.)
   - Develop an introduction that will interest your audience and preview the rest of your presentation. (See the examples on page 281.) Develop the body of your presentation by arranging your major points in order and supporting each one. Develop a conclusion that summarizes your presentation, calls for action, and leaves a lasting impression. (See the sidebar on page 282.)
   - Edit your speech, remembering that it will be heard, not read.
   - Create handouts and activities to sustain audience interest and reinforce the content of your presentation. Create effective visuals for your presentation with PowerPoint. (See the checklist on page 283.)

2. **Practice your presentation (page 284)**
   Rehearse your speech often—preferably in the setting in which you will deliver your presentation and with preliminary feedback from a few listeners.

3. **Present with confidence (page 285)**
   One powerful strategy for preventing and reducing fear of public speaking is to prepare thoroughly. In addition:
   - Arrive early on the day of your presentation to set up.
   - Take a few moments at the beginning of your presentation to collect your thoughts.
   - Create variety in the pace of your presentation by pausing when appropriate.
   - Maintain eye contact with your audience.
   - Avoid contrived gestures.
   - Track the time and plan to finish on schedule.
   - Take specific steps to reduce fear of public speaking. (See the sidebar on page 286.)

♦ Get feedback from audience members on the effectiveness of your presentation.

26. USING COMPUTERS TO PROMOTE YOUR SUCCESS

While you are participating in higher education, learn to use information technology in ways that promote your long-term success.

1. **Bringing a computer to campus: Ask these questions (page 288)**
    Before enrolling in courses, contact an admissions counselor or academic advisor to ask these questions:
    ♦ Do I need to own a computer? Do I need a laptop computer or a desktop computer?
    ♦ Do I need a Windows computer, or can I use a Macintosh?
    ♦ What specifications does my hardware need to meet? What software will I use?
    Also evaluate computer resources at your school. (See the checklist on page 291.)

2. **Expand your learning strategies to include technology (page 290)**
    Integrate information technology with daily study tasks in a variety of ways:
    ♦ Create and maintain an online glossary of key terms for each of your courses.
    ♦ Use outlining software to organize and review your class notes.
    ♦ Use computers for cooperative learning tasks, such as creating mock tests in study groups.

27. BECOMING A MEMBER OF THE ONLINE COMMUNITY

Through Web sites, e-mail, newsgroups, and chat rooms, the Internet puts you in touch with networks of people that extend across your school, across the country, and even worldwide.

1. **Write for online audiences (page 294)**
    Remember that writing for the screen differs from writing for the printed page:
    ♦ Keep messages simple, short, and direct.
    ♦ Use boldface headings, short paragraphs, and other devices to help your readers scan efficiently for the information that they want.
    ♦ Include links to useful Web sites.

2. **Join online communities (page 297)**
    Consider joining e-mail lists, newsgroups, and chat rooms on topics that interest you. If you do:
    ♦ Start by mastering e-mail basics: Send messages only to people who can use them, write an informative subject line, and forward messages selectively.
    ♦ Any time that you're online, observe the principles of "netiquette." (See the sidebar on page 301.)
    ♦ Before enrolling in a distance learning course, consider whether this option will work for you. (See the checklist on page 303.)

chapter 20

Research: Defining What You Want to Discover

A **common mistake** of beginning writers is to hold their noses, close their eyes, and jump into the writing process with both feet and few facts. Avoid this temptation by doing thorough research—that is, by gathering more information than you can include in your final paper or presentation. This allows you to sift through a body of relevant statistics, quotations, and examples and select the gems.

Keep in mind, however, that writing and researching exist in dialogue. The act of writing reveals holes in research. Raising questions leads to answers, which in turn generates new questions. As a creator and refiner of ideas, you'll alternate continuously between writing, speaking, and researching.

Brainstorm Topics

Using your instructor's guidelines for a paper or speech, sit down and make a list of topics that interest you. Write down as many as you can. Unless your teacher has already defined your topic, this is a time to flex your creative muscles using a variety of means. Get started by using the techniques that follow.

Brainstorm with people

There's no need to create in isolation. Forget the myth of the lonely, frustrated artist rehashing ideas alone in a dark Paris cafe. As you search out topics, you can harness the natural creative power of a group to your favor. (For ways to brainstorm ideas in groups, see Chapter 4.)

For example, you might belong to a chat room, newsgroup, or other online community. If so, share your topic ideas and ask for suggestions. Getting online with other members of your classes can be especially helpful.

Use free writing

When you don't know what topic to write about, just list topics randomly. Free associate, letting one thought lead to another. The key is to just keep writing for a certain period of time—say, 10 minutes—without stopping to edit.

Consider free writing on a computer, which offers certain advantages. For example, if you can't think of a particular word or if you forget how to spell it, just type *XXX* in its place and keep writing. Later, you can use the search and replace command in your word processor to fix those spots. A word processor also allows you to alphabetize your list of possible topics and reorganize it in other ways.

Use mind mapping

Mind maps (explained in Chapter 13) offer a visual way to brainstorm. List a broad topic as a key word in the center of a blank piece of paper. Circle that word.

Now, write down any words that pop into your head when you think about that key word. Record each word on a line radiating outward from the key word at the center of the page.

Next, look at any of the words you just wrote and treat them in the same way as your key word: Record related words on connecting lines, one word per line.

Keep going until you fill the page. Feel free to write in different colors and add pictures.

Just start talking

To get topic ideas flowing, start talking. Admit your confusion about a topic for your paper or presentation. Then just think out loud, speaking your first thoughts about possible topics. By putting your thoughts into words, you'll start thinking more clearly. Novelist E. M. Forster said, "Speak before you think is creation's motto."

Refine Your Topic

One way to begin research is to place yourself squarely in the "party scenario." Imagine that you're at a party, and the conversation turns to your writing assignment. Someone asks, "Well, what's your paper all about anyway?" Given the informal nature of this occasion—and the limited attention span of the participants—you've got about 15 seconds to deliver a coherent answer.

If you can do this, then you know your topic. If not, it's time to apply the following suggestions. Keep using them until you know exactly what your research topic is.

example

NARROWING YOUR TOPIC	
TOPICS THAT ARE TOO BROAD	**TOPICS WITH MORE FOCUS**
The Internet	"Dot com" companies during the 1990s
Cancer treatment	Chemotherapy for breast cancer
War	The concept of the "just war"
Feminism	The social impact of Betty Friedan's writing
Agriculture in developing countries	Coffee growers in Latin America

Choose one topic

After you've created a list of possible topics, you'll eventually need to focus on just one. Making this choice is an easy step to put off. However, it is almost impossible to make a wrong choice at the earliest stages of your research. If you're not sure about which topic to research, just choose one. You can choose again later.

Of course, one way to choose a topic is to literally draw ideas out of a hat. Take your brainstormed list of possible topics and use scissors to cut the list into single items. Place them in a box, shake well, and pull one out.

Avoid topics that are too broad or too narrow

A common pitfall is selecting a topic that's too broad. As a topic for a paper in an American history course, for instance, "Harriet Tubman" offers little to guide your research. Instead, consider "Harriet Tubman's activities as a Union spy during the Civil War."

Topics that are too broad create practical problems. You might start your research and say to yourself, *There's so much to say about this that I could write 100 pages.* That's a clear sign that you should narrow down your topic.

Another problem, perhaps less common, is first choosing a topic that is too narrow. After several days of research, you might find yourself still wondering how you'll ever come up with enough material to fill a single page. Or you might write a first draft of your paper and find yourself repeating ideas and examples. In either case, go back to the drawing board and use brainstorming to come up with a more general topic.

Ask leading questions

Asking standard types of questions about your possible topics can help you refine them. Start with the five "journalist questions":

- *Who* are the main people associated with this topic or the major players in this event?
- *What* led up to this event, or what else do I need to know in order to write about this topic?
- *When* did this event happen, or when was this topic first researched?
- *Where* did this event take place, or where has this topic been researched?
- *Why* does this topic or event matter?

Visualize the final product

To gain clarity, state your topic as a working title for your paper or presentation. Visualize that title at the top of a sheet of paper. Then start imagining the words of the first paragraph, or hear the opening words of your speech. If you can see yourself continuing beyond that point with confidence, you probably have a well-defined topic.

Do initial research

At this stage, after first defining your topic, research is not about mining for facts or conducting extensive interviews. That comes later. For now,

▶ sidebar

USING A SEARCH ENGINE TO REFINE YOUR TOPIC

Get on your computer, connect to the Internet, and access a search engine such as AltaVista (http://www.altavista.com), Google (http://www.google.com), or Yahoo! (http://www.yahoo.com). These sites include a directory of Web pages organized by topic.

The first page of a directory includes links to the most general topics. Clicking any link on this page will take you to a page with more specific links. In turn, clicking on any of *these* links will lead you to other pages with even more specific links.

Say that you want to write about alternative medicine—a topic that you know is too broad for a four-page paper:

1. Go to Yahoo!'s first directory page, which includes a link for *Health*; click on this link.
2. Yahoo! will display a new page with *Hot Topics* related to Health where you can find a link to *Alternative medicine*; click on this link.
3. Now a page appears with a list of topics related to Alternative medicine; any one of these would provide you with a more focused topic for your paper.

In summary, the Internet path you followed is: *Health → Alternative medicine → Acupuncture.*

just get an overview. Discover the overall structure of your topic—its major divisions or subtopics. Say that you want to persuade the reader to vote for a certain candidate. Then learn enough about this person to state her stands on key issues and summarize her background.

At this stage, it's fine to do research by using secondary sources, for instance, encyclopedias and almanacs. (For information about the difference between primary and secondary sources, see Chapter 21.)

After digging into your topic for a few hours, consider your prospects for proceeding. If you keep running into the same facts or ideas over and over again, or if you find only dated or sketchy references to your topic, choose a new topic.

State Your Thesis

Clarify what you want to say in your paper or presentation by summarizing it in one concise sentence. This sentence is called a *thesis statement,* and it refines your working title. It also helps in making a preliminary outline.

You might write a thesis statement such as: "Harriet Tubman's activities with the Underground Railroad led to a relationship with the Union army during the Civil War." A sentence such as this, which is clear and to the point, will make your paper easier to write. Remember that it's fine to rewrite your thesis statement as you learn more about your topic.

Write a complete sentence

A thesis statement is different from a topic statement. Like newspaper headlines, a thesis statement makes an assertion or describes an action. It is expressed in a complete sentence, including a verb. *Diversity* is a topic. "Cultural diversity is valuable" is a thesis statement.

A powerful thesis statement can expand on a topic in several ways, such as:

- Making a provocative statement.
- Stating a new relationship between factors that have not been seen as connected.
- Calling the reader or listener to take action.

Students sometimes craft a compelling thesis statement and invest hours in researching, only to find that they've wandered hopelessly off their stated topic. Look for a close fit between your topic and your thesis statement. Place them next to each other and scrutinize their relationship.

Be willing to revise your thesis statement

Getting to the stage at which you've refined your topic, completed some research, and crafted a thesis takes real intellectual effort. Given that investment of time and energy, you might be tempted to see your thesis

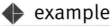 **example**

TOPIC AND THESIS STATEMENTS	
TOPICS	**POSSIBLE THESIS STATEMENTS**
"Dot com" companies during the 1990s	Investors in "dot com" companies during the 1990s failed to predict the problems with online retailing.
Chemotherapy for breast cancer	New drugs for breast cancer chemotherapy may prevent, as well as treat, this common disease.
The concept of the "just war"	Definitions of the "just war" shifted with each generation of new weapons.
The social impact of Betty Friedan's writing	Betty Friedan's book *The Feminist Mystique* paved the way for more women to enter the work force.
Coffee growers in Latin America	Fair-trade policies for coffee growers in Latin America benefit consumers, as well as farmers.

statement as etched in stone. Be aware, however, that your thesis statement can still change. In fact, it's a good idea to change or alter your thesis statement as you do more research and gain more understanding of your topic.

Keep in mind that being *flexible* about your thesis is not the same as being *indefinite*. At any point in your research or writing, make sure that your thesis reflects a clear and definite stand on your topic.

Keep your thesis in front of you

As a way to stay focused and save research time, keep your thesis in front of you—literally—as you work. Write your thesis on an index card and tape it to your computer. Or open up a file on your computer that includes only your thesis statement; keep that window open.

If you're ever in doubt about whether to pursue a certain line of research or include a particular fact in your final paper, ask yourself: Does this relate directly to my thesis? If not, don't use it.

Clarify Your Purpose

Effective writing flows from a purpose. Discuss the purpose of your assignment with your instructor. Also think about how you'd like your reader or listener to change after reading about your thesis.

Consider three types of purpose

Psychologists often speak about three dimensions of personal change:

- **Cognitive** change means adding to your knowledge about a topic or adopting a new point of view.
- **Affective** change refers to feeling differently about something or altering a deeply held attitude.
- **Behavioral** change refers to modifying the way you act.

These terms also point to three different purposes for speaking or writing. Simply put, do you want your audience to *think* differently (cognitive change), to *feel* differently (affective change), or to *act* differently (behavioral change)? Of course, you may initially have more than one purpose in mind. To focus your thinking and make a stronger impression on your audience, choose one of these as your primary purpose.

State your purpose succinctly

To clarify your purpose, state it in one sentence. For instance: "The purpose of this paper is to define the term *success* in such a clear and compelling way that I win a $1,000 scholarship from Houghton Mifflin."

The key word in this purpose statement is *define*, a verb that signals a cognitive purpose: to add to the audience's level of knowledge. Though this is the writer's primary purpose, there's a secondary behavioral purpose as well: to persuade Houghton Mifflin to award the writer a $1,000 scholarship.

> ▶ **sidebar**
>
> ## KEY WORDS FOR PURPOSE STATEMENTS
>
> **FOR A COGNITIVE PURPOSE:**
> Use a verb to describe how you will add to your audience's knowledge, such as:
>
> I intend to *analyze*. . . .
> I intend to *compare*. . . .
> I intend to *contrast*. . . .
> I intend to *defend*. . . .
> I intend to *define*. . . .
> I intend to *describe*. . . .
> I intend to *explain*. . . .
> I intend to *prove*. . . .
> *Note*: Many of these words are identical to the key direction words for essay questions (see page 222.)
>
> **FOR AN AFFECTIVE PURPOSE:**
> Use a verb to describe how you will affect your audience emotionally, such as:
>
> I intend to *convince*. . . .
> I intend to *depict*. . . .
> I intend to *narrate*. . . .
> I intend to *persuade*. . . .
> I intend to *show*. . . .
>
> **FOR A BEHAVIORAL PURPOSE:**
> Use a verb to describe what you want your audience to do after reading your writing or hearing your presentation, such as:
>
> I want my audience to *buy*. . . .
> I want my audience to *call*. . . .
> I want my audience to *go to*. . . .
> I want my audience to *send*. . . .
> I want my audience to *write a letter in support of*. . . .

One way to state your purpose is to begin your thesis statement with the words *I intend to*. Follow this with a key word such as *explain* or *persuade* that clarifies your purpose.

Let your purpose dictate your direction

The direction of your research and writing will be greatly affected by the purpose you choose:

- If you want someone to *think* differently, for example, then make your writing clear and logical. Support your assertions with evidence.
- If you want someone to *feel* differently, consider crafting a story. Write about a character your audience can sympathize with, and tell how she resolves a basic problem.
- If you want the audience to take action, explain exactly what steps to take and offer solid benefits for doing so.

Analyze your audience

Whenever you want the members of your audience to change in any significant way, start by discovering where they stand right now—what they already think or feel about your topic and what actions they usually take based on those thoughts or feelings. Then you can offer convincing reasons for them to adopt your viewpoint or take the actions you recommend.

In addition, you may benefit from discovering other characteristics of your audience as well, such as their:

- Ages
- Educational levels
- Income levels
- Occupations
- Political affiliations
- Race or ethnic groups
- Religious affiliations

Of course, much of your writing in higher education may be directed to an audience of one: the person who assigns and evaluates your work, usually your teacher. Even so, you can still benefit from an audience analysis. In particular, make sure you know the exact terms of your assignment: what your teacher is expecting you to produce in terms of number of words, types of sources, and final format. Also, see if you can determine whether this person has any prior opinions or strongly held feelings about your topic.

List the Questions You Want to Answer

So far, your research process has yielded a carefully defined topic and a thesis statement that says something significant *about* that topic. These are intellectual feats of a high order—and preludes to efficient research.

In order to continue your research, you'll need to expand your thesis statement into a complete paper or presentation. To do this, create a dialogue with yourself by asking and answering questions.

Discover your main question

Every paper or presentation calls on you to answer one question above all others. This is your *main question,* one that gets to the heart of your topic and your purpose. This is the question that will guide and direct your research at each stage.

To discover your main question, simply take your thesis statement and turn it into a question. For example, "Fair trade policies for coffee growers in Latin America benefit consumers, as well as farmers" is a thesis statement. Stated as a main question, it becomes, "How do fair trade policies for coffee growers in Latin America benefit consumers, as well as farmers?"

 example

LISTING RESEARCH QUESTIONS

Topic:
"Dot com" companies during the 1990s

Thesis:
Investors in "dot com" companies during the 1990s failed to predict the problems with online retailing.

Purpose:
I intend to explain how investors in "dot com" companies during the 1990s failed to predict the problems with online retailing.

Main question:
How did investors in "dot com" companies during the 1990s fail to predict the problems with online retailing?

Supporting questions:
- Who were some of the major online retailers and what did they sell?
- How does online retailing differ from other forms of retailing?
- What gaps existed in the marketing plans for online retailers?
- Could anyone have predicted these gaps?
- Did some online retailers succeed? If so, how did they differ from their competitors?

List supporting questions

Chances are that you can think of questions you'll need to answer before you can fully answer your main question. You may also be able to predict the questions that your audience will ask after reading or hearing your thesis statement. These are your *supporting questions.* The next step in your research is to consult sources of information that answer these questions.

 experiment WITH A STRATEGY FROM THIS CHAPTER

Think of a time when you were assigned to write a research paper and were confused about how to begin. In a short paragraph, describe that assignment in the space below, along with your feelings about it:

Next, review the suggestions in this chapter. Could any of them have helped you overcome confusion or save time during the incident you just described? Choose one suggestion that would have been particularly helpful and summarize it here:

Now think of a research assignment that you'll be doing this term. Could the suggestion you just summarized help you in this upcoming assignment? If so, describe exactly how you intend to use the suggestion. If not, review this chapter for a suggestion that you think *will* help and describe how you intend to use it:

In your calendar, make a note to come back to this exercise at the end of the current term. At that time, evaluate how well the suggestion worked for you and whether you plan to use it in the future:

Research: Using Sources of Information

To **many students,** the word *research* conjures up images of a lonely scholar trapped among stacks of decaying, dusty manuscripts—a hermit who's taking notes on subjects that nobody cares about.

If that's your image, think again. The process of research is more like climbing Mount Everest. You'll make observations, gather facts, trek into unfamiliar intellectual terrain, and ascend from one plateau of insight to another. Keen researchers see facts and relationships. They focus their attention on the details, then discover unifying patterns. Far from being a mere academic exercise, research can evolve into a path of continual discovery.

Just as mountain climbers rely on maps, you'll benefit from a research plan. Before digging into the stacks at the library or mining the Internet for information, know what questions you want to answer. (See Chapter 20 for suggestions about defining these questions.) Also, choose the kind of sources you want to consult and evaluate their quality.

Use General Research Strategies

Consider the variety of materials available at a modern, fully equipped library. There are books, magazines, newspapers, scholarly journals, audiotapes and videotapes, microfilm, CD-ROMs—not to mention billions of Web pages and other Internet resources. When you're hunting for information and ideas to answer a question, how do you possibly choose a place to start?

To begin, reduce this encyclopedic range of materials to a few manageable categories. Start with the distinction between primary and secondary sources.

Find primary sources

Primary sources are often the researcher's dream. These are firsthand materials: personal journals, letters, speeches, government documents, scientific experiments, field observations, interviews with recognized experts, archeological digs, and even original works of art.

Primary sources can also include scholarly articles. These are different from the articles you'll find in popular magazines, such as *Time, Newsweek, Wired,* or *Rolling Stone.* Rather, scholarly articles appear in the *New England Journal of Medicine, Contemporary Literary Criticism,* and similar publications. Signs of scholarly articles include:

- Names of authors with their credentials and academic affiliations.
- Lengthy treatment of carefully defined topics.
- Conclusions based on an extensive review of relevant publications, survey research, data collected in a laboratory experiment, or a combination of these.
- Extensive bibliographies and references to the work of other scholars in the form of footnotes (at the bottom of each page) or endnotes (at the end of the article).

If you pick up a magazine with page after page of full-color advertisements and photos of celebrities, you're not dealing with a scholarly journal. Though any kind of publication is potentially useful as a source, scholarly journals and other primary sources are unmatched in depth and credibility.

Find secondary sources

Secondary sources interpret and explain primary sources. Examples are:

- Magazines, such as the *Atlantic Monthly* and *Scientific American,* that have wide circulation and lengthy and substantial treatment of current issues.
- Nationally circulated newspapers such as the *Washington Post, New York Times,* and *Los Angeles Times.*
- General reference works such as the *Encyclopedia Britannica* and their more specialized counterparts, such as the *Oxford Companion to English Literature.*

Secondary sources are useful places to start your research by getting an overview of your topic. They may even be all you need for informal research. But for many of the research projects you'll undertake in higher education—including major papers, presentations, theses, or manuscripts you want to publish—you'll need primary sources to get the information you want.

Think critically about your sources

Critical thinking starts with the basic intellectual tasks of spotting assumptions, analyzing arguments, examining logic, and assessing the evidence offered for a point of view. (See Chapter 3 for guidelines.) The trick is to balance two attitudes that at first might seem contradictory. On one hand, you can benefit by staying open to new ideas from new sources. On the other, you can avoid getting fooled by holding your sources to high intellectual standards.

You can often evaluate print sources by scrutinizing their *front matter* (preface, publication data, table of contents) and *back matter* (bibliography, glossary, endnotes, index). Also scan any headings, subheadings, and summaries you can find. If you have time, read a chapter.

As you do all this, evaluate the source according to three main criteria:

- **Relevance.** Look for sources that deal directly with your research questions. If you're in doubt about the relevance of a particular source, ask: Will this material help me achieve my purpose and support my thesis?
- **Currency.** Notice the published date of your source material (usually found in the front matter on the copyright page). If your topic is time-sensitive, then set some guidelines about how current you want your sources to be. For example, for a presentation about the advantages of low-carbohydrate diets, you might want to consult only sources published in the past five years. Sources published without a date may not be useful for your purpose.
- **Credibility.** Scan the source for biographical information about the author. Look for education, training, and work experience that qualify this person to publish on the topic. Also notice any possible sources of bias, such as political affiliations or funding sources that might color the author's point of view. For instance, you can predict that a pamphlet on gun control policies that's printed with funding from the National Rifle Association will promote certain points of view. Round out your research with more other sources on the topic.

Find Published Sources

In the early days of the Internet, researchers used to distinguish between sources published in print and sources published online. Today that distinction no longer holds so tightly. Many newspapers and magazines publish Web sites with parallel content. Authors of novels and nonfiction books may even have their own Web sites that include excerpts from their work.

☑ checklist

EVALUATE INTERNET SOURCES

Sources of information on the Internet range from the reputable (such the Library of Congress) to the flamboyant (such as the *National Enquirer*). Taking a few simple precautions when you surf the Internet can keep you from crashing into the rocky shores of misinformation.

☐ *Look for overall quality.* Step back and check out the features of that site in general. Notice the clarity of the text and visuals. Also notice how well the site is organized and whether you can navigate the site's features with ease.

☐ *Consider the source.* Avoid commercial Web sites that promote a single product, service, or point of view; offer "miracle" cures; or rely on personal testimonials as evidence. Look for evidence of bias or special interest. If an organization wants you to buy a service, a product, or a point of view, then determine whether this fact colors the ideas and information posted on the Web site. Noticing the domain in the Uniform Resource Locator (URL) for a Web site can give you significant clues about sources of information and possible bias. For example, distinguish between information from a:

- For-profit enterprise (URL ending in .com)
- Nonprofit organization (URL ending in .org)
- Government agency (.gov)
- School, college, or university (.edu)

☐ *Look for documentation.* When you find an assertion on a Web page or other Internet resource, notice the types and quality of the evidence offered. Look for credible examples, quotes from authorities in the field, documented statistics, or summaries of scientific studies. Also search for endnotes, bibliographies, or another way to find the original sources of information. When reviewing medical, scientific, or technical Web sites, look for a board of qualified experts that reviews the content.

☐ *Consider the date.* Look for the date that crucial information was posted and for notices about when each page was updated. Exercise caution about consulting sites that don't publish dates.

☐ *Test links.* Look for links to pages of reputable organizations. Click a few of those links. If they lead you to dead ends, this might indicate a page that's not updated often—and not a reliable source for late-breaking information.

☐ *Double-check.* Crosscheck information by visiting several sites on the same topic.

In addition, you can print out any Web page. And many Web sites also allow you to download documents published in PDF format—documents that are designed to be printed out.

That being said, you can often benefit from starting your research in the school library. In addition to housing print and audiovisual materials, the library may give you access to online sources, including special databases that are not available on the Web.

Use the library

Your campus library has three basic elements:

- **Catalogs**—online databases that list all of the library's accessible sources.
- **Collections** of sources, such as books, magazines, newspapers, audiovisual materials, and materials available from other collections via interlibrary loans.
- **Computer resources**—Internet access; connections to schoolwide computer networks; and databases stored on CD-ROMs, CDs, or DVDs.

To discover the joy of research, pick one library as your first stop for information. Get to know it well. Start with a library orientation session. Step into each room and ask about what's available there. Find out whether the library houses any special collections and provides access to primary sources that are related to your major.

Ask a librarian

Librarians are trained explorers. They know ways to search out information that's located in countless places. They can also guide your own expedition into the data jungle. Their purpose is to serve you. Ask for help.

Remember that librarians have different specialties. Most libraries have a reference librarian who can usually let you know whether the library has what you need. He may suggest a different library or direct you to another source, such as a business, community agency, or government office.

You can save hours by asking.

Search with key words

Print materials, Internet sources, and other online sources are catalogued in searchable databases. The art of searching them lies mainly in using key words to describe what you want to find.

Key words are those that describe your topic and closely related subtopics. Say that you're writing a critical review of *The Brothers Karamazov* by Fyodor Dostoyevsky. Key words you can use include *Dostoyevsky, Brothers Karamazov*, and the names of individual characters, such as *Ivan Karamazov* and *Dimitri Karamazov*.

There's a simple way to tell whether you're using accurate key words: the number of relevant "hits" (catalog listings) you get when you type in your key words. If you get thousands of hits—including many that are unrelated to your topic—use more specific key words. If you get only a few hits, use more general key words or a different search engine or database.

▶ sidebar

REFERENCE WORKS: PRINT AND ONLINE

Encyclopedias. Leading print and online encyclopedias include *Encyclopaedia Britannica* (http://www.eb.com) and *Columbia Encyclopedia* (http://www.bartleby.com). Specialized encyclopedias cover many fields and include, for example, *Encyclopedia of Psychology, Encyclopedia of the Biological Sciences, Encyclopedia of Asian History,* and *McGraw-Hill Encyclopedia of Science and Technology.*

Biographies. Read accounts of people's lives in biographical works such as *Who's Who, Dictionary of American Biography, Biography Index: A Cumulative Index to Biographic Material in Books and Magazines, Contemporary Authors, Dictionary of Literary Biography, African American Biographies, Chicano Scholars and Writers, Lives of the Painters,* and *American Men and Women of Science.*

Critical works. Read what scholars have to say about works of art and literature in *Oxford Companion* volumes (such as *Oxford Companion to Art* and *Oxford Companion to African American Literature*).

Statistics and government documents. Among many useful sources are *Statistical Abstract of the United States, Current Index to Statistics, Handbook of Labor Statistics, Occupational Outlook Handbook,* U.S. Census publications (print and online), and *Digest of Educational Statistics.*

Almanacs, atlases, and gazetteers. For population statistics and boundary changes, see *The World Almanac, Countries of the World,* or *Information Please.* For locations, descriptions, pronunciation of place names, climate, demography, languages, natural resources, and industry, consult *Columbia-Lippincott Gazetteer of the World* and the CIA *World Factbook,* both of which are available in print and online.

Dictionaries. For etymologies, definitions, and spelling, consult *American Heritage Dictionary of the English Language,* 4th edition (one volume), *Oxford English Dictionary* (multiple volumes; useful for detailed etymologies and usage discussions and examples), *Facts on File* specialized dictionaries, and other specialized dictionaries, such as *Dictionary of Literary Terms* and *Dictionary of the Social Sciences.*

Indexes and databases. Databases of articles appearing in periodicals make searching for an article on a specific topic easy. Databases contain publication information and an abstract and sometimes the full text of the article, available for downloading or printing right from your computer. Your library houses print and CD-ROM databases and subscribes to some online databases; others are accessible through online library catalogs or Web links.

Reference works in specific subject areas. These cover a vast range. Examples include the *Oxford Companion to Art, Encyclopedia of the Biological Sciences,* and *Concise Oxford Companion to Classical Literature.* Ask a librarian for more.

Books in print and alternatives. If you want to find a book or to check on bibliographical details, use Books in Print (available in print and online). If your library does not subscribe to the online version, you can use the Amazon.com site (http://www.amazon.com) or any other large commercial online bookseller to look up the details of a book—at no charge.

Periodical articles. Find articles in periodicals (works issued periodically, such as scholarly journals, magazines, and newspapers) by using a periodical index. Use electronic indexes for recent works, print indexes for earlier works—especially for works written before 1980. Check which services your library subscribes to and the dates the indexes cover. Indexes may provide abstracts; some, such as Lexis-Nexis Academic Universe, Infotrac, OCLC FirstSearch, and New York Times Ondisc, provide the full text of articles.

Online library catalogs and home pages of libraries and universities. The Web gives you access to the online resources of many libraries (actual and virtual) and universities, which are good browsing sites. Some useful sites are:
Library of Congress–(http://lcweb.loc.gov);
Smithsonian Institution Libraries–(http://www.sil.si.edu/newstart.htm);
and the New York Public Library–(http://www.nypl.org/index.html).

Search tools on the Web. If you do not know the exact Web site you want, you need to search for the information you need. Try a search engine such as
Excite (http://www.excite.com),
AltaVista (http://www.altavista.com),
WebCrawler (http://www.webcrawler.com),
MetaCrawler (http://www.metacrawler.com),
Google (http://www.google.com),
Yahoo! (http://www.yahoo.com), or
Ask Jeeves! (http://www.ask.com).

Virtual libraries. Internet Public Library (http://www.ipl.org); WWW Virtual Library (http://vlib.org).

For better searches with key words, also experiment with these techniques:

- **Use Boolean terms.** These include the words *AND, NOT,* and *OR.* Use *AND* when you want to find sources that deal with more than one topic (*crime fiction AND Dostoyevsky*). Use *OR* when you're looking for sources that discuss either topic, though not necessarily both (*crime fiction OR Dostoyevsky*). Insert *NOT* in front of a key word for topics that are irrelevant to your research (*crime fiction NOT Dostoyevsky*). Ask a librarian about ways to use other Boolean terms.
- **Try different spellings.** Names for some people and places have several accepted spellings, especially when translated into several languages. For instance, *Dostoyevsky* might also be spelled *Dostoevsky* or *Dostoevski.*

- **Look for a link to advanced search techniques.** Many search engines include their own instructions for using key words.
- **Use your first search results to initiate another search.** Consult some of the sources produced from your first search. Check their tables of contents, glossaries, and indexes for new key words that are relevant to your topic. Also, copy the title of a book, article, or Web site and paste it into a search engine. You may get a whole new list of relevant hits.
- **Contact authors via e-mail.** Authors may include their e-mail address in a book or Web site. Doing so means that it's probably OK for you to contact them. In the process, you may uncover materials unknown to anyone else.

▷ **sidebar**

DIG INTO THE INVISIBLE WEB

As you use the Web for research, remember that some pages may elude conventional search engines. Examples are pages that are searchable only *within* a particular Web site—for example, databases that you can access exclusively from the U.S. Census Bureau site. A popular name for this group of "hidden" pages is the *invisible Web.*

Over time, the size of the invisible Web will shrink as more sophisticated search engines appear. For now, experiment with these:

Academic Info: www.academicinfo.net/index.html
Best Information on the Net:
  http://library.sau.edu/bestinfo/
CompletePlanet: www.completeplanet.com/
Direct Search: www.freepint.com/gary/direct.htm
Infomine: http://infomine.ucr.edu/
Internets: www.internets.com/
Invisible-Web.net: www.invisible-web.net/
The Invisible Web: www.invisibleweb.com/
Librarians' Index to the Internet: http://ipl.org/
Scout Report Archives:
  http://scout.wisc.edu/archives/
Searchability: www.searchability.com/

Turn to People as Sources

Making direct contact with people as you complete your research can offer a welcome relief from hours of solitary library time. Here's your chance to conduct interviews—to pose questions to a real human being rather than a lifeless search engine.

Interview experts on your topic

Your research will uncover the names of experts on your chosen topic. Consider doing an interview with one of these people—in person, over the phone, or via e-mail. To get the most from interviews:

- Schedule a specific time for the interview and a specific place, if you're meeting the expert in person.
- Agree on the length of the interview in advance.
- Enter the interview with a short list of questions to ask.
- Allow time for additional questions that occur to you during the interview.
- If you want to tape-record the interview, ask for permission in advance.
- When working with people who don't want to be taped, be prepared to take handwritten notes.
- Ask experts for permission to quote their comments.
- Follow up on interviews with a thank-you note.

Capture your own ideas

Don't forget one of the most important people to consult: yourself. As you gather and digest the ideas of others, you'll come to conclusions of your own. This is the ultimate goal of the research process. Capture your insights in writing, treating them as notes and citing yourself as the source.

Take Notes on Your Sources

The traditional method of research is to take notes on index cards, with one idea, fact, or quotation per card, along with bibliographic information about the source of that note. (See *Checklist: Create a Working Bibliography*). The advantage of limiting each card to one item of information is that you can easily arrange them according to the sequence of your outline and rearrange them to reflect ongoing changes in your outline.

Taking notes on a computer—using word processing or database software—offers the same flexibility as index cards. In addition, you can take advantage of software features that help you create tables of contents, indexes, graphics, and other elements of your final project.

☑ checklist

CREATE A WORKING BIBLIOGRAPHY

Before you begin taking notes, plan to record certain key information about each source you consult. You'll need this information later in the writing process as you create a formal list of your sources—especially sources of quotes or paraphrased material that are included in the body of your paper or presentation. By keeping track of your sources as you conduct research, you create a working bibliography.

Following are checklists of the information to record about various types of sources. Whenever possible, print out or make photocopies of each source. For books, include a copy of the title page and copyright page, both found in the front matter. For magazines and scholarly journals, copy the table of contents.

For each *book* you consult, record the:
❒ Author
❒ Editor (if listed)
❒ Translator (if listed)
❒ Edition number (if listed)
❒ Full title, including subtitle
❒ Name and location of publisher
❒ Copyright date
❒ Page numbers for passages that you quote, summarize, or paraphrase

For each *article* you consult, record the:
❒ Author
❒ Editor (if listed)
❒ Translator (if listed)
❒ Full title, including subtitle
❒ Name of periodical
❒ Volume number

Choose when to summarize your source

For some of your notes, you may simply want to summarize your source in a few sentences or paragraphs. To do this effectively:

- Read your source several times for understanding.
- Put your source away; then write a summary in your own words.
- In your summary, include only the author's major points.
- Check your summary against your source for accuracy.
- Along with your summary, list the bibliographic information for your source.
- Cite the source that you summarized. (See the Appendices, starting on page 324.)

❐ Issue number
❐ Issue date
❐ Page numbers for passages that you quote, summarize, or paraphrase

For each *computer-based source* you consult (CD-ROMs and Internet documents), record the:
❐ Author
❐ Editor (if listed)
❐ Translator (if listed)
❐ Full title of the page or article, including subtitle
❐ Name of the organization that posted the site or published the CD-ROM
❐ Dates on which the page or other document was published and revised
❐ Date you accessed the source
❐ URL for Web pages (the uniform resource locator, or Web site address, often starting with http//)
❐ Version number (for CD-ROMs)
❐ Volume, issue number, and date for online journals
Note: Computer-based sources may not list all of the preceding information. For Web pages, at a minimum, record the date you accessed the source and the URL.

For each *interview* you conduct, record the:
❐ Name of the person you interviewed
❐ Professional title of the person you interviewed
❐ Contact information for the person you interviewed: mailing address, phone number, e-mail address
❐ Date of the interview

Choose when to paraphrase your source

At times, you may want to take notes that are more detailed than a summary but less lengthy than an exact quotation from your source. In that case, paraphrase your source:

- Read your source several times for understanding.
- Include the author's major points, along with key supporting facts or examples.
- Put your source away; then write the paraphrase in your own words.
- Check your paraphrase against your source for accuracy.

examples

PARAPHRASE WITH SKILL

The art of paraphrasing is to use your own words and sentence structure while capturing another person's ideas. This calls for more than simply changing a few words in the original source material. Consider the following examples.

Original passage
Higher education offers you the chance to learn how to learn. In fact, that's the subject of this book. Employers value the person who is a "quick study" when it comes to learning a new job. That makes your ability to learn a marketable skill.

Ineffective paraphrase
With a college education comes the chance to learn how to learn. Employers want the person who is a "quick study" in a new job. Your ability to learn is a marketable skill.

Effective paraphrase
When we learn how to learn, we gain a skill that is valued by employers.

- Along with your paraphrase, list the bibliographic information for your source.
- Cite the source that you summarized. (See the Appendices, starting on page 324.)

Choose when to quote your source

When an author makes a point in a forceful or memorable way, you may want to use that person's exact words in your notes. When taking a direct quote from one of your sources:

- Verify that you've used the wording exactly as it appeared in the original source.
- Place the quoted material within quotation marks.
- Along with your quote, list the bibliographic information for your source.
- Cite the source that you summarized. (See the Appendices, starting on page 324.)

One option for taking notes on computer-based sources (CD-ROMs, Web pages, and other Internet documents) is to simply copy and paste text from the source into a word processing file on your computer. This can be an efficient way to take notes and an easy way to inadvertently commit plagiarism. To prevent this problem, change any downloaded text to a distinct font, one that's different from the font you will use in your paper. Then choose whether to summarize, paraphrase, or quote this material.

sidebar

AVOID PLAGIARISM

Using another person's words or images without giving proper credit is called *plagiarism*. This is a real concern for anyone who researches and writes, including students. Plagiarism can have big-time consequences, ranging from a failing grade to expulsion from school.

If your paper includes a passage, identifiable phrase, or visual image created by another person, acknowledge this fact. Do the same for any idea that is closely identified with a particular person:

- Put any passage or phrase that you take word for word within quotation marks; cite the source in a footnote or endnote.
- When you summarize or paraphrase ideas from a source, also cite the source.
- When you use the same sequence of ideas as one of your sources—even if you haven't summarized, paraphrased, or quoted—cite that source.
- Submit only your original work, not materials that have been written or revised by someone else.

Note: You do not have to cite sources for statements that represent general knowledge—for example, the dates of well-known historical events.

For guidelines about how to cite your sources in a research paper, see the Appendices starting on p. 324.

Digest your notes

Schedule time to review all the information and ideas that your research has produced. If you view research as a task that you can squeeze into a few hours, then you may end up more confused than enlightened. But when you allow for time to reread and reflect on the facts you gather, you create the conditions for genuine understanding.

In particular, take the time to:

- Read over all your notes without feeling immediate pressure to write.
- Summarize major points of view on your topic, noting points of agreement and disagreement.
- Look for connections in your material—ideas, facts, and examples that occur in several sources.
- Note direct answers to your main and supporting research questions (see Chapter 20).
- Revise your thesis statement, based on discoveries from your research.
- Put all your notes away and write informally about what you want to say about your topic.
- Look for connections between your research and your life—ideas that you can verify based on personal experience.

experiment WITH A STRATEGY FROM THIS CHAPTER

Based on your past experiences with writing papers and preparing presentations, brainstorm a list of the feelings you associate with the word *research*. Examples might range from *stress* or *confusion* to *fun* or *discovery*. Write your list in the space below:

If your feelings about research projects were mainly positive, then you were probably using some of the techniques described in this chapter, or other techniques that were equally effective. Describe any that worked particularly well for you:

If you listed any negative feelings about research, then reflect on the source of those feelings. What one suggestion from this chapter could you use to create a new, more positive experience of research?

Finally, describe how you will use this suggestion in an upcoming assignment. After completing the assignment, use the space below to describe how well it worked for you, and whether you intend to use it again.

Preparing to Write

Writing is not a matter of first *knowing* what you think and then transcribing it on paper. Rather, writing is a process of *discovering* what you want to say. This calls for experimenting, exploring, and following some leads while rejecting others.

Most teachers of writing talk about three stages in this process of discovery:

- **Prewriting** includes all the preparation that precedes the first draft: choosing and defining a topic, reflecting on your purpose, creating a thesis statement, researching, and outlining. (For more on prewriting tasks, see Chapters 20 and 21.)
- **Writing:** producing a complete first draft of your paper or presentation.
- **Revising,** which can range from a quick proofreading for grammar and punctuation to a complete overhaul of your paper and perhaps several more drafts.

Even though most descriptions of writing present the process as a series of steps, remember that writing is also highly personal. You might go through the steps in a different order or find yourself working on several at once.

Plan the Project

Create a file on your computer for planning each writing project. In this file, list the due date for your paper. Then generate a list of all the steps you'll take to meet that goal. Use the numbering feature in your word processing program to arrange these steps in order, set a due date for each step, and enter these dates in your calendar.

To set up a meaningful schedule, get the details of your assignment, including:

- Length
- Number of sources required
- Types of sources required
- Format for title page, footnotes or endnotes, bibliography, and other key aspects of the manuscript
- Final due date and due dates for any interim documents, such as an outline or first draft

☑ checklist

SET UP A WRITING SCHEDULE

You can break your goal—a finished paper or polished presentation—into smaller steps that you can tackle right away. To create a writing schedule, simply list these steps and determine how long you will take to complete each one.

As you plan, be generous with time. Take your initial estimate of the number of hours or days your writing project will take, and then double it. If you finish a step early, you'll find plenty of uses for the extra time.

Common steps in the writing process are listed here. Add other steps as needed to fit the requirements of your assignment. Then set a date to complete each step.

Prewriting
- ❒ Define your topic
- ❒ Consider your purpose
- ❒ Do initial research
- ❒ Create a thesis statement
- ❒ List questions to answer
- ❒ Do in-depth research
- ❒ Outline your paper or presentation

Writing
- ❒ Complete the first draft

Revising
- ❒ Complete the second draft
- ❒ Complete the third draft
- ❒ Proofread
- ❒ Prepare the final manuscript

A rough but useful guideline is to allow 50 percent of your total project time for prewriting and writing the first draft. Devote the remaining 50 percent to revising.

Whenever possible, also allow for breaks between each step. By taking minivacations from your project, you'll come back to writing with renewed energy and a fresh store of ideas.

Create an Outline

An outline is a map of all the prewriting steps you've taken: defining your purpose, choosing a topic, writing a thesis, and researching. (For more details on these steps, see Chapters 20 and 21.) When you follow a map, you avoid getting lost. Likewise, an outline keeps you from wandering off your topic.

Outlining can keep you focused and save you hours of writing time. Problems with organization and content are much easier to fix in a 1-page outline than in a 10-page paper.

Many of the guidelines for taking notes in outline form (see Chapter 14) also apply to outlining your writing. Some additional suggestions follow.

Start with a basic organizing pattern

Your research may yield long lists of facts, examples, quotations, and other material that you can use to support your thesis and accomplish your purpose for writing. Outlining gives you a chance to assemble all this material up front—before you write a first draft—and organize it in a manner that will make sense to your audience.

The most basic organizing pattern is a three-part structure: introduction, body, and conclusion. In the introduction, you grab your audience's attention, present your thesis, and preview the content of your paper or presentation. In the body, you state your key points and support each one. Finally, in the conclusion, you summarize your points, explain their significance, and call your audience to take any appropriate action.

Of these three sections, the body is the longest and often the greatest challenge. To stay organized, you can:

- **Tell a story.** Many novels, plays, and short stories are organized chronologically: The authors narrate incidents in the order in which they occur. You can use this organizing pattern even when writing fact-based, nonfiction material—especially when you describe a series of historical events.
- **Create a map in the audience's mind.** Describe the main features of an object, the main geographical locations relevant to your subject matter, or the arrangement of any elements in space. You use this organizing pattern every time that someone asks you for driving directions. The same basic pattern works even with more sophisticated subject matter.
- **Provide a numbered list.** Much instructional and technical writing, from cookbooks to computer manuals, presents steps that are performed in a certain order to complete a procedure or produce

a result. You may find this organizing pattern useful for all or part of your paper or presentation.

- ***Present your major points one by one, in logical order.*** This pattern of organization is basically a list without numbers. In your outline, include your thesis statement, followed by your strongest supporting point, your next strongest point, and so on. Expand each point with facts, quotations, and examples.
- ***Define your terms.*** Sometimes you can develop large sections of a paper or presentation simply by defining your key terms in a logical order. For tips on writing effective definitions, see the sidebar *Types of Definitions* in Chapter 3.
- ***Create a continuum.*** Say that you're writing a paper on job possibilities for students who major in English. You could present those careers on continuum, beginning with those that pay the least to those that pay the most. Or you could list jobs ranging from those with the most projected openings in the next five years to those with the fewest projected openings. This is another kind of continuum.

▶ sidebar

CREATING AN INVITING INTRODUCTION

As you outline, give careful thought to the introduction to your paper or presentation. Think of the introduction as a kind of transition. The members of your audience are leading busy lives, filled with many objects of attention. Your introduction helps them make the transition from their many concerns to your specific topic.

Grabbing your audience's attention with a "hook" is one way to help them make this transition. A hook is any statement that generates interest, often by delivering a surprise. You can do this by providing:

- A provocative point of view: *One of the most effective ways to care for other people is to be totally selfish.*
- An interesting anecdote: *One of the world's great novelists was a woman who took a man's name: George Eliot.*
- Intriguing questions: *What if you could cut your living expenses in half and enjoy your life even more?*
- Memorable quotations: *Eleanor Roosevelt once said, "No one can make you feel inferior without your consent."*
- Startling statistics: *Nearly forty million people in the United States—many of them children and vulnerable older adults—have no health insurance.*

Note: You might want to write your introduction last, even though this section comes first. One function of the introduction is to preview the body of your paper or presentation. This can be far easier to do when you've already written the body.

- **Organize alphabetically.** This pattern is simple, obvious, and often effective. In certain parts of longer writing projects, such as a book index or glossary, alphabetical organization is virtually a must.

Do an informal outline

An informal outline represents your first attempt to organize your material. This is a prelude to a more formal outline that you prepare later.

Informal, or *scratch*, outlines are often short and done quickly, sometimes literally on scratch paper. One option for creating this type of outline is to use index cards:

- **Gather a stack of index cards and brainstorm.** List topics that you want to include in your paper or presentation. Capture each topic in one word or phrase per card.
- **Group the cards into separate stacks.** Base your stacks on the organizing patterns described previously.
- **Refine the stacks.** Arrange the stacks in a logical order. Next, arrange the cards within each stack in a logical order. Keep rearranging cards until you discover an organization you like.

If you prefer to outline on a computer, explore the outlining feature of your word processing program. This feature allows you to format various levels of headings and rearrange them on the screen in much the same way you'd shuffle index cards.

Draft a formal outline

If you know your topic well, you might be able to draft your paper from an informal outline, especially if the paper is short and the

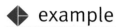 **example**

SCRATCH OUTLINE

Working Title:
The Atkins Diet: Weighing the Pros and Cons

Thesis:
Though the Atkins diet promotes short-term weight loss, the long-term health effects of this diet are still unknown.

Outline:
  I. Intro: Personal testimony from someone on the Atkins diet
 II. Main features of diet
     A. Problem: Carbohydrates and weight gain
     B. Solution: Restricting carbohydrates
III. The program
     A. Induction
     B. Ongoing weight loss
     C. Premaintenance
     D. Lifetime maintenance
IV. Arguments for Atkins diet
     A. Testimonial evidence
     B. Research evidence
 V. Arguments against Atkins diet
     A. Flaws of testimonials
     B. Differences between carbohydrates
     C. Gaps in research
VI. Conclusion: Deciding what works for now
     A. Waiting for more research
     B. Getting a doctor's guidance

◆ example

USE A THESIS STATEMENT TO CREATE A FORMAL OUTLINE

Besides using a thesis statement to clarify the main point you want to make about your topic, you can use this statement as a springboard for creating a formal outline.

To do this, revise your thesis statement so that it indicates the major parts of your paper or presentation. Then summarize each part in a complete sentence. Each of these sentences can become a heading in your outline–and, eventually, the topic sentence of a full paragraph.

Following is an example of this process.

Original thesis statement:
Though the Atkins diet promotes short-term weight loss, the long-term health effects of this diet are still unknown.

Revised thesis statement:
Though the Atkins diet promotes short-term weight loss, the evidence for this diet has three serious flaws: reliance on testimonials, incomplete research, and the possibility of disease.

Formal outline:
I. The Atkins diet promotes short-term weight loss.
   A. Lack of carbohydrates in the diet forces the body to burn fat.
   B. Burning off fat promotes rapid and early weight loss.
II. However, evidence for the Atkins diet has three serious flaws.
   A. It relies heavily on personal testimonials, which are unreliable.
   B. Existing studies examine only short-term effects.
   C. High amounts of fat in the diet may promote heart disease.

topic is straightforward. But if you're writing a longer paper on a more complex topic, then consider converting your informal outline into a formal outline—one that consists of complete sentences.

When you use complete sentences as headings in your outline, you gain clarity. A heading such as "Carbohydrates and weight gain" is a phrase that indicates a point you'd like to make. "A high-carbohydrate diet promotes weight gain" is a sentence that actually makes your point.

After you write a formal outline, test it. Make sure that each word in your outline relates directly to your thesis and purpose. If possible, put your outline away for a day or two and return to it with fresh eyes.

Choose whether to state your thesis and where

Your teachers may have specific requirements about where to place a thesis statement in your paper. If not, then you have two creative choices to make: where to place your thesis statement and whether to include it at all.

Including a thesis statement in the introduction of a term paper or other nonfiction piece can help your reader find your key message right away. Even so, this is not always the optimum placement. At times you may find it more effective to place your thesis in the middle or at the end of your paper. Instead of beginning with your thesis, you can offer a series of examples and facts that imply, support, and build up to it. Then, when you *do* state your thesis, the effect can be dramatic.

Delaying a thesis statement can be an effective choice when members of your audience are opposed to your point of view. Rather than starting off with a statement that generates resistance, you can carefully build your case before asking people to accept your opinion.

Notice that much published writing—especially short stories, poetry, novels, and plays—does not include a thesis statement. Each is a form of fiction in which authors narrate a series of events. Fiction communicates not by *telling* you what to think but by *showing* you what a character thinks, feels, and does. You learn from fiction as you learn from life: by reflecting on concrete experience rather than on terms, assertions, logic, and evidence.

Plan for collaborative writing

Writing is usually seen as a solitary, even tortured process. Yet it doesn't have to be that way. In the work world, writing projects are often collaborative ventures done by teams.

Collaborative writing can be energizing and rewarding, or it can be a draining source of perpetual conflict. The difference lies in the way you structure the writing process. Keep these suggestions in mind:

- **Find tasks that can be done by a group.** Many prewriting tasks can be completed in meetings. Examples are brainstorming topics, drafting thesis statements, and creating informal outlines. Groups can also meet to provide editorial direction, such as guidelines for revising a draft.

- **Assign other tasks for individuals to complete between meetings.** Researching, writing drafts, creating graphics, and revising drafts are usually most appropriate for individuals to complete. You may want to assign these tasks to people with learning styles based on reflective observation and abstract conceptualization (see Chapter 2).

- **Use technology to promote collaboration.** Team members can send outlines and drafts as attachments to e-mail messages. In addition, the entire team can meet to edit drafts in outline mode—a format for viewing documents that shows only headings and sub-headings of a document. In Microsoft Word, the most popular word processor, you can also take advantage of the Track Changes feature—a way for individual reviewers to suggest detailed revisions and record them in a draft. Writers can later review these suggestions and accept or reject them.

experiment WITH A STRATEGY FROM THIS CHAPTER

Recall a writing assignment you were asked to complete this term. In the space below, write a short paragraph describing the major steps you took leading up to your first draft. Examples might include choosing a topic, writing a thesis statement, doing research, and creating an outline:

Evaluate the process you used to complete the writing, listing anything you would like to do differently with your next writing project. For instance, you might want to avoid a last-minute deadline crunch or to use your research time more effectively:

Now review this chapter for any strategies that can help you gain your desired outcomes. List one strategy here and describe how you intend to use it:

Writing a Draft

I f you've completed the prewriting steps explained in Chapters 20 through 22, then much of the hard work involved in creating a paper or presentation is behind you. Now you can relax into writing your first draft.

Reduce Resistance to Writing

Writing a first draft is a kind of performance art. As with other art forms, you develop skill by practice.

One way to ease any difficulty associated with producing a first draft is to practice writing, even when you're not assigned to do so. The following suggestions offer ways to start.

Use free writing

According to Natalie Goldberg, teacher and author of *Writing Down the Bones*, there are only two rules in free writing: Keep your hands moving, and don't think. In other words, write without stopping.

For optimum results, begin your free-writing session by picking any topic that interests you and setting a timer—say, for 10 minutes. Then keep your pencil or pen in motion across paper until the timer goes off. Write anything that pops into your head. Put yourself on automatic pilot until the words start happening on their own.

The trick is to give yourself permission to keep writing—even if you don't think your work is very good, even if you want to stop and rewrite. It's OK if you stray from your initial topic. Just keep writing and let the ideas flow.

Free writing can help you draft a lot of material in a relatively short time. That material will be rough, and you may end up using only a small part of it. Even so, this technique can prevent the writing problem that many students find most difficult: getting started.

Bring variety to your writing experience

Some people find it works well to forget the word *writing*. Instead, they ease into the task with activities that help generate ideas. You can free

☑ checklist

USE A COMPUTER FOR FREE WRITING

A computer can be especially useful for free writing. Experiment with the following steps:

❐ *Review your prewriting material.* This can include your topic, thesis statement, purpose, outline, and notes.

❐ *Set a time limit for the free-writing session.* Experiment to find an optimum length of time for free writing on a computer. Allow enough time so that you fill up at least a page, but not so much time that you run out of steam. If you stop free writing while you still have some intellectual energy left, that primes the pump for your next free-writing session.

❐ *Start typing and keep your fingers moving.* Dim the computer screen while you free write. That way you resist the temptation to stop writing, reread, and fiddle with words.

❐ *Repeat the process.* Take a break, set another time limit, and write again. In a single hour, you can do several sessions of free writing.

❐ *Save your work and make backup copies.* The beauty of free writing on a computer is that you build a body of material on disk. This is material that you can revise and perhaps even paste into assigned papers and presentations.

associate, meditate, daydream, doodle, draw diagrams, visualize the event you want to describe, talk into a tape recorder, babble about your topic to a friend—anything that gets you started.

Techniques such as these work because part of the writing process takes place outside our awareness. Many creative people report that ideas come to them while they're doing something totally unrelated to writing. It's like the composer who said, "There I was, sitting and eating a sandwich, and all of a sudden this darn tune pops into my head." Once you immerse yourself in a topic, you can trust your deep mind. It's writing while you eat, sleep, and brush your teeth.

Other ways to bring variety to your writing are to:

- Write with many tools—on various types of paper, using different kinds of pens or a computer.
- Write in many places—your home, the library, coffee shops, restaurants, and outdoors.
- Write often for short time periods.
- Write informally in a personal journal; use journal entries as seeds for assigned papers and presentations.

Get physical

Writing is physical, like jogging or playing tennis. You can move your body in ways that match the flow of your ideas. While working on the first draft, take breaks. Go for a walk or run. Speak or sing your ideas out

▶ sidebar

USE TECHNIQUES TO OVERCOME WRITER'S BLOCK

- *Write letters.* Instead of writing a draft, write a letter or e-mail message *about* your draft. Describe what your writing project is about and, in general, what you want to say. You can send this message to someone, keep it to yourself, or even trash it; whatever seems most appropriate. The only purpose of your letter is to get unblocked and unleash ideas for your draft.
- *Speak, then write.* Communicate with a friend or family member about your draft as described in the previous suggestion. Instead of writing, however, *talk* about what you intend to write. Encoding your message in speech instead of text activates a different part of your brain—a way to stimulate creativity. Consider asking a friend to take notes as you speak, or run a recorder and transcribe what you're saying.
- *Prime the pump.* End each day's writing session when you're in the middle of a sentence. This lack of closure can induce a sense of creative tension. On a subconscious level, your mind can keep searching for ways to finish that sentence. By the time you begin writing the next day, you'll have a place to start.
- *Go back to prewriting.* Sometimes a problem is diagnosed as writer's block when it's actually lack of preparation. If you sit down to create a first draft and repeatedly draw a blank, go back to a prewriting task. Toying with your outline or rereading your notes may get your creative juices flowing.

loud. From time to time, take a pause to close your eyes, release muscle tension, and breathe deeply.

Write regularly

Inspiration is not part of the working vocabulary for many professional writers. Instead of waiting for inspiration to strike, they simply make a habit of writing at a certain time each day.

You can use the same strategy. Schedule regular blocks of time each week to write. The very act of writing can breed inspiration.

Finish the First Draft Quickly

To create your first draft, just gather your notes, arranged to follow your outline. Now, write about the ideas in your notes. Write in paragraphs, one idea per paragraph. If you have organized your notes logically, related ideas and facts will appear close to each other.

If you created a formal sentence outline (as explained in Chapter 22), you already have the basic structure of your draft in place. Now build on that structure: Expand each sentence in your outline into a full paragraph.

Write a draft before checking your notes

Another option is to write a first draft without referring back to your notes and outline. If you've immersed yourself in the topic, chances are that much of the information is already bubbling up near the surface of your mind anyway. Later, when you edit, you can go back to your notes and correct any errors in what you remembered from your research.

Write sections in any order

Keep in mind that there's no obligation to write straight through, following your outline from the beginning to the end. Some professional writers prefer to write the last chapter of a novel or the last scene of a play first. With the ending firmly in mind, they can guide the reader through all the incidents that lead to it.

You may feel more comfortable with certain aspects of your topic than with others. Dive in where you feel most comfortable.

Write in your own voice

As you write your first draft, let go of the urge to sound "official" or "scholarly." Visualize a member of your audience and express the most important things you'd say to her about the topic. This helps you avoid the temptation to write merely to impress. Write the way you speak.

The other side of this coin is that we can't really write the way we speak. The spoken word is accompanied by facial expressions and gestures, as well as changes in voice tone, pitch, and volume. Slang expressions and incomplete sentences used in everyday speech are not appropriate in academic writing. Rather, the key message behind the advice to "write the way you speak" is to express yourself directly and honestly, without hiding behind a facade.

Remember that you can revise later

Many writers prefer to get their first drafts down quickly. Their advice is to just keep writing until you finish the entire draft, or least a large section of it. You can pause occasionally to glance at your notes and outline. But avoid stopping to edit your work. You will revise this rough draft several times, so don't worry if the first draft seems rough or choppy.

In particular, let go of grammar, punctuation, and spelling. You can fix those things later, as you revise. To begin, write as if you were explaining your topic to a friend. Let the words flow. The very act of writing can release creative energy.

It's perfectly all right to crank out a draft that you will later heavily rewrite or even throw away. The purpose of a first draft is simply to generate lots of material to give you something you can work with—that's all. For most of us, that's far better than facing a blank page.

Save your drafts

Preserve your first draft and later drafts of each paper or presentation. Save each draft in a separate word processing file, make backup copies, and periodically print out hard copies, as well. In addition, keep an archive of passages that you cut from each draft.

Saving all this material offers two benefits. First, while writing a second or third draft, you may want to restore passages from your first draft. When you have backup copies, you can do that.

Second, you might be able to use material from earlier writing projects in future assignments. Professional writers know the value of recycling earlier material, when appropriate. Though you may need to revise previously written material, you can save time by having it on hand rather than creating it from scratch.

Respect writer's "high"

There may be times during a first draft that you feel ideas come without stopping. It may feel as if the ideas are just flowing through you, circulating from head to hand without conscious effort on your part. This is a natural "high" similar to states that accomplished athletes, musicians, and artists have reported.

Such moments can happen after you've been grappling with a passage, have reached a point at which you feel stuck, and feel ready to give up. Welcome getting stuck, and don't give up. A breakthrough may not be far behind.

Get Some Distance From Your Draft

When your first draft is finished, put it away for at least several hours—several days, if you can afford the time. Then, reread your draft straight through with fresh eyes and without editing. Put yourself in the place of your teacher or another potential reader of your paper and imagine how you might react to the draft.

The key suggestion here is to let yourself get some distance in time and space from your first draft. Time brings useful perspective. On Tuesday night, you might think your writing sings the song of beautiful language. On Wednesday, you will see that some words, like the phrase "sings the song of beautiful language," belong in the trash.

Plan to revise a paper or presentation two or three times. Make a clean copy of those revisions, and then let the last revised draft sit on a shelf for a few days. Your brain needs that time to disengage itself from the project and rest. Grammatical mistakes, awkward constructions, and lapses in logic will become apparent only if you can reread your draft with fresh eyes. Before you begin the process of revising your draft—a process described in the next chapter—give yourself time to step back.

experiment WITH A STRATEGY FROM THIS CHAPTER

Describe exactly what happens when you start to write. What thoughts or images run through your mind? Do you feel any tension or discomfort in your body? Where? Let the thoughts and images come to the surface without resistance. Complete the following statement:

When I begin to write, I. . . .

Next, review the suggestions given in this chapter for one that could dramatically affect your experience of creating a first draft. Describe that suggestion here, including how you intend to use it for your next writing assignment:

I intend to. . . .

After using this suggestion, reflect on how well it worked for you. If it did work well, consider making it a regular part of your writing routine. However, if you can think of another technique that would work better, describe that technique by completing the following sentence:

I intend to. . . .

Revising Your Draft

One definition of a writer is simply anyone who rewrites. People who write for a living might rewrite a piece seven, eight, or even more times. Ernest Hemingway rewrote the last page of *A Farewell to Arms* 39 times before he was satisfied with it. When asked what the most difficult part of this process was, he said, "Getting the words right."

People who rewrite care. They care about the reader. They care about precise language and careful thinking. In addition, people who rewrite care about themselves. They know that the act of rewriting teaches them more about the topic than almost any other step in the creative process.

There's a difference in pace between writing a first draft and revising it. Keep in mind the saying "Write in haste, revise at leisure." When you edit and revise, slow down and take a microscope to your work.

Get Feedback About Your Writing

Ultimately you are responsible for revising your writing. No one else can really enter your mind and heart to do the job for you. However, revision does not have to be a lonely process. You can get valuable feedback from independent, objective readers.

Before you start revising, consider sharing your first draft with a few people and asking them for feedback. Ask teachers, classmates, or other members of your target audience to review your draft. Look for people who are tactful *and* frank enough to tell you what they really think.

This takes courage, but the results are often worth it. By the time you finish a draft, you'll be so immersed in your writing project that you can easily forget how newcomers to your topic will respond. You might take certain connections between ideas for granted—connections that may not be obvious to your audience. Getting feedback can help you fill in the gaps.

▶ # sidebar

ASKING FOR FEEDBACK ON YOUR WRITING

When showing a draft to reviewers, you can request feedback in a variety of ways. For example,
ask them to:

- State your thesis in their own words.
- Tell you how well you supported your thesis with
  logic and evidence.
- Place a checkmark or question mark in the margin next to passages that "stopped" them while
  reading—paragraphs that seemed out of order
  or sentences that seemed unclear.
- Circle passages that they found especially vivid
  or interesting.
- Circle passages that they found repetitive, unnecessary, or uninteresting.
- Suggest possible topics, points, or details to add.
- List specific questions.
- Offer at least one suggestion for improving your
  paper.

Look for two types of feedback

To get the most value from feedback on your writing, separate it
into two broad categories.

The first is macroscopic, or "big
picture," feedback. At this level, you
consider the overall scope and
structure of your paper. Find out
if your thesis statement is clear to
readers and convincingly sup-
ported by evidence. Also discover
how readers respond to the organization of your paper—whether the
major sections seem to follow a
logical sequence and whether transitions between sections seem clear.

The second category deals with
microscopic, or "little picture,"
concerns. These are revisions to
make at the level of individual
sentences and words—corrections
to spelling, punctuation, and
grammar. Listen to what your
readers say about diction (your choice of words) and syntax (the variety
of sentence structures in your draft).

Some of your readers might not distinguish between these two levels
of feedback. Often their impulse is to fix spelling and punctuation
rather than tell you whether your paper as a whole hangs together and
makes sense. Listen to what these readers have to say, and ask questions
that help them lift their eyes to the bigger picture.

Use technology to assist feedback

Using a computer makes it easy to revise and distribute multiple copies
of your paper. Instead of sending out paper copies, you can send reviewers a copy of your word processing file.

Also take advantage of software features that allow reviewers to enter
suggestions right into your documents. Using the comment feature in
Microsoft Word, for example, you can flag individual comments from
different reviewers, reject comments that you disagree with, and incorporate ideas that you like directly into a new draft.

Welcome feedback

Keep in mind that when other people criticize or edit your work,
they're not attacking you. They're just commenting on something

you wrote. By remembering this distinction, you can learn to welcome feedback.

To reduce your sensitivity to feedback, reflect on the fact that there's much more to you than what you wear, where you go to school, or what you do for a living. These are just external considerations that don't get to the essence of who you are.

In the same way, you are more than your draft. If you don't like the clothes you're wearing, you can change them. And if you don't like your first draft, you can change it. In either case, your feelings of self-worth don't have to get involved.

Learn to give constructive feedback

One way to *get* constructive feedback is to *give* it. Fellow students and colleagues at work might ask you for feedback on their writing. When they do, start from a positive frame of mind. Instead of looking for errors right off the bat, focus on parts of a draft that you like. And rather than making negative comments ("You really lost me in the third paragraph"), offer suggestions ("I'd like to see a clearer topic sentence in the third paragraph"). Using *I*-statements can make your feedback much easier to receive.

Consider the Scope of Your Writing

After sifting through reviewers' comments on your first draft, read straight through the entire piece again with fresh eyes—preferably after you've been away from it for several days. Resist any urge to stop and rewrite passages. Your aim at this point is simply to get an overall impression of your work and register a gut reaction.

Eventually the feedback you've received will gel with your own responses to your writing. You'll get a clear sense of what you want to revise.

To bring some clarity to the task of revision, think of it as a process that focuses on three different aspects of your writing: *scope, structure,* and *style.* If you begin by clarifying the overall scope of your paper or presentation, you may find that problems of structure and style are much easier to fix.

Count words

One key aspect of scope is quantity: the total number of words and images in your paper or presentation. Your teacher may specify the length of your paper by limiting it to a certain number of words. If you develop a habit of staying within the specified limits, teachers will be grateful— as will editors if you ever choose write for publication.

Most word processing software includes a command that calculates the total number of words in a document. This feature can be a big help in assessing the scope of your writing. You can also select individual sections of your document and get word counts for each section.

Read your paper out loud

Another effective way to revise the scope of your paper is to read it out loud. The eyes tend to fill in the blanks in our own writing. The combination of voice and ears forces us to pay attention to the details.

As you read, mark any places where you hesitate or feel that something is missing. These are sections you might want to expand, delete, or eventually reword.

Look for material to cut

At the level of scope, the most common type of revision is to cut passages that don't contribute to your purpose or support your thesis. At this point, don't worry about polishing individual words, phrases, and sentences. That time will be wasted if you choose to delete them. Rather, decide now which passages you want to let go. Then come back to what remains and polish it.

Approach your rough draft as if it were a chunk of granite from which you will chisel the final product. In the end, much of your first draft will be lying on the floor. What is left will be the clean, clear, polished product.

Note: For maximum efficiency, make the larger cuts first—sections, chapters, pages. Then go for the smaller cuts—paragraphs, sentences, phrases, words.

Keep in mind that cutting a passage means just for now, for this paper, for this assignment. Keep a file of deleted passages and save them for future use.

Look for material to add

Though the bulk of revision consists in choosing what material to leave out, you may come to points in your draft that cry out for expansion. Perhaps you have the space to add a major point to your argument or a major event to your narration. Or perhaps you can enliven the material by adding a vivid quotation, a telling example, or a key fact. If so, add this material now, before you turn to matters of structure or style.

Also, go back to your main research question and list of supporting questions (see Chapter 20). Determine whether your draft answers each question. If not, you may need to go back to your notes, look for relevant answers, and integrate them into your next draft.

Consider the Structure of Your Writing

Structure is all about flow—putting the sections of your paper in a logical order and crafting smooth transitions between them. If your draft doesn't hang together, then you may need to reorder your ideas. Imagine yourself with scissors and glue. You're going to cut the paper into scraps, one scrap for each point and its supporting material. Then you're going to paste these points down in a new, more logical order.

Create a new outline

Students and teachers tend to think of outlining only as a prewriting step. Actually, outlining can also be an effective tool for revising—especially for clarifying the structure of your draft after you cut or add material.

To experience this benefit of outlining, approach your draft as if it's an assigned reading and take notes on it in outline form. (See Chapter 14 for suggestions on outlining.) You can create either a topic outline or a sentence outline, though a sentence outline may give you a more precise view of your paper's main points and their development.

Another option is to make a *topic sentence outline*. Simply copy the topic sentence from each paragraph of your paper and paste these sentences—in order—into a separate document.

Revise your draft to match your outline

Using an outline to reduce your draft to its essentials enables you to take a macroscopic view and look for logical connections between sections and paragraphs. If you find gaps in logic or organization, this is an ideal time to fix them.

At this stage, you can test new structures simply by playing with your outline. This is easier and more efficient than trying to rearrange whole sections of your paper or presentation. Read your list of topics from beginning to end and see if the thread of ideas makes sense. Put your topic sentences in several different sequences and see if they create a more logical flow. Then consider revising your draft to match your revised outline.

Consider the Style of Your Writing

After you've revised your draft for scope and structure, you can focus on style. The main concerns here are effective word choice, variety in sentence structure, and fixing errors.

Refine word choices

In general, write with nouns and verbs. Using too many adjectives and adverbs weakens your message and adds unnecessary bulk to your writing.

Use nouns to point out specific details. Put verbs in the active rather than the passive voice. Simply by doing these two things, you'll find that

◆ examples

EFFECTIVE WORD CHOICES

Instead of writing with vague nouns:
The speaker made effective use of the television medium, asking in no uncertain terms that we change our belief systems.

You can include specifics:
The reformed criminal stared straight into the television camera and shouted, "Take a good look at what you're doing! Will it get you what you really want?"

Instead of writing in the passive voice:
A research project was begun.

You can switch to the active voice:
The research team began a project.

Instead of piling on adverbs and adjectives:
The diminutive woman had enough strength to quickly propel objects over vast, almost unimaginable, distances.

You can cut words and create an image in the reader's mind:
She stood only five feet tall, but she could throw a baseball from home plate into the stands over right field.

your writing becomes leaner and more forceful.

Look at sentence length and variety

As you read your first draft, take a microscope to your sentences. Look first at their length. Long sentences (25 or more words) can induce reader fatigue, especially if they occur in a series. For variety, periodically throw in a short sentence. Remember that a sentence can be as short as two words (*He cried*) or even one (*Wow!*).

You can also inject variety into your style by experimenting with the placement of key word elements. A classic sentence structure is subject → verb → object—for example:

- *Jane hugged Dick.*
- *Our local newspaper won a Pulitzer Prize.*
- *Iris Murdoch won recognition as a philosopher and novelist before developing Alzheimer's disease.*

However, you can sometimes achieve an intriguing or dramatic effect by inverting the order of subjects, verbs, and objects:

- *The person seen hugging Dick was Jane.*
- *The Pulitzer Prize—our local newspaper editor could hardly believe that her staff had won it.*
- *The mind of a philosopher, the sensibility of a novelist, and the delusions of Alzheimer's disease—all merged in the mind of Iris Murdoch.*

Proofread for mechanics

When applied to writing, *mechanics* is a word that refers to the details of grammar, punctuation, and spelling. To revise at this level, keep a dictionary handy. In addition to listing spellings and defini-

examples

SIX COMMON SENTENCE ERRORS

Run-on sentence

Original: Cassandra Wilson's vocal range is stunning, her only peer in the history of jazz singers is Ella Fitzgerald.
Revised: Cassandra Wilson's vocal range is stunning. Her only peer in the history of jazz singers is Ella Fitzgerald.

Sentence fragment

Original: Wilson's peer in jazz history: Ella Fitzgerald.
Revised: Wilson has a notable peer in jazz history: Ella Fitzgerald.

Comma missing after a long introductory phrase

Original: As a jazz musician who combines the talents of vocalist and pianist Diana Krall has few peers.
Revised: As a jazz musician who combines the talents of vocalist and pianist, Diana Krall has few peers.

Dangling modifier

Original: Ambling down the city street, the parking ramps seemed so dingy.
Revised: Ambling down the city street, I noticed that the parking ramps seemed so dingy.

Disagreement between pronoun and antecedent

Original: Each citizen should pay the full amount of income tax that they owe.
Revised: Each citizen should pay the full amount of income tax that he or she owes.
Revised again: Citizens should pay the full amount of income tax that they owe.

Disagreement between subject and verb

Original: The problem with her drafts are structure.
Revised: The problem with her drafts is structure.

tions for thousands of words, many dictionaries offer pointers for proofreading.

To catch errors in your drafts, proofread on paper. It's easy to miss errors in spelling and punctuation when your text dwells on the screen. Print out your manuscript double-spaced, grab a pencil, and mark up your draft at a location away from your computer.

The spelling checker bundled into your word processor will compare each word in your draft to a built-in dictionary and flag any unrecognized words. Remember, however, that spelling checkers cannot take context into account. This makes it possible for them to miss certain errors. For example, you might type the word *witch* and spell it correctly, even though you actually intended *which*. Use your spelling checker, but carefully review the results it gives.

Prepare your work for submission

In a sense, any paper is a sales effort. If you hand in a paper with wrinkled jeans, its hair tangled and unwashed, and its shoes untied, your instructor is less likely to buy it. To avoid this situation, present your paper in an acceptable format for title pages, margin widths, fonts, footnotes or endnotes, and bibliographies.

Check with your teacher for requirements for each of these elements. Also see the Appendices starting on page 324 for guidelines for documenting sources.

☑ checklist

POLISHING YOUR DRAFT: EFFECTIVE REVISION IN A NUTSHELL

Scope
- ❏ Your introduction captures the audience's attention, states your topic, and previews the body of your paper or presentation.
- ❏ Your writing presents a clear thesis statement or narrates a series of events unified by a consistent point of view.
- ❏ Your writing answers the main questions implied by your title and thesis statement.
- ❏ You support each of your main points with adequate details—quotations; examples; statistics; and vivid descriptions of people, places, or things.
- ❏ Your conclusion leaves the reader or listener with a sense of resolution without sounding mechanical or forced.

Structure
- ❏ The major sections of your paper or presentation flow in a logical sequence.
- ❏ The paragraphs of your paper or presentation flow in a logical sequence.
- ❏ Your paragraphs include topic sentences that are developed in a clear and logical way.

Style
- ❏ Your writing is concise, purged of needless words.
- ❏ Your sentences are filled with action verbs and concrete, specific nouns.
- ❏ You use variety in sentence structure.
- ❏ Your sentences are free of mechanical errors.

experiment WITH A STRATEGY FROM THIS CHAPTER

Think about how you typically respond when faced with the task of revising your writing. If you could instantly create one new outcome relating to the way you revise your writing, what would it be? For instance, you might want to catch more sentence errors, or simply complete the whole process in a much more efficient way. In the space below, describe a specific change you'd like to make:

Now list one suggestion from this chapter that could help you make the change you listed:

Next, describe a way to use this suggestion for a writing task that you now face:

Imagine that you are going to teach a course in effective writing. What is the single most important thing you would tell your students about the process of revision? Write your answer in the space below.

Making Effective Presentations

Presentations make a difference. Presentations can move people to change their opinions, change their votes, or change their lives. Democracy rests on the free exchange of ideas, accomplished largely by the power of the spoken word.

Polishing your speaking and presentation skills can help you think on your feet, communicate clearly, establish credibility, and build community. These skills will promote your success in higher education and in any career you choose.

As you read this chapter, keep one point about terminology in mind. The word *presentation* includes the traditional topic of public speaking, as well as elements used to supplement and support the spoken word: handout materials, group discussions and exercises, and visual elements that are created and displayed with audiovisual equipment.

Plan Your Presentation

Sometimes, listeners tune out during a speech. Just think of all the times you've listened to instructors, lecturers, politicians, and other public speakers. Think of all the wonderful daydreams you had during their speeches. Your audiences are like you. The way you plan and present your speech can determine the number of people in your audience who stay with you until the end.

When the choice is yours, talk about topics that hold your interest, and offer something of value for your audience. Whenever possible, weave personal experiences into your presentation. Your enthusiasm will reach the audience.

Choose your topic and thesis

Chapters 20 through 24 offer guidelines for selecting a topic, defining your purpose, doing research, and writing. All of these chapters can help you as you plan a presentation on your chosen topic.

With presentations, it's especially important for you to summarize your message in one concise sentence: your thesis statement. This is the bottom line or take-away message, the one thing that you want your audience to remember after they applaud, stand up, and walk out of the room.

When you communicate by writing, the members of your audience can reread your words as often as they like. When you communicate by speaking, your listeners don't have that luxury. They have to fully comprehend your message the first time that they hear it. If you carefully define your topic and emphasize your thesis, you'll create a more forceful and memorable impression.

Analyze your audience and purpose

To make an effective presentation, be precise about your purpose. Speeches can inform, persuade, motivate, or entertain. Choose what you want to accomplish, and let your audience know what you intend.

Choosing your purpose means analyzing your audience. Find out as much as you can about these people, including demographic data such as their ages, political affiliations, and levels of education. Above all, discover:

- What they already *know* about your topic.
- How they *feel* about your topic—including attitudes that could lead them to resist your message.
- What you want them to *do* after your presentation—anything from simply expressing agreement with your ideas to plunking down their hard-earned money for your service or product.

Consider setting and length

Also consider the setting in which you and your audience will meet. Settings can vary from a three-minute talk in front of a small group of classmates to a formal presentation in front of hundreds of scholars. Think in terms of three basic options:

- ***Short and sweet for a small audience.*** For some presentations, you may have little time to prepare. If so, you can plan to be informal or even speak impromptu, with few notes.
- ***Longer and for a bigger audience.*** This option probably calls for more preparation on your part, including more extensive research and notes in the form of a detailed outline.
- ***Longest for a meeting of specialists or scholarly audiences.*** This is the most formal setting and generally involves the longest presentation. As such, it calls for the most careful preparation. You'll probably want to write out your speech word for word. You may even be required to submit the manuscript beforehand.

As you consider the length of your presentation, plan on delivering about 100 words per minute. This is only a general guideline, however, and you may want to refine this estimate by timing yourself as you practice your presentation.

In any case, aim for a lean presentation—enough words to make your point, but not so many that you make your audience restless. Be brief, be seated, and leave your listeners wanting more.

Choose a format for your speaking notes

Some professional speakers recommend that you speak from key words or phrases written on a series of index cards. If you use this option, number the cards so that you can quickly put them in order again if you drop them. As you speak and finish with the information on a card, move that card to the back of the pile. Write information clearly and in letters large enough to be seen from a distance.

One disadvantage of this system is that it involves a lot of card shuffling. Another option for speaking notes is mind mapping (see Chapter 13). You can mind map even an hour-long speech on one sheet of paper.

☑ checklist

FORMATS FOR SPEAKING NOTES

Option 1: A bare-bones outline
When your presentation is short and the setting is informal, prepare with a brief outline:
❏ Write out your opening in a complete sentence.
❏ Summarize each of your major points in a key word or short phrase.
❏ Write out your closing in a complete sentence.

Option 2: A detailed outline
For longer and more formal settings, consider making a detailed outline:
❏ Write out your introduction and conclusion word for word.
❏ List each major point in a complete sentence.
❏ If you include quotations, statistics, or technical details, also write these out completely and include their sources.
❏ Number each page of notes.

Option 3: A full manuscript
This option is for speeches in formal settings, such as presentations of research results at an academic conference. To promote your comfort on the podium and make your presentation more natural, make your manuscript easy to read:
❏ Print out the text triple-spaced in a large font that's easy to read.
❏ Print key words and phrases in bold so that you remember to emphasize them.
❏ Use ellipses (. . .) to indicate any spots where you plan to pause.
❏ Number each page of notes.

Even if you plan to give a brief presentation on a topic that you know well, consider the benefits of writing out your speech. Writing is the method par excellence for clarifying what you want to say, assembling evidence to support your point of view, and detecting gaps in logic. To experience these advantages, commit your entire speech, or key parts of it, to writing. From this complete manuscript you can make briefer notes in the form of cards or mind maps.

Develop your introduction

Though some members of an audience begin to drift during a speech, most people pay attention at the beginning. So the first few sentences of your speech are crucial. Use the introduction to reveal your topic, announce your thesis, and explain how your audience can benefit from what you have to say.

The trick is to capture your audience's attention—something that's done most effectively in the first few seconds of your presentation. Start out with a memorable quotation, a personal anecdote that your audience can identify with, a startling statistic, or an attention-getting question.

Develop the body of your presentation

The main body of the speech is the content—70 to 90 percent of most speeches. To develop this section of your presentation, ask yourself what questions your introduction is likely to raise in the minds of your audience members. Arrange those questions in a logical order and answer each one in turn. In your answers, include facts, descriptions, expert opinions, statistics, and other concrete details to help you hold audience attention.

Structure your presentation so that, at any point, an alert listener

 examples

CRAFTING AN EFFECTIVE INTRODUCTION

Start with a bang! Compare the following two introductions to speeches on the subject of world hunger.

Example #1: "I'm honored to be here with you today. I intend to talk about malnutrition and starvation. First, I want to outline the extent of these problems, then I will discuss some basic assumptions concerning world hunger, and finally, I will propose some solutions."

Example #2: "More people have died from hunger in the past five years than have been killed in all the wars, revolutions, and murders in the past 150 years. Yet there is enough food to go around. I'm honored to be with you today to discuss the problem."

Preview your presentation. Reveal your point up front. The following introduction reveals that the speech to follow has three distinct parts: "Cock fighting is a cruel sport. I intend to describe exactly what happens to the birds, tell you who is doing this, and show you how you can stop this inhumane practice."

Note: Keep it brief. Audiences appreciate a preview—as long as it's short. If you keep talking about what you *intend* to talk about during the body of your presentation, people may get bored or restless. Get the audience's attention, get them oriented, and then get to the point.

could summarize what you've said so far and predict what topic you'll cover next. Give your audience a signal when you change topics: "The second reason hunger persists is. . . ." Also, recap from time to time and preview the topics you plan to cover next.

Develop your conclusion

At the end of the speech, summarize your points and draw your conclusion. You started with a bang; now finish with drama. Use the conclusion to call people to action.

Make it clear to your audience when you've reached the end. Avoid endings such as "This is the end of my speech" or "Well, I guess that's it." A simple standby is "So, in conclusion I want to reiterate three points: First. . . ."

Again, keep your conclusion short. When you are finished, just stop talking.

Edit for the ear

As you prepare each part of your presentation, remember the differences between the written word and the spoken word. When writing, you can craft longer sentences with a variety of lengths and structures.

▶ sidebar

THREE WAYS TO PERSUADE YOUR AUDIENCE

Aristotle, the ancient Greek philosopher, wrote a text on rhetoric (the art of persuasion) that is still widely quoted. He recommends that any persuasive speech include three main elements, presented in the following order.

First, establish credibility. Ethos is a Greek word for character. Aristotle believed that audiences want to know whether a speaker is credible and honest. So your first goal is to establish that you know what you're talking about and that you can be trusted. Do this by telling humorous stories about yourself and mentioning your association with people whom your audience already trusts. Ironically, you can sometimes gain credibility by being modest about your qualifications—a quality that audiences may perceive as honesty.

Next, engage emotions. Aristotle also spoke about *pathos,* the Greek word for passion or emotion. Human beings have instinctive desires for security, appreciation, recognition, pleasure, and love. Whenever possible, tie your presentation to one of these basic drives. Show that adopting your ideas or acting on your recommendation will help audience members get something that they want. Deliver a benefit that people feel strongly about.

Finally, provide reasons. Logos, the Greek word for logic, comes last in Aristotle's system. Aristotle believed that rational arguments in favor of your point of view have little force unless your audience first trusts you and feels emotionally engaged. Logic and evidence are important, but for maximum impact, present them after you've already established *ethos* and *pathos.*

When speaking, however, you can often be clearer by using shorter sentences with simpler structures.

Also consider word choice. Steer clear of technical terms and professional jargon (unless your audience knows them). Opt for shorter, familiar words. And when possible, use personal pronouns: *I, you, we.* Such words foster a sense of inclusion.

Create handouts and activities

Especially when your presentation will last more than an hour, give your audience some paper to hold. Consider sharing your speaking notes with your audience. Even a simple list of the topics you plan to cover can help your audience stay oriented.

On your handouts, leave enough space for people to take notes on your presentation. Also, distribute handouts before you speak rather than interrupt your presentation to distribute them.

☑ checklist

KEY POINTS ABOUT POWERPOINT

Use slides generated with presentation software such as PowerPoint to *complement* rather than *replace* your speaking. If you use too many slides—or slides that are too complex—your audience may focus on them and forget about you. To avoid this fate:

❏ *Keep text simple.* Limit the amount of text on each slide. Stick to key words presented in short sentences and bulleted or numbered lists. Use a consistent set of plain fonts that are large enough for all audience members to see.

❏ *Keep colors simple.* PowerPoint offers a wide spectrum of colors that you can combine in countless patterns. Don't feel obligated to use all that computing power. To create clear and memorable slides, stick with a simple, coherent color scheme. Use light-colored text on dark background, or dark text on a light background.

❏ *Maintain consistency.* Make sure that the terminology you use in your speaking, in your handouts, and in your slides is consistent. Inconsistency can lead people to feel lost—or to question your credibility.

❏ *Proofread.* Check for spelling errors yourself. Then ask someone else to proofread your slides as well.

❏ *Watch your timing.* Show each slide at an appropriate point in your presentation. If you're showing a chart or graph and want the audience to notice a particular piece of information, then point to it. When slides are no longer relevant, change them or fade the screen to black.

❏ *Stay out of the way.* As you start feeling comfortable on stage, you might get enthusiastic, gesture freely, and start moving around. That's fine, but don't stand in front of your slides. Keep to the side of the screen while maintaining eye contact with your audience.

For lengthy presentations, plan to let your audience get into the action. Leave time for questions and comments. Break large audiences into small groups for discussions and role-playing exercises. If you make people sit still for more than a half-hour, you risk losing them to fatigue or boredom. Let them stretch, stand, talk, and move. This will wake everyone up—and engage people with learning styles that favor concrete experience and active experimentation.

Practice Your Presentation

The key to successful public speaking is repeated practice. Rehearse your presentation in front of friends or while looking in the mirror. Speaking often before small groups builds confidence. (In fact, it can be just as demanding as talking in front of a large group.) You can also practice by speaking up often in class.

When you rehearse your presentation:

- *Practice in the room where you will deliver your speech.* Hear what your voice sounds like over a sound system. If you can't practice your speech in the actual room, at least visit the site ahead of time.
- *Use your imagination.* As you speak—even if it's to an empty room—visualize a full audience sitting in front of you. Gesture just as you would before a real audience.
- *Project your voice.* Speak at your normal speed, but do so loudly enough to fill the room. Your voice sounds different when you talk loudly, and this can be unnerving. Get used to it before the big day.
- *Practice using equipment.* If you plan to use slides or other audiovisual equipment, then practice with them. Make sure any materials you will need for your presentation will be available when you want them. Double-check equipment to make sure it's in good working order.
- *Record your presentation and listen to it.* Better yet, videotape your presentation. Many colleges and universities have video equipment available for students' use.
- *Listen for repeated phrases.* Typical culprits are *you know, kind of, really,* plus little *uh*'s, *umm*'s, and *ah*'s. To get rid of these mannerisms, simply tell yourself that you intend to notice every time they pop up in your daily speech. When you hear them, tell yourself that you don't use those words anymore.
- *Unless you plan to read your manuscript word for word, avoid dependence on your notes.* Diligent practice relieves you of having to rely heavily on your notes. Know your material and present the information in a way that is most natural for you.

- ■ ***Plan how to dress.*** If you want to get your message across, dress appropriately. Dress up to speak before the Association of University Presidents—unless they're having a picnic. If you plan on a formal wardrobe, then consider dressing up even while you practice.

Present with Confidence

If you feel nervous before you make a presentation, then you're normal. One powerful strategy for preventing and reducing anxiety is to prepare thoroughly. If you know your topic inside and out, you'll create a baseline of confidence.

In addition to careful preparation, you can use the following suggestions to enhance your delivery.

Set the stage

On the day of your presentation, arrive early to set up. Before you begin, be sure you have the audience's attention. If people are still filing into the room or adjusting seats, they're not ready to listen.

If you notice a side conversation in the room during your presentation, continue speaking and look directly at the people who are **talking.** You will usually regain their attention when you do this.

Begin with grace

The first few moments can set the tone for your entire presentation. After you're introduced, stand up and approach the front of the room at a natural pace. Take a moment to look at your notes before you begin speaking; there's no need to rush. You may find that allowing a few seconds to collect yourself helps you relax.

Pause when appropriate

Beginners sometimes feel they have to fill every moment of a presentation with the sound of their voices. Don't give in to that temptation. Take a deep breath from time to time and allow a moment of silence. This will let your audience take a mental deep breath as well.

Maintain eye contact

When you look at people, they become less frightening. Remember that it is easier to listen to someone who looks at you. Find a few friendly faces around the room. Smile, and imagine that you are talking to them individually.

Notice your gestures

Be aware of what your body is telling your audience. Contrived or staged gestures will look dishonest. Be natural. If you don't know what to do with your hands, notice that. Then don't do anything with them.

Track the time

You can increase the impact of your words by keeping track of the time during your speech. Better to end early than run late. The conclusion of your speech is what is likely to be remembered, and you might lose this opportunity if people are looking at the clock.

Get feedback on your presentation

Review and reflect on your performance:

- Did you finish on time?
- Did you cover all the points you intended to cover?
- Was the audience attentive?
- Did you handle any nervousness effectively?
- What can you do to improve your performance and delivery next time?

Also welcome evaluation from members of your audience. Ask some of them directly for feedback.

Most of us find it difficult to hear criticism about our speaking. Notice such resistance on your part, then let it go. Every piece of feedback that you take to heart will increase your skill at making presentations.

▶ sidebar

REDUCE FEAR OF PUBLIC SPEAKING

Nervousness at the prospect of public speaking is common. You can deal with it by noticing it. Be totally in the present moment. Notice how the room feels. Notice the temperature and lighting. See the audience. Look at them. Make eye contact. Notice all your thoughts about how you feel and gently release them. Tell yourself, "Yes, my hands are clammy. I notice that my stomach is slightly upset. My face feels numb." Allow these symptoms to exist. Experience them fully. When you do, those symptoms often become less persistent.

In addition to using the power of awareness:

- Look for opportunities to speak briefly and frequently in public.
- See public speaking simply as an extension of one-to-one conversation.
- Choose topics that excite your passion.
- Use stress reduction techniques such as slow, deep breathing before and during your speech.
- Focus on the audience and the content of your presentation rather than on your own comfort level.
- Look at your audience and imagine them all dressed as clowns; if you lighten up and enjoy your presentation, so will the audience.

▶ experiment WITH A STRATEGY FROM THIS CHAPTER

Think back to a time when you were called on to speak before a group. In the space below, write down what you remember about that situation. For example, describe the physical sensations you experienced before and during your presentation, the overall effectiveness of your presentation, and any feedback you received from the audience:

Based on what you wrote above, what would you like to do differently the next time you speak? Describe one key change you'd like to make:

Now, review this chapter for a suggestion that could help you produce the change you just described. Summarize that suggestion here and describe how you intend to use it:

Using Computers to Promote Your Success

Information technology pervades our lives. Computers are not only found on our desktops, in our libraries, and on our laps, but they are also embedded in cars, appliances, automatic teller machines, and grocery checkout lanes.

While you are participating in higher education, you may use computers to:

- Research and write papers and presentations using library catalogs and the Internet.
- Collect and analyze laboratory data.
- Collaborate on group projects.
- Stay in touch with friends, family, and teachers via e-mail.
- Participate in newsgroups and other online communities.
- Register for classes.
- Take distance-learning courses.
- Download course materials.

These activities offer you a chance to master computer technology in ways that relate to your long-term interests. This factor may be as critical to your personal and professional life as the ability to think, read, write, listen, and speak well.

Bringing a Computer to Campus: Ask These Questions

There's more to computer literacy then just showing up at school with a computer. Start by contacting an admissions counselor or academic advisor and asking the following questions.

Do I need to own a computer?

Many schools have computer labs with equipment that's available for anyone to use for free. Even so, you may find that it's more convenient to own your own computer and printer. If you decide to buy this equipment, find out whether your school sells hardware and software at a student discount. Also ask about getting an extended warranty with technical support.

Do I need a laptop computer or a desktop computer?

Laptop computers have the obvious advantage of portability. They also take up less space—a key consideration if you live in a dorm room. Yet laptops tend to be more fragile and more expensive than desktop computers. In addition, desktop models often have more potential for technical upgrades—an alternative to buying a new computer in the near future.

Do I need a Windows computer, or can I use a Macintosh?

The majority of personal computers used in higher education and business settings are Windows based. However, most schools accommodate Macintoshes. If you use a Macintosh, look for software that freely exchanges files with Windows.

What specifications does my hardware need to meet?

To find a personal computer that supports your academic success, think about technical specifications. These are the requirements that computers must meet in order to connect to the school network and run software applications commonly used by students. In particular, ask about requirements for your computer's:

- **Operating system.** This is the built-in software that keeps track of computer files and allows you to run software applications. Be sure to keep the CDs that contain backups of files of your operating system software and upgrades.
- **Random Access Memory (RAM).** Many people refer to RAM simply as *memory*. In either case, this is a temporary storage area for data that you use, such as word processing or database files. RAM is measured in megabytes (MB). Consider installing extra RAM when you buy your computer—as much as you can afford.
- **Processor.** The processor is the piece of hardware that actually carries out the operating system's commands. Processor speed is measured in megahertz (MHz) or gigahertz (GHz). One GHz is about the same as 1,000 MHz. The higher this rating, the faster your computer will run.
- **Hard drive.** The hard drive stores the operating system, along with all the other files you save and use. Space on a hard drive is measured in gigabytes (GB). One gigabyte equals about 1,000 megabytes. Again, the more, the better.

- ***Ethernet card.*** This is sometimes called a network adapter or network interface card (NIC). It allows you to connect your computer to campus networks and the Internet. The speed of an Ethernet card is measured in megabits per second (Mbps). Find out what speed is recommended for your school. You may want to buy this piece of hardware and have it installed after you get to school.

- ***Optical drive.*** This piece of equipment is built in to newer computers, though you can buy it separately. An optical drive allows you to read and write data to compact discs (CDs), digital video discs (DVDs), or both. Use optical drives to make backup copies of all your working files. If you do not have access to an optical drive, consider using a zip drive and zip disks to create backups.

What software will I use?

Many students find that a package such as Microsoft Office—which includes a word processor, spreadsheet, and presentation software—meets their needs. Find out what's recommended for your school. Also ask whether your school provides Internet and virus protection software.

Expand Your Learning Strategies to Include Technology

You can integrate information technology with daily study tasks in a variety of ways. Experiment with the following and invent more of your own.

Create course glossaries

One way to review for tests is to create and maintain a glossary of key terms for each of your courses:

- Every time you encounter a key word or technical term in your course notes or textbooks, key that word into a word processing or database file.
- Create a separate file for each of your courses.
- For each term, write a definition and a sentence using the word in context.
- Sort the words in alphabetical order.
- Update your glossary files once weekly, based on that week's class work and assigned readings.
- Each time you update a glossary file, print it out.
- Keep a current printout in your backpack or briefcase to study while you are waiting in line or for appointments.

☑ checklist

EVALUATE COMPUTER RESOURCES ON CAMPUS

No matter what your major, you'll find yourself using information technology to complete course work. You'll also use information technology to handle many of the administrative details of higher education, such as registering for courses and checking grades. You can even use computers to connect to virtual and "real-time" communities based at your school.

Pose the following questions to advisors, librarians, and the staff of your campus computer center. These are especially useful questions to ask when you apply to a college or university or when you transfer to a new school.

- ❐ Does the school require a level of computer competency for graduation or for completing specific majors?
- ❐ How many public access computers are available at school?
- ❐ What computer support and troubleshooting services are available at school?
- ❐ What library resources are available online, and are they accessible from remote locations such as residence halls?
- ❐ Can students receive credit for distance learning—courses taken online from other schools?
- ❐ Is the school catalog available online?
- ❐ Can students access grades and other personal information online?
- ❐ Can parents access student information, and under what conditions?
- ❐ Does the school offer free e-mail accounts to students?
- ❐ Can students register for classes, drop classes, and add classes online?
- ❐ Can students handle financial transactions online—for example, tuition payments, financial aid, and bookstore purchases?
- ❐ Does the school use "smart cards" or "debit cards" to provide identification and to help students access services?
- ❐ Are students allowed to create personal Web pages and online portfolios?
- ❐ What policies govern the use of computers on campus and activity in online communities?
- ❐ Does the school post Web sites for student organizations?
- ❐ Do faculty members distribute course materials online and accept assignments submitted via e-mail?
- ❐ Does tuition include a technology fee? If so, what services does it cover?
- ❐ Does the school provide high-speed Internet connections in residence halls and class buildings?
- ❐ Does the school charge for printing from public access computers?
- ❐ Does the school regularly update its own information technology?

Capture your notes on disk

Outlining software offers many possibilities for organizing and reviewing your notes on textbooks and lectures:

- Take lecture notes directly on a laptop, or take handwritten notes and key them into your computer after class.
- Divide chapter or lecture notes into sections; then write a heading to capture the main point of each section.
- For a greater level of detail, use several levels of headings, ranging from major to minor.
- To save time when you review, just display the headings and scan them as you would scan the headlines in a newspaper.
- Use outlining to review: View headings only and recite (verbally or in writing) what you can remember of the body text under each heading.
- Use the drawing and painting features embedded in word processing software to create maps, charts, diagrams, and other visuals to enhance your notes.

Use computers for cooperative learning

Information technology can help you study with other people:

- Use your computer to create and maintain essay, short-answer, and true-false questions based on your textbooks and lecture notes.
- Create study groups for your courses and ask members to share their practice test questions, along with sample answers.
- Go to your school library or media center and find computer-based tutorials in specific subject areas.

☑ checklist

PROTECT YOUR COMPUTER FILES

It's been said that the two most important words about using a computer are *backup* and *save*. This refers to the fact that power surges and loss of electricity can destroy data. Computer users tell stories about losing hours' worth of work in a millisecond. To prevent this fate, take these simple but powerful steps:

❒ While you're creating or editing a computer file, save your work every few minutes. Your computer manual will explain how. (Some software does this automatically.)
❒ Make backup copies of your files on separate storage media, such as zip disks or CDs.
❒ Make backups of your backup disks to store separately.
❒ Find out how to shut down and restart the computer if it "crashes" or "freezes"—that is, suddenly quits or refuses to respond to anything that you type.
❒ Make sure that the computer you're working on has software to detect viruses and repair the damage they can do. Update this software regularly.

▶ experiment WITH A STRATEGY FROM THIS CHAPTER

Think of a persistent academic challenge that you face. It could be frustration with your current level of skill in reading, writing, note-taking, or test-taking. Or your challenge might relate to the content of a specific course—English, a foreign language, science, math, or a course required for your major.

In the space below, describe the biggest academic challenge you face right now:

Next, review this chapter for a suggestion about using technology that could help you meet the academic challenge you just described. *Note:* You may need to modify one of the suggestions in this chapter to make it work for you. Or you could invent a technology strategy of your own.

Describe your strategy, including details about what tasks are involved and when you will complete them:

After using your strategy for at least one week, write about how well it worked:

Becoming a Member of the Online Community

Through Web sites, e-mail, newsgroups, and chat rooms, the Internet puts you in touch with networks of people that extend across your school, across the country, and even worldwide. But thriving in these communities calls for much more than technical savvy. When you join any community, you're more likely to thrive by learning the official policies and unspoken rules that influence relationships among group members. This principle applies in specific ways to online communities.

Write for Online Audiences

Today's information technology allows you to manipulate text and images in ways that were unheard of just a few years ago. Even so, you are subject to limitations imposed by the computer screen. Those limitations relate especially to the workhorse of online communication—good old-fashioned alphanumeric characters, also known as plain text.

Keep messages simple, short, and direct

The computer screen is a poor medium for presenting lengthy text. Jakob Nielsen, a distinguished engineer with Sun Microsystems and author of several books on Web site design, notes that people read text 25 to 50 percent more slowly on screen than on paper. Lengthy sentences and long paragraphs can sometimes be effective in print, but on the screen they turn people off.

To communicate effectively online, get to the point quickly and keep the word count down. The following techniques will help you do that:

- When creating an e-mail message or Web page, write about half the words you would use on a printed page.
- Whenever possible, keep your text to one screen or less.

- Use short words, short sentences, and short paragraphs.
- Write sentences with simple structures; avoid compound and complex sentences.
- Set short line lengths—no more than 65 characters.
- Write in the second person; address the reader as "you."
- Use active verbs and write in the present tense.
- Avoid "fluff," such as clichés and the language of advertising; stick to essential ideas and verifiable facts.
- Whenever possible, use short, concrete, and familiar words; eliminate jargon and define technical terms in plain English.
- Include long documents in an attachment that recipients can print out.
- When replying to someone else's message, include only the parts of the original message that are relevant to your reply.

Help your readers scan

Research indicates that when people sit at their computers, they don't read word for word. Instead, they scan. And many of them will not scroll downward past the first screen of text.

Assist online audiences by giving your text a visible structure. Include features to help readers quickly find what they want and take in relevant details at a glance:

- Think in terms of a three-part structure for each page of text: Make your main point in the first sentence of the first paragraph. Add another paragraph with key details to support that point. End with a paragraph that clearly explains what response you want the reader to make.
- Break up your text with headings printed in boldface; when writing online you can sometimes insert a heading before each paragraph.
- Keep headings short.
- To clarify the structure of your text, use minor headings as well as major headings.
- Write headings that are informative enough to make sense when displayed out of context, such as in a list of "hits" from a search engine.
- Break up paragraphs with bulleted lists, numbered lists, and graphics.
- Keep lists short.
- Highlight important key words or phrases, but don't overdo it.

Include links

Links to external Web sites allow readers to go beyond your message and follow a train of thought in depth. Adding timely and relevant links can also enhance your credibility, showing that you've taken the time to research your topic. To help readers get the most from links:

- Highlight the link; display the key words in color, and underline them.
- Describe briefly what readers will find when they click on the link; give them enough information to choose the links that interest them.
- Too many links can be confusing, so include them selectively.
- Place links at the end of paragraphs, where they will not impede the flow of text.

▶ sidebar

DESIGNING YOUR OWN WEB SITE

Applications such as Netscape Composer and Front Page allow you to create pages of text and graphics for online display and link them together in a Web site. To use these applications effectively, remember some basic principles of Web site design:

- *Start with your purpose.* Clarify why you want to start a Web site in the first place: What results do you want to create? What are the key messages you want to provide? Can you provide them better in a medium other than the Web?
- *Analyze your audience.* Get a clear mental image of the people who are likely to visit your Web site. Ask a lot of questions about them: What do they already know about the topic of your site? What new things do they want to learn? How do they feel about your site topic? And how will they use the information your site provides?
- *Consider structure.* Ask how you will design your site so that visitors can navigate it clearly. Create a site map—a list of all your individual pages grouped in categories. Visit Web sites you like, study their site maps, and notice how pages are designed.
- *Make your site easy to use.* Keep your pages simple, attractive, and uncluttered. Include graphics, but keep them simple enough to download quickly.
- *Consider limitations up front.* The way your pages appear on your screen and the way they appear on someone else's screen can be surprisingly different. This difference is due to variations in hardware and software. To anticipate these differences, set your monitor resolution to the basic setting of 800x600 characters; make sure all page content is visible in this display area. Think twice before using special features such as Java scripts and applets.
- *Plan for maintenance.* If your Web site has dynamic content—text and images that need revision—allow time for updating your site. Make sure that links still work. At the bottom of each page, note the last date that the page was revised.
- *Let people reach you.* Include your e-mail address and ask visitors to send suggestions for your site.

Join Online Communities

Online communities come in many varieties. Many of them adhere to three basic formats:

- E-mail lists
- Newsgroups
- Chat rooms

Start by mastering e-mail basics

To begin, master the basis of communication in most online communities—e-mail.

With a computer and modem, you can send e-mail to anyone who's also connected to the Internet. Using e-mail can save paper, time, and postage. By sending e-mail messages, you can avoid playing "phone tag." Used ineffectively, however, e-mail can waste time and cause a host of other frustrations. To get the most from this medium of communication, consider the suggestions that follow.

Target your audience. Write an informative subject line—one that invites the recipient to read your message. Also be conscious of the amount of e-mail that busy people receive. Send e-mail messages only to the people who need them, and only when necessary.

Consider how long your message might be stored. Your message could dwell in a recipient's in-basket for weeks or months. Think carefully about the impact of your message, both in the short and the long term. When composing e-mail, ask for what you want; at the same time, be courteous. Edit sentences written in the heat of a strong emotion—sentences that you might regret later. Also, remember that it's easy to send a message to the wrong person. Don't include a statement in any e-mail message that would embarrass you if this happens.

Before you hit the "send" button, proofread. Every message you send, even the shortest, most informal message, says something about your attention to detail. Put your best electronic foot forward. If you plan to send a long message, draft it in a word processing program first so that you can take advantage of spelling checkers and other editing devices. Then copy the text and paste it into the body of an e-mail message.

Use text formatting carefully. Boldface, italics, underlining, smart quotes, and other formatting options may not transfer well across e-mail programs. On your recipient's computer, special characters may appear as nonsense characters. If your message will be widely circulated, use generic (ASCII) characters that any computer can read.

For example, use asterisks to *emphasize* words. Place titles within plain quotation marks. Don't indent the first line of a paragraph. Instead, insert a "hard return"—a blank line—between paragraphs. Use two hyphens (--) in place of a dash (—). Avoid using special symbols such as ©, or use an alternative such as (c).

Forward messages selectively. Think twice before forwarding generic messages from other sources—cartoons, joke files, political diatribes, and "inspirational" readings. Your recipients may already have in-baskets overflowing with e-mail, leading them to view forwarded messages as irritating clutter.

Test attachments. If you plan to send an attachment, do a dry run first. You may find that it takes a couple of tries to get attachments sent in a format that your recipient can read. For instructions on how to format attachments, see the help feature in your e-mail program.

As an alternative, see if you can save your attachment as "text only," copy it, and then paste it into the body of an e-mail message. Send this message separately from the attachment.

Note: Attachments sometimes come with computer viruses that can damage your hard disk. Open attachments only from people you know, and use antivirus software. Forward attachments with extreme care.

Protect your privacy. Treat all online communication as public communication. Include only content that you're willing to circulate widely. Share personal data with caution.

Prevent bounced messages. Bounced e-mail includes messages returned to you automatically because they are undeliverable. The problem could be an incorrect e-mail address for your recipient.

Stay on top of your in-basket. Tame the e-mail tiger. Read and respond to e-mail promptly. If there's little chance that you will refer to a message in the future, then delete it.

Investigate e-mail lists

E-mail lists—sometimes called mailing lists or "Listservs"—consist

▶ sidebar

USE ACRONYMS WITH CARE

Acronyms that appear in e-mail messages are shorthand expressions for common phrases. Use them cautiously; your recipient may not understand them. Examples are:

- **2l8** too late
- **btw** by the way
- **cul** see you later
- **fwiw** for what it's worth
- **iow** in other words
- **irl** in real life
- **kwim** know what I mean
- **lol** laughing out loud
- **tia** thanks in advance
- **tnx** thanks
- **ttfn** ta ta for now
- **ttyl** talk to you later

of e-mail addresses for groups of people who want to automatically receive messages on a certain topic. There are thousands of these lists, both public and private. Most are free; some charge a fee for joining.

When you subscribe to an e-mail list, you can send a message to a posting address at any time. Everyone who subscribes to the list will receive your message. Likewise, you will receive e-mails that other subscribers send to the posting address. Some lists are highly active, generating dozens of messages daily.

To get the most from e-mail lists:

- Remember that each list has two addresses, one for subscribing and a separate one for posting messages.
- Save the first message you get when you subscribe to a list; this message contains instructions for posting messages and how to suspend or cancel your subscription.
- Read the instructions message for ways to control the number of messages you receive.
- Before posting your first message, spend some time browsing through the list's archive of past messages.
- Find out if your list allows you to send messages to individual members rather than to all subscribers.
- Write courteous messages that are informative and relevant to the list topic.

Consider newsgroups

Newsgroups—also called Usenet newsgroups, Web forums, and bulletin boards—allow members to post and read messages. Unlike e-mail lists, all messages sent to a newsgroup are posted at an Internet address that anyone can access.

Newsgroups usually focus on a particular topic—anything from astronomy to Zen Buddhism. Some groups are moderated by a person or group that screens messages. Other groups are a free-for-all, open to any message from any person.

To access a newsgroup, you'll need special software. Today that software is often bundled in to a Web browser, such as Internet Explorer, or an e-mail program.

To get the most from newsgroups:

Expect anarchy. With many newsgroups, no one is truly in charge. Although a few groups have moderators, most are free-for-alls that accept any message from any subscriber. Messages run the gamut from fascinating and insightful to malicious and ill informed.

Don't believe everything you see. Anyone can start a newsgroup, and people who post messages have a wide range of expertise. Don't assume that the information presented is accurate or timely. Check facts against other sources, such as current encyclopedias and other credible reference works.

Learn the ground rules. Many newsgroups have written policies about what kinds of messages are permitted. Often you'll receive e-mail with these rules when you subscribe. Look for a "frequently asked questions" (FAQ) file that explains the policies of the group. These files have names such as *newusers.questions* or *newusers.faq.*

"Lurk" before you post. When you're new to a newsgroup, spend a little time "lurking"—reading posted messages without replying to them. By observing what people write and what they don't, you'll learn the unwritten rules for that group. When you post your first message, give a little background about yourself as it relates to the group topic.

Avoid attachments. Group members may have trouble downloading or opening them. Also, don't copy and paste Web pages into your document. Just copy and paste in the full URL (the page's Web address).

Consider chat rooms

Chat rooms allow computer users to send and receive messages live, in "real time." This is as close to a live conversation as most computer users get while they're online. To join in, you'll need special software, such as AOL Instant Messenger or a similar application, bundled in to your Web browser.

Some chat rooms are set up for specific audiences and for special purposes. Rooms may be ongoing or planned to last only for a limited time. For example, newspapers and magazines may create chat rooms that allow readers to discuss feature articles. Your teachers may also set up chat rooms in which you and your classmates can take part in digital exchanges for the duration of a course. You may even do group exercises and role-playing via chat rooms.

Chat rooms might be called MUDs (multiuser domains) or MOOs (multiuser domains, object oriented). Whatever their name or purpose, chat rooms call on you to abide by the same principles that apply to communication in e-mail lists and newsgroups. In addition, see the following box for a short course in online courtesy.

> ▶ **sidebar**

WAYS TO FIND E-MAIL LISTS, NEWSGROUPS, AND CHAT ROOMS

You can access most online communities via Web sites that explain how to join them. To find newsgroups on topics that interest you, use several search engines. Examples are:

CataList: www.lsoft.com/lists/listref.html
DejaNews: www.dejanews.com
Liszt: www.liszt.com
Reference.COM: www.reference.com
Egroups: www.egroups.com
ListBot: www.listbot.com
MudConnect: www.mudconnect.com

▶ sidebar

A BRIEF GUIDE TO "NETIQUETTE"

Certain kinds of exchanges can send the tone of online communications into the gutter. To promote a cordial online community, abide by the following guidelines.

- **Respect others' time.** People often turn to the Internet with the hope of saving time, not wasting it. You can accommodate their desires by typing concise messages. Adopt the habit of getting to your point, sticking to it, and getting to the end.
- **Use emoticons with care.** *Emoticons* are combinations of keyboard characters that represent an emotion, such as :›). (Turn the book sideways to see a smiling face at the end of the last sentence.) Emoticons may not be appropriate for some Internet-based communications, including exchanges with a prospective employer.
- **Fine-tune the mechanics.** Proofread your message for spelling and grammar, just as you would for a print message. Give your readers the gift of clarity and precision. Use electronic communications as a chance to hone your writing skills.
- **Avoid typing passages in ALL UPPERCASE LETTERS.** This is the online equivalent of shouting.
- **Design your messages for fast retrieval.** Avoid graphics and attachments that take a long time to download, tying up your recipient's computer.
- **Respect copyrights.** If you want to quote at length from another person's work, get that person's permission. (See the information on avoiding plagiarism on page 253.) If you do quote, credit the original source and tell readers where to find it.
- **Don't dish out spam.** *Spam* refers to unsolicited messages, often meant to advertise a product or service, that are sent indiscriminately to large numbers of computer users.
- **Can the sarcasm.** Use humor—especially sarcasm—with caution. A joke that's funny when you tell it in person might fall flat or even offend someone when you reduce it to writing and send it down the computer wires.
- **Put out flames.** Flaming takes place when someone sends an online message tinged with sarcasm or outright hostility. To create positive relationships when you're online, avoid sending such messages. If you get one, do not respond in kind.
- **Add your signature.** End messages with your name and e-mail address. Most e-mail software allows you to create a "signature file" with this information that will appear automatically at the end of every message you send.

   The bottom line: Remember that behind every computer is a person. The cornerstone of netiquette is to remember that the person on the other end is a human being. Ask yourself one question whenever you're at the keyboard and typing messages: Would I say this to the person's face?

Investigate distance learning

Distance learning takes place when teachers and learners are separated geographically but communicate by the Internet or other technology.

In former days, the term *distance learning* referred to correspondence courses in which teachers and students exchanged materials by old-fashioned "snail mail." Now participants in distance learning stay in touch through fax, e-mail, Web sites, chat rooms, and teleconferencing.

Besides exchanging print materials, students and instructors who are engaged in distance learning often share computer files, videotapes, audiotapes, and other audiovisual materials. Sometimes distance learning involves students' traveling across the state or across the country for in-person interactions.

Through distance learning, students with limited mobility, such as those with physical disabilities, gain greater access to higher education. So do older students with full-time jobs and busy family lives.

Your school may offer distance-learning courses for full or partial credit. You can also find online courses by entering the key words *distance learning* in any search engine on the World Wide Web.

☑ checklist

ARE YOU READY FOR DISTANCE LEARNING?

❏ *Before signing up for a distance-learning course, consider whether this medium fits your learning style*. If you thrive on face-to-face interaction with peers and instructors, then distance learning may not work for you. Besides removing the chance to meet regularly with other people, some forms of distance learning erase the nonverbal signals that you pick up by watching an instructor lecture. Often those signals relay important information—such as clues about what will be covered on the next test.

❏ *Do some research up front*. Contact the instructor ahead of time. Ask to review the course materials before you sign up. See if you can talk with someone who has already taken the course. Get a sense of whether distance learning will be a fit for you. Also consider the credibility of any organization offering distance-learning programs. These programs vary in quality, so shop carefully.

❏ *Scope out the necessary hardware and software*. Find out what equipment you'll need for distance learning. Also, learn to use required hardware and software before the course starts. When classes begin, you can then focus on content instead of fumbling with equipment.

❏ *Find out how the instructor wants you to submit your work*. If you can do this via e-mail or fax, you might be able to send papers and other assignments on the same day that they're due. But if you need to use the regular mail or an overnight service, allow enough time for delivery.

❏ *Remember that no technology works perfectly at all times*. Sometimes a power surge or other mishap sends computer messages into the digital void. Keep backup copies of all assignments you submit. Be prepared to send duplicates if one is lost in the mail or in data transmission.

❏ *Be prepared to work independently*. When it comes to doing required reading, completing assignments, and preparing for teleconferences, distance learning requires you to act largely on your own. All learning, but especially distance learning, relies on your initiative.

experiment WITH A STRATEGY FROM THIS CHAPTER

List and briefly describe any online communities in which you currently participate. If you haven't joined one before, then describe an online community that you might like to participate in:

Now, review the suggestions in this chapter for an idea that could make your online exchanges more effective. Describe that suggestion here, including details about when, where, and how you will use it:

After actively using the suggestion, reflect on how it worked for you:

Finally, consider the possibility of setting up your own online community. Describe the type of community you would form. Also, list the policies you would set up to govern exchanges between members:

SUCCEEDING IN MATH AND SCIENCE

Chapter 28   Mastering Math and Science
Chapter 29   Reducing Math and Science Anxiety

Quick Reference Guide to SUCCEEDING IN MATH AND SCIENCE

28. MASTERING MATH AND SCIENCE

Math and science courses can help you acquire job skills, understand new technology, and think critically.

1. **Make early choices to promote your success (page 307)**
   Success in math starts before you set foot in a classroom, with the choices you make about courses and teachers:
   - Take courses in a logical sequence and in consecutive terms.
   - Find teachers with an approach that matches key aspects of your learning style.

2. **Make the most of class time (page 309)**
   Success in math and science depends on your active, day-to-day involvement in class:
   - Review your notes and readings daily.
   - Take complete and accurate notes that integrate material from text and class. (See the example on page 310.)
   - Get regular feedback on your performance and ask for help as soon as you become confused.

3. **Use textbooks effectively (page 310)**
   To succeed in math and science, redefine the word *reading* to include problem solving:
   - Math and science courses are often text driven, so devote plenty of time to reading.
   - Read actively, pausing periodically to work problems or recite key concepts.
   - Read slowly when appropriate, digesting material sentence by sentence and even word for word.
   - Focus on three types of material in textbooks: general principles, specific examples, and sample problems.

4. **Gain skill at solving problems (page 312)**
   Develop a body of techniques for solving math problems:
   - Review previous problems that you've solved.
   - Divide problems by type and isolate those that are most difficult for you.

   - Read each problem several times before trying to solve it.
   - Translate problems into plain English. (See the examples on page 313.)
   - After reading a problem, list what you know and what you want to find out.
   - Choose what arithmetic operations (addition, subtraction, multiplication, division) and formulas you will use.
   - Play with possible solutions, looking for alternative ways to solve a problem.
   - Check your work for precision and accuracy.
   - Prevent common errors on math tests. (See the sidebar on page 315.)
   - Celebrate your growing mastery in problem solving.

5. **Get the most from science courses (page 315)**
   Think critically about scientific results by understanding in general how scientists work:
   - Check the basics of the scientific method, which is based on testing hypotheses by making observations and publicly sharing results.
   - See science as an extension of the decision-making processes you use in daily life.
   - When reading scientific articles, pay special attention to the introduction and conclusions.
   - Before a lab session, gather appropriate materials and understand what you're supposed to observe and measure.

29. REDUCING MATH AND SCIENCE ANXIETY

Overcoming math and science anxiety can open you up to new courses—and even new careers.

1. **Open up to math and science (page 319)**
   Notice and rethink stereotypes about mathematicians and scientists:
   - Look for assumptions about math and science that prevent you from fully participating in these courses.
   - Think critically about those assumptions.

2. **Create a plan to master math and science (page 320)**

To overcome obstacles to success in math and science, work at the levels of your thoughts, feelings, and actions:

- ◆ Accept your current level of proficiency in math and science, whatever it is.
- ◆ Release inflexible, irrational thoughts, such as, *I'll never be any good in math.*
- ◆ Notice how feelings of anxiety surface as physical sensations, and observe those sensations in a detached way.
- ◆ Use systematic desensitization to defuse anxiety. (See the checklist on page 322.)
- ◆ Create a plan to fill specific gaps in your knowledge and skills related to math and science.

Mastering Math and Science

The work of scientists and mathematicians will change the way you live. For example, the mapping of the human genome may result in new medical treatments that could save your life someday. Advances in computer technology could render your current job obsolete or create entirely new careers for you to pursue. Yet such developments will remain a mystery to you unless you understand core mathematical concepts and the basics of the scientific method.

Besides furnishing the raw material for the most recent technology, math and science teach a process of thinking that is valuable in itself. Even basic algebra will show you ways to gain skill at critical thinking, problem solving, and decision making.

This chapter focuses on suggestions for mastering math courses. Because math is crucial to many science courses, these suggestions can promote your success in both areas. Also see the final section of this chapter for specific tips on mastering science.

Make Early Choices to Promote Your Success

Success in math starts before you set foot in a classroom, with the choices you make about courses and teachers.

Choose courses with care

The pacing and sequence of your math courses can make a huge difference in your grades and in the way you feel about these subjects. Set the grounds for early success by remembering to:

- **Assess your course readiness.** Before enrolling in a math course, make sure you have the background to understand it. Review your notes and textbook from your most recent math course. Also, preview the assigned text for your next math course. If you have any doubts about your readiness for the course, meet with the teacher.

- *Take courses in sequence.* Math and science courses are often cumulative: The content of one course builds on the content of another. Talk to a math teacher or your advisor about what courses to take and in what order.

- *Take math courses "back to back."* You may find it tempting to take a break between required math classes. That's understandable, but this choice can make it harder for you to succeed. Think about math in the same way you think about learning a foreign language. If you take a year off between Spanish I and Spanish II, you won't expect to gain much fluency. To master a language, you take courses back to back. It works the same way with math—a kind of foreign language in itself.

- *Beware of short courses.* Courses that you take during summer school or another shortened term are, by necessity, condensed. You can find yourself doing far more reading and homework each week than you do in longer courses. If you enjoy math, then the extra intensity can provide a stimulus to learn. If math is not your favorite subject, then give yourself the gift of extra course time. Enroll in courses with more calendar days.

Choose teachers with care

Whenever possible, find a math teacher whose approach to math matches key aspects of your learning style. One way to do this is by trial and error: You simply try several teachers until you find one whom you enjoy. However, this approach takes time and could lead to needless frustration. Instead, ask around and discover which teachers have a gift for making math understandable. To do this:

- Look for math courses that tend to fill up early and find out who teaches them.
- Notice the office hours posted for math teachers; some may be more available to answer questions than others.
- Ask your academic advisor to recommend math teachers.
- Ask friends to name their favorite math teachers and to explain why they view these teachers as favorites.

Of course, you may not always have a choice in math teachers. Perhaps only one teacher is offering the course you need during a given term. If so, there's still plenty you can do to learn from this teacher, no matter what that person's style is. Consider the possibility that the teacher could open up a whole new way of learning math for you. Also form a study group early in the course and ask for help at the first sign that you're failing to understand an assignment.

Make the Most of Class Time

Success in math and science depends on your active involvement. Attending class regularly, coming to class with homework finished, speaking up when you have a question, and seeking extra help when you need it are all crucial. In addition, experiment with the following strategies.

Review class work daily

Some students assume that they'll never be any good in math and science and then behave in a way that confirms that belief. Get around this mental trap by giving at least the same amount of time to math and science that you give to other courses. If you want to succeed, make daily contact with these subjects. Warm up for each class session by reviewing the previous assignments, listing questions, and solving some extra problems.

Take useful notes

Taking notes in math courses calls for specific planning. You might try a few different note-taking formats before discovering one that works for you. Whatever format you choose, remember to:

- **Integrate material from classes and textbooks.** In math courses, concepts that are taught in class tend to mesh tightly with concepts presented in assigned readings. Take notes in a way that helps you make the connections. In your math notebook, leave several blank pages between each day's class notes. Fill these pages with summaries of terms, definitions, equations, formulas, examples, and sample problems from your textbooks.
- **Take complete notes.** Success on math hinges on step-by-step learning. When your teacher works a problem in class on the board, copy each step exactly. Avoid skipping a step in your notes because it seems obvious. During a review session hours or days later, the gap in your notes could leave you scratching your head.
- **Create a calculator handbook.** When a math class relies extensively on use of a calculator, create a section in your notebook to record keystroke sequences for key formulas. Also note the context—the kinds of equations and problems for which these sequences are useful.

Get regular feedback and ask for help

Ask questions fearlessly. In any subject, learning is enhanced when you ask questions. And there are *no* dumb questions.

Ask for help as soon as you're confused. The rapid pace and sequential nature of math courses makes it essential for you to get help at the first sign of trouble.

example

THREE-COLUMN NOTES FOR MATH COURSES

Adapted from Paul D. Nolting, Math Study Skills Workbook *(Houghton Mifflin, 2000), p. 51. Copyright © 2000 by Houghton Mifflin, Inc. Used with permission.*

- Record key words and concepts in the "Key Words" column.
- Record each problem step in the "Examples" column.

- Record the reasons for each step in the "Explanation/Rules" column.
- To study from your notes, cover up the "Examples" and "Explanations/ Rules" sections and recite out loud the meaning of the key words or concepts.

KEY WORDS	EXAMPLES	EXPLANATIONS/RULES
Natural numbers	$1, 2, 3, 4, 5, \ldots$	You can count them.
Whole numbers	$0, 1, 2, 3, 4, 5, \ldots$	Natural numbers and zero
Integers	$\ldots -2, -1, 0, 1, 2, \ldots$	Negative numbers and whole numbers
$-n$	$-(-10) = 10$	Count the number of signs; an even number of signs results in a positive number
$-n$	$-(-15)(-15)$	Count the number of signs; an odd number of signs results in a negative number

Help is available in many forms—your teacher, a math tutor, a study skills center, supplementary textbooks, computer-based tutorial programs, and more. Chances are that help is free and all yours simply for the asking.

Use Textbooks Effectively

To succeed in math, redefine the word *reading*. In this new context, reading means more than passing your eyes over the pages or even taking detailed notes. Math textbooks typically contain fewer words and more graphics and illustrations than assigned readings for your other courses. In most cases, the text is simply an introduction to solving problems and other forms of practice.

You learn math by *doing*, much as you learn guitar by actually picking up an instrument and playing it. You would not expect to learn the guitar simply by reading a book *about* playing the guitar. The same principle applies to math.

Make your text a high priority

In a history, an English, or an economics class, the teacher may refer to some of the required readings only in passing. In contrast, math and science courses are often text driven. That is, class activities follow the format of the book closely.

Read chapters and sections in order, as they're laid out in the text. Master one concept before going to the next and stay current with your reading.

Plan on reading at least one supplementary text in each math course. Ask your teacher to recommend one. Getting a different take on the material can be a big help. Also, save textbooks from previous courses as reference and review materials.

Read actively

While reading your math textbooks, stop at strategic points to reinforce your understanding of the material. At these points you can:

- Create a written list of key terms and translate each one into plain English.
- Copy diagrams, formulas, or equations.
- Work problems even if they're not assigned.
- List questions to ask in class.
- Close your book and mentally reconstruct the steps of an experiment or a mathematical proof.

Read slowly

It's ineffective to breeze through a math or science book as you would the newspaper. To get the most out of your text, be willing to read each sentence slowly and reread it as needed. A single paragraph may merit 15 or 20 minutes of sustained attention.

Focus on three types of material

Most math textbooks—no matter what their subject matter or level of difficulty—are structured around three key elements:

- **Principles.** These are the key explanations, rules, concepts, formulas, or proofs. Read these carefully, in the order in which they're presented.
- **Examples.** For each general principle, find at least one example of its application, such as a sample problem with a solution. See if you can understand the reason for each step involved in solving the problem. Then cover up the solution, work the problem yourself, and check your answer against the text.
- **Problems.** In your study schedule for math courses, build in extra time for solving problems—lots of them. Solve all the assigned

problems, then do more. Group problems into types, and work on one type at a time. To promote confidence, take the time to do each problem on paper and not just in your head.

The key is to remember that these three elements are facets of the same diamond. If you try to isolate one from another—by focusing only on principles or by skipping problems, for example—you disrupt the unity of your text and create a source of confusion.

Gain Skill at Solving Problems

Because problem solving is so important to succeeding at math, develop a body of techniques that you can rely on. Start with the following suggestions and develop more techniques of your own.

Review problems you've solved before

Look over assigned problems and more. Make up your own variations on these problems. Work with a classmate and make up problems for each other to solve. The more problems you review, the more comfortable you're likely to feel solving new ones.

Divide problems by type

Make a list of the different kinds of problems and note the elements of each. By dividing problems into type or category, you can isolate the kinds of problems you have that are difficult for you. Practice those more and get help if you need it.

Read each problem several times

Read the problem at least twice before you begin. Read slowly. Be sure to understand what is being asked. Let go of the expectation that you'll find the solution right away. You may make several attempts at solving the problem before you find a solution that works.

Sometimes the sound of your voice will jar loose the solution to a problem. Talk yourself through the solution. Read equations out loud.

Translate problems into plain English

Putting problems into words aids your understanding. When you study equations and formulas, put those into words, too. The words help you see a variety of applications for each formula. For example, $c^2 = a^2 + b^2$ can be translated as "the square of the hypotenuse of a right triangle is equal to the sum of the squares of the other two sides."

List what you know and what you want to find out

Survey each problem for all of the givens. Look for what is to be proved or what is to be discovered. Consider using three columns labeled "What I already know," "What I want to find out," and "What relates the

◆ example

ENGLISH EXPRESSIONS AND THEIR MATHEMATICAL EQUIVALENTS

Adapted from Paul D. Nolting's Math Study Skills Workbook, *Houghton Mifflin, 2000, p. 67.*

A number added to 5	$5 + x$
A number decreased by 7	$x - 7$
A number increased by 13	$x + 13$
Difference between 3 and x	$3 - x$
Difference between x and 3	$x - 3$
Five times the difference of a number and 4	$5(x - 4)$
Five times the sum of x and 2	$5(x + 2)$
Five is 3 more than a number	$5 = x + 3$
One-half a number is 10	$x/2 = 10$
Quotient of 3 and x	$3/x$
Quotient of x and 3	$x/3$
Seven is greater than x	$7 > x$
Ten more than x	$x + 10$
Ten percent of x	$0.10x$
Ten subtracted from 10 times a number is that number plus 5	$10x - 10 = x + 5$
Ten times x	$10x$
The product of 2 and a number is 10	$2x = 10$
The sum of 5x and 10 is equal to the product of x and 15	$5x + 10 = 15x$
The sum of two consecutive integers	$(x) + (x + 1)$
The sum of two consecutive even integers	$(x) + (x + 2)$
The sum of two consecutive odd integers	$(x) + (x + 2)$
Twice a number	$2x$

two." This last column is the place to record a formula that can help you solve the problem.

For clarity in problem solving, reduce the number of unknowns as much as you can. You may need to create a separate equation to solve each unknown.

Draw an elaborate colored picture or a diagram if you are stuck. Sometimes a visual representation will clear a blocked mind.

Decide how you will solve the problem

Before you start crunching numbers or punching a calculator, take a moment to plan your approach. Choose what arithmetic operations (addition, subtraction, multiplication, division) or formulas you will use.

In addition, reread the section of your textbook that includes problems like the one you're trying to solve. Study the examples in your book and then return to your unsolved problem.

Play with possible solutions

There's usually not one "right" way to solve a problem. Several approaches or formulas may work, though one may be more efficient than another. Be willing to think about the problem from several angles or to proceed by trial and error. Remember that solving a math or science problem is like putting together a puzzle. You may work around the edges for a while and try many pieces before finding one that fits.

Check your work for precision and accuracy

One way to check your work is to estimate the answer before you compute it. Then ask yourself if the answer you actually got seems in the ballpark. In addition:

- **Use common sense.** Step back and ask if the solution seems reasonable at first glance. Reread the problem and remind yourself of the key question it asks. For example, if you're asked to calculate a discount on an item, then that item should cost less in your solution.
- **Keep units of measurement clear.** Say that you're calculating the velocity of an object. If you're measuring distance in meters and time in seconds, then the final velocity should be in meters per second.
- **Perform the opposite operation.** If a problem involves multiplication, check your work by dividing; if it involves addition, use subtraction; if factors, then multiply; if a square root, then figure the square; if differentiation, then integrate.
- **Put your answers to the test.** Plug your answer back into the original equation or problem and see if it works out correctly.

Savor solutions

Celebrate the times when you're getting correct answers to most of the problems in the textbook. Relish the times when you feel relaxed and confident as you work or when you look over the last few pages and they seem easy. Then remember these times if you feel math or science anxiety.

▶ sidebar

PREVENTING COMMON ERRORS ON MATH TESTS

Adapted from Carol Kanar, *The Confident Student,* p. 387. Copyright © 2004 Houghton Mifflin, Inc. Used with permission.

Math tests usually require you to solve problems. Following are three common kinds of problem-solving errors and ways to avoid them.

A *concept error* is a mistake you make when you do not understand or know which principle or rule to use when solving a math problem.

Example: You analyze the errors on three or four tests and find that you missed every problem that required you to factor. Review factoring concepts and work as many practice problems as you need to until you're sure that you can factor.

An *application error* is a mistake you make when you know what concept applies to a problem, but you are unable to apply it correctly. You may make application errors when trying to solve word problems that require you to derive a formula. To eliminate application errors, anticipate what formulas you will be asked to use on a test; then practice solving those kinds of problems.

Example: You understand the concept that rate equals distance divided by time ($r = d/t$). However, you read a word problem that gives you the rate and time and asks you to figure the distance involved.

Careless errors are needless mistakes you make when you do not proofread your work before handing in a test. To reduce your chances of making careless errors, plan your test-taking time to include five or more minutes at the end to check for mistakes, such as forgetting to add a sign, not reducing to lowest terms, or adding or subtracting incorrectly. Determine what kind of careless error you make most often so that you will be conscious of it.

Example: You multiply $-2x$ by $2x$ and arrive at the answer $4x^2$. The correct answer is $-4x^2$.

Get the Most from Science Courses

Science is based on the premise that we can make meaningful predictions about the natural world—everything from the timing of a volcanic eruption to the kind of medication that will alleviate clinical depression.

The word *science* describes both a process and a result. Scientists use a fairly standard *process* called the *scientific method* to describe, explain, and predict events. The *results* produced by this method create the core findings of physics, chemistry, biology, psychology, and other sciences.

Perhaps you're planning on a career in a scientific field. If so, you may get directly involved in research. Even if you're not planning to become a scientist, you can think critically about scientific results only by understanding in general how scientists work.

Understand the scientific method

Major steps in the scientific method include:

- **Creating a hypothesis.** A hypothesis is a statement that can be true or false. A hypothesis answers a question, and each term in a hypothesis can be defined precisely. Examples of hypotheses are: *Water boils at 32 degrees F; light can be measured as particles, as waves, or both;* and *people with Alzheimer's disease will develop abnormal plaques in their brain tissue.* In contrast, a statement such as *Ambition corrupts people* could be true *and* false, due to the differing ways that each word in this sentence could be defined. As such, this statement does not make a scientific hypothesis.

- **Designing experiences to test the hypothesis.** A hypothesis implies an actual situation in which the statement can be tested: You could heat a pot of water to 32 degrees F and see if it boils; a doctor could perform an autopsy on people diagnosed with Alzheimer's disease to see if abnormal plaque is present in their brains. During such situations, scientists make observations and collect data. With nonscientific statements, it is difficult—perhaps impossible—to consistently set up testing situations. With a statement such as *Ambition corrupts people*, scientists could reasonably disagree about which observations are relevant to this statement and what kind of measurements, if any, would be meaningful to make while testing it.

- **Analyzing the data and reflecting on the hypothesis.** After scientists collect data, they analyze it to see if it confirms the hypothesis. If the data and the hypothesis conflict in significant ways, then scientists may reject the hypothesis. Remember that no hypothesis in science is ever *proved* once and for all. All statements made as a result of the scientific method are tentative and subject to revision as new data appears. In fact, the whole process of science can be viewed as setting up a hypothesis and then diligently searching for ways to *disprove* it.

- **Making findings public.** Science takes place in community. Researchers publish their work. In these publications, scientists describe in detail how they tested a hypothesis, collected data, and made measurements. Their aim is to make these instructions so complete that one of their colleagues could set up the same conditions to test the same hypothesis. When many scientists get the same results from the same testing procedure, the hypothesis gains even more credibility. Eventually scientists may integrate this hypothesis with others to form a scientific theory or law.

See science as extension of discoveries in daily life

The scientific method may sound like a complex process that can take place only in the laboratory. However, you use the same basic steps to arrive at conclusions and solve problems in your daily life.

For instance, consider the process you used to select the school that you currently attend. You made some preliminary observations about yourself and about some prospective schools. Then you created a hypothesis about which schools offered the closest fit for your interests. You probably tested this hypothesis by visiting several schools. On the basis of these experiences, you accepted or rejected your hypothesis.

Science differs from such cases mainly in:

- The *complexity* of the events it seeks to explain.
- The amount of *control* that scientists exert when setting up events to observe.
- The degree of *precision* that scientists use in making observations and taking measurements.

Use specific strategies to read about science

Unless you choose to become a scientific researcher, most of your learning about science will come from readings and discussions of those readings. Remembering the basics of the scientific method, look for answers to the following questions as you read primary sources (articles in scholarly journals):

- What question or problem led to the research?
- What hypothesis did the researchers propose?
- What events were set up to test this hypothesis?
- What data was collected and how was it analyzed?
- Did the researchers confirm the hypothesis?
- Have other researchers using similar methods produced similar results?

When you read scientific articles, look for headings that signal places in the text to find the answers to these questions. Typical headings include "Introduction" (a statement of the problem, key question, or hypothesis), "Methods" (conditions set up to test the hypothesis), "Data" (measurements taken), and "Conclusions" (reflections on the validity of the hypothesis).

You may find most of the information you want from a scientific article in the introduction and the conclusions section. To put an article into larger context or to find a plain-English explanation of its conclusions, look for reputable secondary sources on the same topic. Some options are nationally circulated newspapers with weekly science features and popular magazines with long, substantial articles about current scientific research. Ask a librarian to recommend such sources.

Get the most from lab sessions

Laboratory work is crucial to many science classes. To get the most out of these sessions, be prepared:

- Determine in advance what procedures you'll be doing and what materials you'll need.
- Memorize, or have close at hand, any formulas you will need during the lab session.
- Know what you're supposed to observe and measure.
- If possible, visit the lab before your assigned time and get to know the territory.
- Find out where materials are stored and where to dispose of chemicals or specimens.
- Bring your lab notebook and worksheets to record and summarize your findings.

experiment WITH A STRATEGY FROM THIS CHAPTER

Think about all the times that you apply math or science concepts in daily life. Examples are comparing prices and making decisions about what to buy (especially purchases with a big sticker price, such as tuition or a car) and choosing between alternative forms of medical treatment.

In the space below, brainstorm some possible benefits that can result from your success in math and science courses. Think of ways that you could apply math and science in your daily life:

Next, choose one suggestion from this chapter that you will commit to use in your math or science courses. Complete the following sentence:

I intend to. . . .

Reducing Math and Science Anxiety

When they open books about math or science, some capable students break out in a cold sweat. This is a symptom of two conditions sweeping over students across the world—math anxiety and science anxiety.

Think of the benefits of overcoming math and science anxiety. Many more courses, majors, jobs, and careers could open up for you. Knowing these subjects can also put you at ease in everyday situations: calculating the tip for a waiter, planning your finances, working with a spreadsheet on a computer. Speaking the languages of math and science can also help you feel at home in a world driven by technology.

Open Up to Math and Science

Sometimes what keeps people from succeeding at math and science is their mental picture of scientists and mathematicians. Often that picture includes a man dressed in a faded plaid shirt, baggy pants, and wingtip shoes. He's got a calculator on his belt and six pencils jammed in his shirt pocket.

Such pictures are far from the truth. Succeeding in math and science won't turn you into a nerd. Not only can you enjoy school more, but you'll also find that your friends and family will still like you.

Notice assumptions about math and science

Our mental pictures about math and science can be funny. At the same time, they have serious effects. For many years, science and math were viewed as fields for white males. That excluded women and people of color. Promoting success in these subjects for all students is a key step in overcoming racism and sexism.

Sheila Tobias, author of several books on overcoming math anxiety, points out that people often make faulty assumptions about how math and science are learned. These assumptions can include:

- *Math calls only for logic, not imagination.*
- *There's only one right way to do a science experiment or solve a math problem.*
- *There is a magic secret to doing well in math or science.*
- *Math and science don't allow for imagination.*
- *Math and science are only useful for certain careers.*
- *Only some people succeed at math and science.*

Think critically about those assumptions

The ideas listed here can be easily refuted. To begin, mathematicians and scientists regularly talk about the importance of creativity and imagination in their work. At times they find it hard to explain how they arrive at a particular hypothesis or conclusion. And as far as we know, the only secret they count on is hard work. With some time and extra thought, you can think of more ways to refute half-baked assumptions about math and science.

Create a Plan to Master Math and Science

To overcome obstacles to success in math and science, work at the levels of your thoughts, feelings, and actions. All three areas are related, and changing one will promote change in the others.

Accept your current level of proficiency

Math and science are cumulative. Concepts tend to build on each other in sequential order. If you struggled with algebra, for example, you will probably have trouble with trigonometry or calculus.

To ensure that you have an adequate base of knowledge, tell the truth about your current level of knowledge and skill. Remember that it's OK to continue your study of math and science from your current level of ability, whatever that level might be.

Release irrational thoughts

When students fear math and science, they often say negative things to themselves about their abilities in these subjects. Many times this self-talk includes statements such as: "I'll never be fast enough at solving math problems"; "I'm one of those people who can't function in a science lab"; "I'm good with words, so I can't be good with numbers."

You can deal with this kind of self-talk in three steps:

- **Get a clear picture of such statements.** When they come up, speak them out loud or write them down. When you get the little voice out in the open, it's easier to refute it.

- ***Next, do some critical thinking about these statements.*** Look for the hidden assumptions they contain. Separate what's accurate about them from what's false. Negative self-statements are usually based on scant evidence. They can often be reduced to two simple ideas: "Everybody else is better at math and science than I am" and "I don't understand it right now, so I'll never understand it." Both of these are illogical. Many people lack confidence in their math and science skills. To verify this, just ask other students. Also ask about ways they overcame confusion.
- ***Start some new self-talk.*** Use statements that affirm your ability to succeed in math and science: "When learning about math or science, I proceed with patience"; "Any confusion I feel now will be resolved"; "I learn math and science without comparing myself to others"; "I ask whatever questions are needed to aid my understanding"; "I am fundamentally OK as a person, even if I make errors in math and science."

Notice one characteristic of effective self-talk: It cultivates something that psychologists call an *internal locus of control*. This means that you see your own intentions and behaviors as the main sources of the results you create in math and science courses (and in your life as a whole). "I will do better in math courses by asking for help when I'm first confused" is a statement based on an internal locus of control. "I flunked because my math teacher hates me" is not.

Face feelings of anxiety

Notice your body sensations. Math or science anxiety is seldom just a "head trip." It registers in the human body, too. Examples are a tight feeling in the chest, sweaty palms, drowsiness, or a mild headache.

Let those sensations come to the surface. Instead of repressing them, open up to them. Doing so often decreases their urgency.

Remember that your emotional state will fluctuate as you change the focus of your attention. During moments of anxiety, you tend to focus on yourself and the unpleasant sensations you're experiencing. Instead, consciously shift your attention to planning and action—to the next thing you will *do* to increase your skill at math and science.

Fill specific gaps in your knowledge and skill

Before you register for a math or science course, seek out the assigned texts for the class. Look at the kind of material that's covered in early chapters. See if you can answer the questions and solve the problems included at the end of each chapter. If that material seems new or difficult for you, see the instructor and express any concerns you have. Ask for suggestions on ways to prepare for the course.

☑ checklist

USE SYSTEMATIC DESENSITIZATION TO DEFUSE ANXIETY

See anxiety as a learned response—one that you can "unlearn." You might be able to do this through a process that's sometimes used by people in psychotherapy. This process is called *systematic desensitization*:

❑ List some specific situations that trigger your math or science anxiety—for example, running out of time to answer all the questions on a test.

❑ Create a mental picture of yourself reacting in a new way to this trigger—such as budgeting your test time and finishing all the questions with time to spare.

❑ Next, set up a situation that *simulates* the situation you fear; for instance, create a mock test with the same number and kinds of questions that you anticipate will appear on your next test.

❑ Put yourself squarely in that simulated environment; for example, take your mock test in the actual exam room.

❑ Use relaxation techniques such as deep breathing at any time you feel nervous.

❑ If your level of fear prevents you from functioning in your simulated situation, then back off a little and create a less demanding situation, such as a mock test with fewer or simpler questions.

Your academic advisor or a counselor at your student health center may be able to help you use systematic desensitization. Ask for help, especially if your worries about math or science courses interfere with your daily life.

Also consider cooperative learning. Math and science are often seen as solitary endeavors in which students either sink or swim on their own. This does not have to be your experience. Instead of going it alone, harness the power of cooperative learning. Study math and science with others. That way you can learn about different approaches to reaching solutions.

By studying with others and creating an environment in which it's OK to make mistakes, you can overcome a variety of fears. From the first day of a math or science course, be on the lookout for potential study group members. You can start to associate math and science with the fun of group interaction.

experiment WITH A STRATEGY FROM THIS CHAPTER

Most of us can recall a time when learning became associated with anxiety. For many people, this happened early with math and science. One step to getting past this anxiety is to write a math or science autobiography.

Recall specific experiences in which you first felt stress over these subjects. Where were you? How old were you? What were you thinking and feeling? Who else was with you? What did those people say or do?

Describe some of these experiences in the space below. Continue on separate paper if needed.

Now reflect on these experiences to see if there is any pattern to the difficulties you experienced in math or science courses. Complete the following sentence:
I discovered that my biggest barrier in math or science is . . .

Finally, based on your reading of this chapter, list one action you will take to overcome any anxiety you feel about math or science.
I intend to. . . .

Appendix 1: Documenting Sources with MLA Style

The Modern Language Association (MLA) publishes a manual of style with guidelines for *citing* (giving credit to) the sources you use in writing research papers. The process of citing your sources is called *documentation*, and it includes:

- **In-text citations:** the last name of the author and the page number for each source; these are included in the body of your paper.
- **A works-cited section** at the end of your paper that lists full information about your sources.

Note: When researching a paper, you might read some sources but not refer to them directly in your paper. List these sources in a bibliography, *not* in a works-cited section.

For guidelines about which sources to cite, see the sidebar "Avoid Plagiarism" in Chapter 21, page 253.

Following are some key points about MLA style. For complete MLA guidelines, see the latest version of the *MLA Handbook for Writers of Research Papers* (Modern Language Association of America).*

MLA style for in-text citations

For in-text citations, identify the author and page number of each source. The first time you mention an author in your text, give his or her full name. After that, just use the author's last name. At the end of your text sentence, give only the page number(s) in parentheses, followed by the sentence period. Do not include *p.*, *pp.*, or the word *page*. Cite inclusive page numbers as follows: 35–36; 257–58; 100–01; 305–06; 299–300.

*The following is adapted from Ann Raimes, *Keys for Writers,* 3rd ed. (Boston: Houghton Mifflin, 2002), pp. 125–151. Adapted with permission.

Style for an author named in your introductory phrase. The following example includes a quotation from the author, followed by the page number of the source:

Joyce Johnson's interviews with young women provide examples of what she sees as the "American post-modern dream" (19).

Style for an author not named in your text. If you do not mention the author while introducing the reference, include the author's last name in the parentheses before the page number, with no comma between them:

Interviews with young women provide examples (Johnson 19).

Style for two or more authors. For a work with two or three authors, include all the names, either in your text sentence or in parentheses:

Interviews with young women provide examples (Johnson and Sidel 19).

Author with more than one work cited. You can include the author and title of the work in your text sentence:

Joyce Johnson, in her book *Young Women in the Labor Movement*, provides examples of what she sees as the "American post-modern dream" (49–51).

If you do not mention the author in your text, include in your parenthetical reference the author's last name, followed by a comma, an abbreviated form of the title, and the page number:

Interviews with young women provide examples (Johnson, *Young Women* 49–51).

Electronic and Internet sources. Electronic database material and Internet sources have no stable page numbers. In this case, simply provide the author's name:

Joyce Johnson's interviews with young women provide examples of what she sees as the "American post-modern dream."

If no author is given, include the title of the source.

MLA style for the list of works cited

The references you make in your text to sources are brief, usually only the author's last name and a page number. This allows people to read through your paper without interruption. For complete information about the source, readers can use your brief in-text citation as a guide to the full reference in the list of works cited at the end of your paper.

In your list of works cited, alphabetize the list by authors' last names. Alphabetize by the exact letters in the spelling. For example, *MacKay* precedes *McHam*.

Basic form for a book with one author

Sidel, Ruth. *On Her Own: Growing Up in the Shadow of the American Dream*. New York: Penguin, 1990.

Note that the second line of the citation is indented five spaces.

Book with two authors. Use authors' names in the order in which they appear in the book. Separate the names with commas. Reverse the order of only the first author's name:

Lakoff, George, and Mark Johnson. *Metaphors We Live By*. Chicago: U of Chicago P, 1980.

In this example, *U of Chicago P* stands for *University of Chicago Press*.

Book with four or more authors. Either list all the names or use only the first author's name followed by *et al.* (Latin for *and others*):

Bellah, Robert N., et al. *Habits of the Heart: Individualism and Commitment in American Life*. Berkeley: U of California P, 1985.

Edited book. Use the abbreviation *ed.* or *eds.*, preceded by a comma, after the name(s) of the editor or editors:

Gates, Henry Louis, Jr., ed. *Classic Slave Narratives*. New York: NAL, 1987.

Article in a scholarly journal. For journals in which each issue begins with page 1, include the issue number after the volume number, separated from the volume number by a period. (*Volume* refers to the year in which an issue is published.)

Ginet, Rami. "The Soviet Unions and the Syrian Ba'th Regime: From Hesitation to *Rapprochement*." *Middle Eastern Studies* 36.2 (2000): 150–71.

Some journals use consecutive pagination throughout a volume. For example, if the first issue ends at page 175, the next issue starts at page 176. For these publications, omit the issue number.

Article in a magazine. For a magazine published every week or biweekly, give the complete date (day, month, and year, in that order, with no commas between them). For a monthly or bimonthly magazine, give only the month and year. In either case, do not include volume and issue numbers. If the article is on only one page, give that page number. If the article covers two or more consecutive pages, list inclusive page numbers.

> Cooper, Marc. "Arizona: The New Border War." *Nation* 17 July 2000: 20–24.

Internet and electronic sources. With the fast pace of change in the electronic world, standards are continually evolving for citing sources. For updated information on citing Internet sources, refer to the MLA Web site at http://www.mla.org.

With whatever system of documentation you use, the basic question to ask is: *What information does my reader need in order to access the same site and find the same information I found?* Internet sites vary in the amount of information they provide, and with some you need to go to the home page or search the site to find information. Also scroll to the end of a page; the date of posting often lurks there.

For all of your sources, *do* provide the date when you found the material (your date of access) and the URL.

Appendix 2: Documenting Sources with APA Style

The American Psychological Association (APA) publishes a manual of style with guidelines for *citing* (giving credit to) the sources you use in writing research papers. The APA guidelines are often used by students and researchers in the social sciences. The process of citing your sources is called *documentation*, and it includes:

- **In-text citations:** the last name of the author and the year of publication for each source; these are included in the body of your paper.
- **A references section** at the end of your paper that lists full information about your sources.

Note: When researching a paper, you might read some sources but not refer to them directly in your paper. List these sources in a bibliography, *not* in a references section.

For guidelines about which sources to cite, see the sidebar "Avoid Plagiarism" in Chapter 21, page 253.

Following are some key points about APA style. For complete APA guidelines, see the latest edition of the *Publication Manual of the American Psychological Association.**

APA style for in-text citations

One author. If you mention the author's last name in your own sentence, include the year in parentheses directly after the author's name:

Wilson (1994) has described in detail his fascination with insects.

If you do not name the author in your sentence, include both the name and the year, separated by a comma, in parentheses:

---

*The following is adapted from Ann Raimes, *Keys for Writers,* 3rd ed. (Boston: Houghton Mifflin, 2002), pp. 162–178. Adapted with permission.

The role of the Educational Testing Service (ETS) in designing, evaluating, and promoting the test has been harshly criticized (Owen, 1985).

If you use a direct quotation, include in parentheses the abbreviation "p." or "pp." followed by a space and the page number(s). Separate items within parentheses with commas:

Memories are built "around a small collection of dominating images" (Wilson, 1994, p.5).

Two authors. For a work by two authors, name both in the order in which their names appear on the work. Within parentheses, use an ampersand (&) between the names, in place of *and:*

Kanazawa and Still (2000) in their analysis of a large set of data show that the statistical likelihood of being divorced increases if one is male and a secondary school teacher or college professor.

Later reference:

Analysis of a large set of data shows that the statistical likelihood of being divorced increases if one is male and a secondary school teacher or college professor (Kanazawa & Still, 2000).

Three to five authors. For a work with three to five authors or editors, identify all of them the first time you mention the work. In later references, use only the first author's name followed by *et al.* (for *and others*) in place of the other names.

Jordan, Kaplan, Miller, Stiver, and Surrey (1991) have examined the idea of a "self."

Later reference:

Increasingly, the self is viewed as connected to other human beings (Jordan et al., 1991).

Electronic or Internet source. Give author, if available, and title, followed by the year of electronic publication or of the most recent update. If no year of publication is available, give the date on which you accessed the material. If you cite an e-mail message (personal, bulletin board, discussion group, or Usenet group), cite it in your text as a personal communication; do not include it in your list of references.

Guidelines for the APA list of references

The APA *Publication Manual* and Web site provide guidelines for submitting professional papers for publication, and many instructors ask students to follow those guidelines in order to prepare them for advanced work. Check with your instructor, however, as to specific course requirements for the reference list—especially about indenting the second line of references.

Order of entries in the reference list. Use alphabetical order, and alphabetize letter by letter. Treat *Mac* and *Mc* literally, by letter. For example, *MacKay* comes before *McCarthy*.

If you include several works by the same author, then list the author's name in each entry. Arrange entries chronologically from past to present.

Book with one author

Wilson, E. O. (1994). *Naturalist.* Washington: Island Press.

Edited book

Denmark, F., & Paludi, M. (Eds.). (1993). *Psychology of women: A handbook of issues and theories.* Westport, CT: Greenwood Press.

Article in a scholarly journal. For journals in which each issue begins with page 1, include the issue number in parentheses after the volume number. (*Volume* refers to the year in which an issue is published.)

Ginat, R. (2000). The Soviet Union and Syrian Ba'th regime: From hesitation to *rapprochement. Middle Eastern Studies, 36* (2), 150–171.

Some journals use consecutive pagination throughout a volume. For example, if the first issue ends at page 175, the next issue starts at page 176. For these publications, omit the issue number.

Internet and other electronic sources. For the latest guidelines from the APA on citing electronic sources, refer to its Web site at http://www.apa.org/journals/webref.html. List as much of the following information about your electronic sources as available:

- Author(s)
- Date of work (*n.d.* if no date is provided)
- Title of the work
- Any information about the publication as it appears in print form
- Name of the source and any document number, publication date, or revision date (update)
- For an online source, the date you found the material (access date) and the URL

With whatever system of documentation you use, the basic question to ask is: *What information does my reader need in order to access the same site and find the same information I found?* Internet sites vary in the amount of information they provide, and with some you need to go to the home page or search the site to find information. Also scroll to the end of a page; the date of posting often lurks there.

MASTER Student Index